Frank & Co

JAWBONE

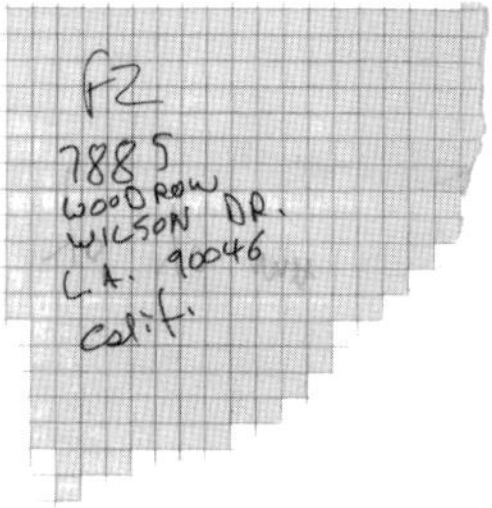

FOR LINDE, JASMIJN ZIVA & FABIAN JACOBUS

Frank & Co
Conversations with Frank Zappa 1977–1993
Co de Kloet

A Jawbone book
Published in the UK and the USA by Jawbone Press
Office G1
141–157 Acre Lane
London SW2 5UA
England
www.jawbonepress.com

Published by arrangement with Haver Productions
haverproducties.nl

ISBN 978-1-911036-81-4

Printed by Short Run Press, Exeter, Devon

1 2 3 4 5 26 25 24 23 22

Contents

Dweezil Zappa. *Sven Doornkaat*.

Foreword
by Dweezil Zappa

THE BOOK YOU'RE ABOUT TO READ WILL ELUCIDATE THE IMPORTANT CHARACTERISTICS OF A LASTING FRIENDSHIP BETWEEN MY FATHER, FRANK ZAPPA, AND THE AUTHOR CO DE KLOET. The respectful and edifying conversations between them have been magnetically preserved by Co, and they reveal playful ease at times. This is quizzically uncustomary considering my father's disdain for being interviewed. My father was more notoriously greeted with fear and trembling from lesser journalists as his comportment toward them appeared to grow more menacing in response to their aimlessly regurgitated questions. However, conversations with my father in 'journalist'-free zones were very different. He was very curious, open, and anthropological. He was fascinated by people and the folklore surrounding their proclivities. His musical text is only a hint at his keen perception of humans in the wild. Some of his songs have content that could be ripped from today's news headlines even though they may have been written more than fifty years ago. His countless interviews reveal an even deeper understanding of the underpinnings of society and his ability to predict foreboding world events. Fake news is not a new invention and he wanted people to be aware of their need to be critical thinkers at all times.

Since Co de Kloet is not necessarily a journalist by trade, rather more of a mysterious practitioner of inventive alliances, he was able to develop a rapport with my father, stratified with unusual regularity. Co has manned various positions in the world of production for music, radio, and television. Among other talents, he has a remarkable ability to create opportunities for atypical artists to work in the realm of orchestral music. He's been described as a creative catalyst in that regard.

He's been operating from 'a secret conurbation of coastal dunes' for decades and has found a way to consistently include my father's musical works in broadcasted radio specials and other important events. Because of his pure love of my father's music and other non-conformist tendencies, he's an enigmatic character. I'm grateful that he understands and appreciates the things that make my father's music different and that he has the enthusiasm and ability to articulate the significance and value of those differences, in comparison to other entertainment. I'm glad he got to know my father as a person. That further informed his understanding of the Sisyphean undertaking it was for my father to create his work.

This book is somewhat analogous to a documentary movie for your brain. The details that unfold are sourced from authentic recordings of interviews over a period of more than twenty years. Whether my father is expressing his views of religion and politics as well his opinions of their ill-advised enmeshment or his bleak opinion about some of his former employees playing his music in public, he gives it to you straight. Well, he gave it straight to Co, and now he's giving it to you! There are many things waiting to be uncovered by you during your exploration of this book.

For example, did you know that some of you consume music improperly? My father has thoughtfully described the existing problem:

> *The main way of consuming it is you don't listen to it—You dress up to it. The music reinforces your wardrobe. And so, by the music being like this, it gives people the chance to act out this fantasy of how modern they think they are.*

What about other practical advice from my father? How about an idea called NEST, which stands for National Emergency Security Trust. He developed the idea back in the '80s, but unfortunately it was not implemented.

> *Yeah, you start with a trust fund where all the people who advertise in the United States would put in one percent of their yearly advertising budget and if you started the fund off with that amount of money you could probably begin with a billion, a billion and a half dollars in the fund. And when there is an emergency someplace, the idea is that Congress always takes too long to appropriate the money, but the emergency fund would put the money out and Congress would in its*

> *time reimburse the fund, and of course the fund is gathering interest when it's not being used.*

You'll also find succinct explanations of world events through his theological filter such as this:

> *Most of the world is endangered today—there are only certain places where people have comfortable lives, and everyplace else there's nothing but imminent danger and death and destruction and pestilence and just horrible stuff going on. Well, who can we blame for that? Because if you blame the devil then you have to think that the devil is more powerful than that guy on the cloud. If the guy on the cloud is the boss, he's the boss, he is making it happen. So what does he think? I don't know. If he likes what he has created as it is said at one point, he was satisfied with what he built, then I am sure he is delighted. He is probably doing a little breakdancing up there.*

Some people that like my father and his music are considered to be unusual. If you're reading this book you're probably one of them. When you see Co, thank him in person for keeping the unusual music we love accessible on the airwaves.

DWEEZIL ZAPPA

HELLO THERE

[illegible]

by

Co de Kloet jr.

(a personal fantasy)

Prelude to the afternoon of writing a book

IT'S FEBRUARY 26TH, 1979. I'm sitting in Frank Zappa's room in the Amstel Hotel in Amsterdam. Next to Frank sits a large cassette recorder, a suitcase full of cassette tapes, and a two-liter thermos of coffee.

Frank used to start his concerts with an amiable 'Hello there!' I tell him that would be an appropriate title, if I were ever to write a book about him. I suggest that he should design the cover, as a sign of approval. He laughs, grabs my pen and paper, and writes:

Hello There
Frank Zappa
by
Co de Kloet Jr.
(a personal fantasy)

Apparently, that 'sign of approval' wouldn't be as easy to come by as I'd thought. That alone is reason enough to limit this book to actual quotes and conversations recorded, as it were, on the record. The 'personal fantasy' elements are my memories of experiences with Frank. Fortunately I have an eidetic memory, and with every experience with Frank being an event unto itself, the memories are more or less self-refreshing.

IT'S OCTOBER 31ST, 2009. Halloween.

I'm in a car with George Duke, driving past Amsterdam's Concertgebouw. We're working together on a production with the Metropole Orkest, featuring George and Napoleon Murphy Brock.

I tell George that it was in that building, on September 9th, 1973, that I first saw Frank Zappa and The Mothers Of Invention perform live. Of course, George was in the band! Wide-eyed, he tells me that—despite his long history of working in Zappa's bands—there's only one Zappa poster in his home studio: a promo for that exact same concert. He promises me that he'll make a scan of it when he gets home and send it to me. That poster, that day, that concert—it was the start of a musical journey that continues to this day.

THIS BOOK DESCRIBES MY TIME WITH FRANK ZAPPA. I had the privilege of knowing him, of calling him a friend, and of working for him both in the media and otherwise. I've never stopped loving the man or his music, and still work hard to bring him into the spotlight. Working with such important musicians as Bruce Fowler, Napoleon Murphy Brock, Terry Bozzio, George Duke, Todd Rundgren, Gary Lucas, Dweezil Zappa, Mike Keneally, Tom Trapp, and Steve Vai also helps affirm my respect for the 'Zappa tradition.'

This book is far from exhaustive. Some memories are too personal, and some anecdotes told by others are perhaps recalled in a different light, so many years later. Emotions play a curious role when you're dealing with someone as charismatic as Frank.

Another reason why this book isn't exhaustive is that I'm busy working on future projects involving Dweezil and Steve. However, I'd like to include my accounts of four projects that hold a special place in my heart, all of which took place after Frank's sadly premature death: the Holland Festival 2000, my four-hour documentary about *Freak Out*, my Dweezil project with the North Netherlands Symphony Orchestra, and my 1993 collaboration with Don Van Vliet, aka Captain Beefheart.

1973

Take-off on radio

RADIO STATIONS WERE ALREADY A FAMILIAR SCENE FOR ME IN 1973. As a kid, I'd accompany my father (my namesake—he'd produced the first pop music program on Dutch public radio) to the VARA broadcasting complex on Heuvellaan in Hilversum. When I was about ten years old, I played in a youth radio orchestra called *De Muzikantenclub*. I was invited also to work as an interviewer on various programs for school radio. Every time I was there, I felt a sense of magic in those long corridors, the weird doors with strange little round windows, the reel-to-reel machines and microphones. And then there were the colorful characters—the programmers, the musicians, the actors, the bohemians—people from all walks of life, all forms of worship, both religious and sexual: the tone-setters who made this media world so magnetic and special.

One of the programs my father produced was called *Z.O.*: an initialism for *Zaterdagochtend* or 'Saturday Morning.' I was fourteen in August 1973. For my very first foray into radio, I joined the show's presenters, Herman Stok and Letty Kosterman, to talk about my idol Frank Zappa, who had an upcoming performance in Amsterdam's Concertgebouw a few weeks later. My recollection of what I said is blurry, but I remember that I was allowed to play a few tunes, so I chose 'Mr. Green Genes' and 'Uncle Meat.' I was rewarded for my appearance with two tickets to the show, and so it was that on September 9th, 1973, I was sitting in the main hall of the Concertgebouw and saw Frank Zappa and The Mothers Of Invention for the first time. One of the band members that day was a pianist with whom I went on to work as a radio producer years later: George Duke. More on that follows later in this book.

I'd been turned on to FZ by Tessel Blok, a girl in first grade with me (who went on to work in radio also). Through her father, she'd discovered an album by The Mothers Of Invention called *Freak Out*. I recognized the title—my father had the same album. I went home, put it on, and experienced what so many experience when they first hear it: my musical perception was completely changed forever. I was already quite fanatical by then about playing the recorder (and later, saxophone). I loved baroque and 'normal' pop music, and frequently heard music by Sinatra and similar artists at home. In spite of this solid foundation, I still felt like I'd been thrown into the deep end—especially when I first heard *200 Motels*, my second Zappa album. The tone had been set.

Herman Stok, the host of my father's *Z.O.* show, lived with his partner Kees van Maasdam in a magnificent house at Prinsengracht 714, on one of Amsterdam's historical canals. He ran his company Popstudio from the basement. It was a small space, bursting at the seams with LPs, all organized by alphabet. It also contained a handsome stereo installation and a state-of-the-art four-channel headset. My parents and I were frequent visitors, and during those visits I would be dumped (not entirely against my wishes) in the basement, where I'd spend hours on end playing albums. More often than not, it was Zappa that I listened to. It was on that headset that I first heard 'Billy The Mountain.' All the Zappa albums were in mint condition, as I was the only one who ever played them. One day, my 'uncles' told me it would best if I took the LPs home with me—it would clear out some much-needed room in the basement. In a single afternoon, I acquired a complete FZ collection.

So that's how something began, back in 1973, that would become a cornerstone of my professional life: I professed my love for Frank Zappa's music (even though I didn't completely understand it) on the radio. What I couldn't possibly have foreseen was that I'd get the opportunity, just a few short years later, to shake his hand—catalyzing a personal and professional friendship with my hero.

1974

Gaining status in high school

IN HIGH SCHOOL IN HILVERSUM, I WAS INTERESTED IN LEARNING ENGLISH MOSTLY TO BETTER UNDERSTAND THE LYRICS TO THE SONGS ON ALL THE ALBUMS I WAS LISTENING TO AT HOME. A 'progressive' bookstore in Hilversum sold illegal books full of lyrics, sloppily thrown together and full of typos (as well as misheard lyrics, as I later discovered). They also had some Zappa books. Even with all the mistakes, they gave me something to study and collect. I knew about two special documentaries made by Roelof Kiers for broadcaster VPRO. The first had been recorded in Zappa's home and on his US tour, and the second was filmed at Pinewood Studios in England while Zappa was recording *200 Motels*, a movie that was casting more and more of a spell on me. Although I'd unfortunately missed the original broadcast, a very kind lady at VPRO (whose name I've regrettably forgotten) arranged for me to visit one of the broadcasting station's villas (one of several located on 's-Gravelandseweg in Hilversum) one day after school.

Seated at an actual editing table with a small screen, I got to watch both documentaries. There I sat, by myself, watching two films that would leave an indelible impression on me—even if most of the actual subject matter went over my head. I saw Zappa working on scores, Flo & Eddie in top form, and Frank confessing how much he loved to share his bed with ladies on tour. I watched the now-infamous scene from his house where he places the nozzle of a vacuum cleaner (while it's still running) over his nipples, and then over Miss Lucy's, of the GTOs. Then he shoves the vacuum between her legs, declaring, 'It also works on pie.' Lucy catches her breath enough to reply, 'It does!' Fascinating television for young and old alike—and in fact it led to questions in Dutch parliament about the 'adult' nature of the films, and VPRO found itself in hot water for a while.

Controversy notwithstanding, the documentaries helped to establish

Zappa's name as a permanent fixture in the Dutch television landscape. I was captivated by this whole new world, and a lot of that had to do with the concept of 'freedom.'

1975

Collecting

I STARTED TO COLLECT EVERYTHING I COULD LAY MY HANDS ON, AND SPENT A GOOD PORTION OF MY MODEST MEANS ON BOOTLEGS, SCORED FROM STORES ALONG UTRECHT'S OUDE GRACHT CANAL. I still have one of those LPs: a green vinyl concert recording called *Zubin & The Jets*, featuring the Los Angeles Philharmonic with Zubin Mehta at the helm and a few of the Mothers. Most of the material would later be reused on *200 Motels*. In the hall at that show were two singers who formed the group The Turtles: Mark Volman and Howard Kaylan (Kaylan was also related to Zappa's manager Herb Cohen). Years later, I spoke with Mark and Howard about that night—but that's another story, which I tell later in the book.

1976

Napoleon

I CAN'T REALLY EXPLAIN WHY, BUT I DIDN'T SEE ZAPPA PERFORM AGAIN UNTIL 1976. When I did, it was a fantastic concert in Amsterdam's Jaap Edenhal on March 6th. The band that night again included some people with who I went on to work later: Napoleon Murphy Brock ('Napi') and Terry Bozzio. Zappa was on guitar, Napi wore a mask, and on bass (from the very first Mothers lineup) was Roy Estrada—who I feel is still an underappreciated musician. I was seventeen by that time, my English was coming along nicely, and I had the night of my life. My father had gotten free tickets, but it wasn't really his kind of music (he'd rather have gone to see the other Frank perform), so he gave them to me. Since I didn't have a driver's license at that age, I went to the concert with a local primary school teacher called Willem Degekamp. After seeing this spectacular performance, I knew I'd never miss another Zappa show in Holland—and I didn't. I was fortunate enough to see every show from that night right up until May 4th, 1988—Zappa's final Dutch appearance.

TV guide *Varagids* ran an announcement: on November 19th, at 10:45pm, German TV station ZDF would broadcast a Zappa concert as part of its show *Vernissage*. In the band were Ruth and George, who were also on stage for the performance I'd seen in 1973. It's impossible to imagine nowadays, but back then we couldn't receive German television channels in Kortenhoef, the tiny village where I lived, so that evening I got on my bike (with my dinky little cassette recorder and a handheld microphone) and rode over to my grandparents' house in Hilversum. I parked myself in front of the screen of their enormous television that received German channels, dangled my mic in front of the speaker, and sat down to enjoy both the amazing show and Bruce Bickford's wonderful Claymations. That KCET TV special has held a special place in my heart ever since. George Duke told me later that Herb Cohen still had hours of unused material from the show—I have no idea where that material is now.

I have many fond memories of this time. I ended up cultivating an enduring professional and personal relationship with Napoleon Murphy Brock. I consider his concerts with the Metropole Orkest, and especially the 2009 show with George Duke, to be some of my best work.

1977

The first interview

1977 WAS A PIVOTAL YEAR. Zappa was playing in Holland; I was eighteen and about to graduate from high school. I'd built up a reputation already among my friends as the great Zappa ambassador. My record collection was growing all the time, thanks to his absurdly prolific output, and through Frank I'd discovered other music also, for example the orchestral works of Edgard Varèse. Frank too had his idols; he too was an ambassador.

I had a dream, one that I shared with so many fans: I wanted to meet Zappa in person and interview him. Easier said than done: by that point, Zappa had been hiring bodyguards for years, and it was around this point in his career that he became genuinely busy. He'd abandoned the name 'Mothers Of Invention,' even 'Mothers,' and the band now simply went by the name 'ZAPPA.' He'd fired his manager Herb Cohen and was wrapped up in a series of lawsuits with his record label, Warner Bros.

In Holland, his records were distributed by WEA, whose Head of Promotion was Jan Bult—a legendary figure in the Dutch media land of Hilversum, who passed away too soon. My father knew Jan, and WEA boss Henk Penseel. Through them, I managed to wrangle a brief moment to talk with Frank. I was ridiculously excited, of course, but in fact too young and inexperienced to know what to do with the precious time I'd been allotted.

I boarded the train on February 4th anyway, and 'signed in' at the Pulitzer Hotel in Amsterdam. Jan told me that Frank wasn't there yet, and that I'd have to wait in the bar. It took forever (or maybe it just seemed that way), and I wandered out of the bar and took a seat in the lobby, by the elevator. Soon, a group of men passed me to take the elevator, and I recognized drummer Terry Bozzio and bass player Patrick O'Hearn. They were followed shortly afterwards by a pair who I didn't recognize, but who immediately picked up on my fandom. They were part of the crew: Coy Featherstone and Tex Abel. By then I was doubting whether I'd ever get my Zappa interview, so I asked if I could interview them in the meantime. They agreed, and I went to their hotel room and recorded a short conversation.

Afterwards, I went back downstairs to the empty lobby and sat down again to wait. There wasn't a soul in sight—suddenly a man was standing next to me, waiting for the elevator. His hair was drawn into a tight ponytail (no curls), his face was shaved except for a small imperial moustache and goatee, he was wearing a designer jacket, and he had a briefcase in his right hand. He fixed me with a glare, his eyes clearly saying, 'Who are you, what are you doing here, and where is my bodyguard?' It was just me and my idol alone in a room, and all I could manage to say was, 'Are you Frank Zappa?' What a stupid thing to say—if there was one question I could have answered myself, it was that. He smiled and replied, 'I sure am.' The elevator doors opened, he disappeared, and I called after him, 'See you later!'

Half an hour passed. Jan Bult appeared and told me to follow him. We went to a room where Zappa was already being interviewed by a lady named Brenda. There were pictures being taken and I joined in—Jan said it was fine. Everyone left and Jan said to Frank, 'This is Co, he's a friend of mine. His father is a radio producer and Co's a huge fan. He'd like to tape a short interview.'

Zappa fixed me with that glare again, and said, 'Really? And you still had to ask whether or not it was *me* when you saw me in the lobby?' Then he broke into a grin and shook my hand, and with that I'd learned a valuable lesson: don't fuck up when dealing with this man.

'You were just being careful, huh?'

The following are a few excerpts from that first taped conversation with FZ.

JAN The last thing we do is, we'll have dinner. At your request dinner will be ready in the restaurant when we get there.

FRANK What time is it now?

CO Ten past six.

JAN In thirty-five minutes from now we'll have the car ready. Tonight, you have one more journalist coming and one radio guy. And then you have the photo session with Claude, who sends his regards.

'Claude' was Claude Vanheye, who has since become a close friend of mine, and we've worked together on numerous projects. That day, he made a portrait of Frank that would go on to become quite famous: Frank is smoking—no surprise there—and wearing a white shirt that George Harrison had worn in a shoot with Claude earlier that month.

This was Frank's last photo session with Claude: their relationship was complicated by the fact that Claude's representative in California was Herb Cohen. At the time, Frank and Herb were embroiled in a lawsuit, and Frank's relationship with Warner Bros. was best illustrated by the slides Frank showed on stage—and, of course, by the T-shirts he sold with the message 'Warner Bros sucks!' In terms of Frank's Dutch friends, I 'took up the baton' from Claude, in a sense. It would be wonderful to have a 'Frank and Claude' book, because the splendid photos that Claude took deserve a publication all of their own.

I met Claude again in 2011, during a project I was producing with Todd Rundgren. At the time, I wasn't aware that this little piece of recording from 1977 would be so prophetic.

CO The name you chose for your new group is just 'Zappa.'

FRANK Yes—like Montrose.

CO Is there a special reason for it?

FRANK Yes, it's easier to remember.

CO Is it?

FRANK You'll always think of the guy sitting on a toilet.

CO Was that a commercial joke?

FRANK Actually, it was an accident. It was designed to be a picture to go with an article in the *International Times*, you remember, that magazine from England? And it was supposed to be used as publicity for our first concert in 1967. But the photographer who took it made a poster and sold it for his own profit, and that poster was bootlegged all over Europe and then eventually went into the United States, and millions of them were sold and I couldn't stop him from doing it.

CO You couldn't?

FRANK No, because in London the photographic copyright laws are different than in the United States. If somebody takes your picture in the US they can't make commercial use out of it without your permission. But in England, if somebody takes your picture, the photographer owns it and he can do what he wants with.

CO When you look at pictures of yourself doing projects with quite large orchestras, like *Lumpy Gravy* or *200 Motels*, you always seem to be quite happy. Do you like working with big orchestras, and if you do—?

FRANK Well, the process of working with an orchestra is very exasperating because orchestras hate music. People in orchestras do not like music, they only like money and they only like their pensions. They couldn't give a fuck about your music, doesn't make any difference whose music it is, they hate music. It's a job, it's just like going in there to saw a piece of wood when they're playing their violins.

CO Are they terrible to work with?

FRANK Yeah, except for one thing. I happen to like the way orchestras sound. And I am crazy enough to put up with that other bullshit just so I can hear something that I write for an instrumental combination. It's more fun to play with a small group that likes what they're doing than to work with the biggest orchestra in the world that's sitting there waiting to collect their pension and take their union break.

Later that afternoon I saw a completely different side to Zappa. Jan Bult wanted to see if he could sell the TV special that Frank had recorded in L.A. (the same KCET special that I'd seen on German television) sliced up in short segments. This triggered Frank's increasing irritation with Warner Bros., while my little tape recorder was still running.

JAN There's one question I would like to ask you. There's a video with animation in it, a beautiful show and I'd like to sell it to Dutch TV. Claude Knobs gives you his regards, he serviced me with a Sony cassette of it, but the thing is we don't have any pop programs that run that long. If I could give you the time that it should run, could you edit it down yourself?

FRANK No.
JAN No way of editing it?
FRANK No way, I will not cut it down.
JAN OK.
FRANK First of all, it's not a pop program. It's a piece of video art! And it shouldn't be judged as a pop program, a pop program is something—
JAN But it's not up to me to judge that.
FRANK But that's—if I was going to sell it to the television station, I would have to explain it to them that way. Just because I'm working in pop music doesn't mean anything in regard to that show, because the music in it isn't especially pop and the video effects that are in it are on a very high artistic level. It's a beautiful show.
JAN It is!
FRANK And when it was shown in France the people went crazy over it.
JAN I know, but the thing is, in our television situation it's very hard to fit it in.
FRANK Well, what can I say?

After a long silence, Frank indicated that I could proceed.

CO Why was 'Black Napkins' censored in, uhm—
FRANK Canada?
CO Yeah.
FRANK Because the guy that put the—You know how they censor, they took a piece of paper tape and put it on the record, and they just covered up 'Black Napkins' and 'The Torture Never Stops.'
CO And they didn't give you any reason?
FRANK Well, they thought that the screams on 'The Torture Never Stops' would arouse Canadians to, uhm—
CO Canadians get aroused by that?
FRANK Yeah, to unwanted heights of passion!
CO And are you allowed to play numbers that have been censored on records, can you play them wherever you like in Canada?

FRANK You mean on the stage?

CO Yeah.

FRANK Of course I play them on the stage. Not only that, we have a tape of the screams from 'The Torture Never Stops' that we use in the concert. It's the second song in the show.

A few hours after my interview, FZ was in the studio with Claude!

After my meeting with Frank, I was in the elevator with Terry Bozzio and Patrick O'Hearn. Talking about Bozzio, Frank had just told me, 'The fact that he is cute doesn't mean he can't play!' I used those exact words (albeit in a different order) in the liner notes to my 2003 CD production with Terry and the Metropole Orkest, conducted by Dick Bakker. The album came out on Favored Nations/NPS OUTPUT, a collaboration between the NPS and Steve Vai's label.

So there it was. I'd met my hero. I had the tapes and the photos. It was another step in what was to become a long journey. The concert the next day was phenomenal, and the last time Frank ever played the Jaap Edenhal. In fact, it was the last time Zappa ever performed in Amsterdam.

1978

Fuck you, Captain Tom!

FEBRUARY 13TH: AFTER AMSTERDAM, ZAPPA WAS BACK IN ROTTERDAM'S AHOY VENUE. The city was blanketed in snow. We were in my uncle's DAF—the car got a flat tire right outside Ahoy, and we missed the first five minutes of the show.

A shirtless Frank appeared onstage. He still believed that 'Ahoy is the stupidest name for a concrete building.' The band was unbelievable, and he introduced us all to his latest discovery: Adrian Belew. I was surprised to see Belew back in Ahoy a few months later, this time featuring on guitar for David

Bowie. Brian Eno later told me that he and Bowie were in the audience that fateful night in Berlin. They hated the show, but Adrian's performance blew them away. Only Adrian knows what really went down, but there's an infamous quote by Zappa, allegedly speaking to Bowie in a restaurant or nightclub in Berlin that they both happened to be surreptitiously visiting at the same time: 'Fuck you, Captain Tom!'

1979

Olive?

ZAPPA WAS WITH CBS BY NOW. Their promotion department had an office in Hilversum, and I was doing a lot of freelance work for the radio. I got an invitation to a press conference on February 26th, in the gorgeous room at the top of the Okura Hotel in Amsterdam. This time, I had a real Nagra instead of my dinky cassette recorder. The room was full of journalists, photographers, and booze. Zappa came in, and someone offered him a drink. He asked for a coffee, but no one had considered that possibility, so one of the CBS guys was sent off to fetch Frank's favorite drink. So much for doing their research. The press conference, scheduled to discuss a few items but mainly to promote the release of the *Sheik Yerbouti* album, was a disaster: the questions were stupid, Frank was bored, and several awkward silences fell. I was sitting next to Frank, and he knew I was a big fan. He asked me why I wasn't asking any questions, and without thinking I gave the best possible answer: that I was there, unpaid and on my own time, to record him for my radio show—but that my show wouldn't be broadcast for a few more weeks. I explained that I didn't want to see his answers to my questions published the next day by journalists who couldn't be bothered to do their homework. Not very supportive of my fellow journalists, perhaps—but it was true. He smiled, and said, 'Come to my hotel later and we'll record it. I can also play you some new tapes with my ghetto blaster.' He told me that his whole band was going to Amsterdam's Carré theater to see the Jacksons perform, and that he was 'of course not going. I'm only here to make music!'

In a nutshell, the press conference went like this:

GIRL Frank, you want an olive?
FRANK No thanks, I had one yesterday. It was really exciting.
CO There have been titles, I think it was in the *Melody Maker*, and one of them was *Zappa Orchestral Favorites*, another one was *Martian Love Games*. Can you tell us what happened to those titles?
FRANK Yeah, an album called *Zappa Orchestral Favorites* is still in the possession of Warner Bros., although they haven't paid me for the tapes. Nor have they paid for the tapes of *Studio Tan*, *Sleep Dirt*, or *Zappa In New York*. I delivered these tapes to them as finished albums in order to conclude my contract with them. And they didn't pay me for them and so there is a lawsuit filed over that, and they still have the tapes for *Zappa Orchestral Favorites* and that probably will be released the next time I release another album on CBS. Just like they released this *Sleep Dirt* album at the same time as *Sheik Yerbouti*.
CO Is it true that the song on *Sleep Dirt*, 'Filthy Habits,' was originally planned for *Zoot Allures*?
FRANK Yeah, and also 'The Ocean Is The Ultimate Solution.' Both of those things—in fact all the material on that album was recorded between '74 and '76.
CO Can you give us more specific details about the personnel on that?
FRANK Yeah, 'Filthy Habits' is me on guitar, Terry Bozzio on drums, and Dave Parlato on bass, and I am doing all the keyboard overdubs and stuff. And 'The Ocean Is The Ultimate Solution' is Bozzio on drums, Patrick O'Hearn on bass, and me on guitar. And 'Regyptian Strut' is Chester Thompson on drums, Bird Legs Youman on bass, Ruth Underwood on percussion, George Duke on keyboards, and Bruce Fowler playing all the horns and stuff. And I am also playing percussion. And on 'Spider Of Destiny' and 'Flambay' and that stuff, it is Ruth and George and Chester and Patrick O'Hearn, overdubbed bass.

CO Is Warner still in possession of the *Martian Love Games* tapes?
FRANK No, no, *Martian Love Secrets* was the original title for the *Sheik Yerbouti* album. I changed the name of the title when they took that picture because I thought that would be a better title for it.
CO Was the name *'Sheik Yerbouti'* something that you made before, or did you do it after seeing the picture?
FRANK Well, I made the name up a long time ago, and when they took that picture and I saw the way it came out, I thought, 'That's what's gonna be on it.'

One of the awkward silences was broken by a rather grim interaction between Frank and one of the other journalists present, who was making a big deal out of the fact that Frank's new vocalist singer Ike Willis was taking over the parts originally sung on the album by Napoleon Murphy Brock. The general argument was that, in the journalist's eyes, Willis was a poor imitation of Brock. After FZ put him down sternly, and defended Willis, it seemed the perfect moment to ask about Zappa's song 'Packard Goose.'

CO Is it true you made a song about rock'n'roll journalists?
FRANK Yeah.
JOURNALIST Like so many other rock'n'roll stars.
FRANK Huh?
JOURNALIST Like so many other rock'n'roll stars!
FRANK Well, it's a good thing to do, you know. It's nice to commemorate them. Because the only other way a rock'n'roll journalist has of being famous is to dress weird, form a group himself, or herself. It's pretty difficult to distinguish yourself with a typewriter, you know. So, it's better just to be an asshole and wait for a group to write a song about you.

Understandably, the silences grew longer and more awkward after that. And then the press conference was over. Frank said, 'See you in the Amstel Hotel.' I asked if I could bring a friend (guitarist Jos Houniet), and Frank replied, 'Sure!'

I announced myself at the hotel that evening, and Jos and I were escorted in by Frank's bodyguard (not Smothers, he was sick). We poured ourselves some coffee and got to talking.

I was making a program for broadcasting station VARA at the time, working for Willem van Beusekom. We kicked off with a station call.

FRANK OK ... hello, this is Frank Zappa talking to you on *ElpeeTuin*.
CO Great! Well, a question that is asked by listeners as well is, 'Why do you never or almost never use the Stratocaster when you are on stage?'
FRANK I have two guitars on stage in case I break a string and it's a different playing style to use a Stratocaster and I'll use it—

[Tape check]

CO Hello, that's OK. You've said in interviews that you like particular guitar players in the past, like Johnny 'Guitar' Watson on some records.
FRANK Mm-hmm.
CO Do you have any new likes in guitar playing nowadays?
FRANK Well, I've heard a few things that I liked. I like some of the stuff that Brian May plays, and I like ... who's the guy that plays with ZZ Top? I like that way he sounds.
CO Mm-hmm?
FRANK That's about it. Oh, there's a jazz musician I think is good, what was his name? Pat Martino.
CO And another item that you talk a lot about in interviews is cynicism, being cynical.
FRANK Mm-hmm?
CO Most people would say that you are very cynical in your lyrics, and the very frequent answer that you give is that being cynical is the only way to survive.
FRANK Well, I think that cynicism is a positive value, and if you think that it's not then that's your misfortune. I think that being cynical is the only rational behavior.

CO Yeah. You also said in a Dutch interview that politics, religion, and items like that is not something that you discuss in public. You still have that opinion? Or—?
FRANK Well, I'll talk about them if I have to, but I always think that it's boring.
CO You just still believe—as you said early in interviews in the '60s and beginning of the '70s, that you still believe in personal freedom?
FRANK I believe that personal freedom starts at home, that is to say if you want to be free it starts inside of you. It's not something that somebody legislates.
CO Mm-hmm . . . and the subjects on the new album, *Sheik Yerbouti*, they're all still very English-orientated. I mean, 'Flakes' is very personal experience-like.
FRANK Mm-hmm.
CO And on other albums you have more things that are more abstract or just made up. And this is, again, real, everyday life. Do you intend to do that more frequently in the future, or what?
FRANK No, I'll do whatever I feel like.
CO Mm-hmm, is that what you always do?
FRANK Yeah.
CO Do you think that—could you tell us about your coming events on CBS or another record company?
FRANK Well—
CO Titles or what?
FRANK What, you mean the name of the next album and stuff like that?
CO Yeah.
FRANK I could tell you, but I'm not going to.
CO Is that because you feel like it? Or is it—?
FRANK It's because you should pay attention to this record and don't worry about the next one.
CO Mm-hmm! Did you . . . the recording and the mixing, was that done in America?
FRANK Yes, the mixing was done in America.

CO And the live tapes that you used were only from the Hammersmith Odeon and some of—?

FRANK No, there's a couple from New York City and two from the Deutschlandhalle in Berlin, and another one from a hall just outside of Nuremberg, and the rest of them are from the Odeon Hammersmith.

CO You did an English tour last month or this month.

FRANK Yeah.

CO That was through England or was it mainly London?

FRANK No, it was through England.

CO And how did the English—

FRANK How did they respond? They responded like English people.

CO How is that?

FRANK Well, English people don't respond. You know, they just kind of sit there. Except for the last audience at the Odeon Hammersmith. They got quite excited. And we also recorded there again.

CO Again?

FRANK Yeah, and we're also recording here in Holland. We're recording all these concerts.

CO You're recording everything you do?

FRANK Yeah.

CO And the big guitar pieces now, from every concert, like 'Rat Tomago'?

FRANK Yeah.

CO And the piece 'Yo Mama'?

FRANK Yeah.

CO Now, I think you just pick the good one from all the concerts and you then put it on the record if you can use it, of course.

FRANK Yeah.

CO That is so?

FRANK Yeah, I mean, there are other ones that are better than that, but they weren't done with that band. I tried to keep only the things that were done with that band. Because there are a lot better ones now that I have on tape.

CO I think the last one you did in Rotterdam last year—

FRANK Yeah.

CO Was very good in 'Yo Mama.'

FRANK Oh yeah?

CO Excellent, yeah.

FRANK I listened to the cassette of it and I don't think that it was as good as the one from Neuenkirchen.

CO No?

FRANK No. Well, it was OK, but not as good as that other one.

CO You told us last year, on stage, that you had some nasty experiences with the direction of the Ahoy Hall. You know, they forced you to have an intermission and stuff like that. How much does that effect your behavior on stage? How much do you worry?

FRANK I don't worry about it, but it interrupts the show. The show is designed to be played straight through, and so at the end of the show there's a certain experience that you have from that.

CO Mm-hmm?

FRANK But if you have to stop it in the middle, and everybody goes out and gets their popcorn, or whatever, and they come back, then you have to start building the show all over again and it interferes with my structure.

CO And tomorrow night, is there another break in there?

FRANK Probably.

CO You don't know yet?

FRANK Don't know yet.

CO It's not planned?

FRANK No.

CO You have a show that's designed again for playing straight through?

FRANK Well, that's the way we always do it. It's always straight through.

CO Yeah, in some shows you have, if you look at the overall buildup of a show, some shows have a very strong comic character.

FRANK Mm-hmm.

CO Like you did in '76, and '77, with the poodle kind of thing and all that. And then again you come back with long instrumental phrases. What do you think the overall buildup will be tomorrow night?

FRANK Well, the structure of this show is basically vocals. There's very little talking to the audience. There is very little instrumental music, because the only solos in the main part of the show are the guitar solos that I play and then one solo that Denny plays.

CO Yeah?

FRANK And other than that it's all vocals and it's mostly songs that people are familiar with. If they know the albums then they'll know these songs. And then about thirty to forty percent of the show is stuff that hasn't been recorded yet.

CO Something that always shows up again is that many people who are really fond of your music and listen to it quite a lot and have all your albums and all that . . . most of the time also like the albums of David Bowie. Do you find any stage appearance—things that you have in common with him? I mean, what do you think in general about his way of making music?

FRANK I don't know anything about it. I've only seen him live one time, and I only stayed for about fifteen minutes. The only records I ever heard of his were singles that were played on the radio.

CO You're not really, uh—

FRANK No.

CO You don't really know his stuff? Your guitar player that you had with you last year went to him.

FRANK Yeah.

CO Did he leave your group for that, or had you finished the tour by that time?

FRANK He went directly to work for Bowie as soon as our tour was done because Bowie offered him twice as much money. Simple American arithmetic.

CO Is Belew an American, by the way?

FRANK Yeah.

CO There have also been letters sent to me and to others at events from a guy in, I believe it was London, who says that there is a very heavy story behind the inside cover of your *Live In New York* album. He says that there is some sort of religious message behind that. I mean, do you put things like that in your covers?

FRANK Absolutely not. Don't believe anything an English person tells you, and especially anything an English person tells you about me.

CO They have a very characteristic and own way of responding to your—everything you do.

FRANK What, the English?

CO Yeah.

FRANK Yeah, they do, they are really specialized.

CO You called them once 'the most eccentric, the only real eccentric people that there is.'

FRANK No, I think that I would modify that to say that there are probably a few eccentric people elsewhere in the world, but I think that there's probably more eccentric people per square foot in that country than any place else. Except for Los Angeles, and the number has gone up in Los Angeles because so many English people have moved there.

CO What we would like to ask you is, the fretless guitar I talked to you about earlier this afternoon—

FRANK Yeah.

CO What type was it?

FRANK It was a prototype that was made by, you know the Acoustic amplifier company?

CO Mm-hmm?

FRANK At one time they tried to make guitars, and this was a prototype for a fretless guitar that they wanted to manufacture. And I found it in a store in Hollywood, I paid seventy-five dollars for it. The guy says, 'I'll sell it to you but you have to take the name off.' You know? Because the company didn't want anybody to know that—because they didn't make any more after that, it was never popular, you see. So they took this chisel and scratched the name off the end and I bought it.

CO This latest album is very—it has a very direct sound. I mean, the *Studio Tan* album and the *Sleep Dirt* album, as for the selection on them, seem just music, but some vocals on this album seem like you are just standing in the room with us and talking to us. For instance, at the end of 'Dancin' Fool,' how do you do that? Is it just very—?

FRANK Well, one way that—one reason why the Warner Bros. records don't sound right is because they have the master tapes, but they don't have the master tones. You know what that is?

CO No.

FRANK A tone is a . . . well, when you go to put the tape onto the disc, you have to align the machine that's playing back the tape to a set of specifications so that the sound coming off of that playback machine onto the disc is correct. And you do this with a piece of tape called the master tones, and they don't have the master tones. Moreover, I wasn't there in the disc-cutting room at the time that the discs were cut, so I couldn't supervise it and I couldn't make it perfect, see? They just took the tapes, didn't pay me, and made these records out of it. And so they don't sound as good as the stuff that I spend all my time working on. On the *Sheik Yerbouti* album, I did everything up to the point where it goes to the factory, I'm with it all the way. When they are putting it on the disc I'm there putting the final touches on it. And that's why it sounds that way.

CO They didn't pay you for those albums?

FRANK No, they haven't.

CO No?

FRANK Nope.

CO But there's still a lawsuit going on isn't there? That's what I understood.

FRANK Yes, it's still going on.

CO You've also said in interviews when some journalist was talking about you about the Wild Man Fischer things, and the Lenny Bruce tapes—

FRANK Mm-hmm?

CO That you are also planning an album about the killing of John F. Kennedy. What ever happened to that?

FRANK No, it wasn't the—it was the killing of Robert Kennedy.

CO Robert Kennedy.

FRANK A man came to us with some tapes. He had been making a documentary album about the assassination of Robert Kennedy, and he'd interviewed all these people and he put together this really fantastic album. That was when we had the Bizarre label. And the deal with Warner Bros. on the Bizarre label was, we could bring projects to them and they had the right to refuse 'em.

CO Mm-hmm?

FRANK And they heard that and refused it, and that's why it never came out.

CO Were they too afraid of—?

FRANK They were afraid of it. Yeah.

CO The effects it could eventually have?

FRANK Yeah, they wouldn't touch it.

CO I think you were sorry about that, weren't you?

FRANK Well, I think everybody should have been sorry about it. It was a pretty frightening album. I mean, it's not something that's gonna make the hit parade, but it had a lot of interesting things in there that you didn't know before. But Warners wouldn't touch it, they wouldn't distribute it.

CO I've also read that with the Lenny Bruce tapes there would be intermissions between his talking, played by your old Mothers formation.

FRANK No, in the Lenny Bruce tapes the original idea that was offered to me in around 1966, when we were recording with MGM, they had some Lenny Bruce tapes and they wanted me to make music to go with the tapes so they could release an album that was *Lenny Bruce & The Mothers*, you see? And I thought about it and I said, 'That man doesn't need my music to make his ideas go,' so I refused to do it.

CO Yeah, that's why—And you only brought out one album on your label, only the *Berkeley*?

FRANK Yeah.

CO And what's the original title for that? *Our Man In Nevada*?

FRANK *Our Man In Nirvana*.

CO Nirvana?

FRANK Yeah.

CO Or is that something different?

FRANK No, *Our Man In Nirvana* was the title for the album that they wanted me to do with music.

CO With the Mothers?

FRANK Yeah.

CO You still own the name 'Mothers' of course, but do you have any intention of using that again?

FRANK No.

CO That's finished?

FRANK That's right. That's for the archives now.

CO And you must have a lot of material recorded in those days. What's going to happen with that if the Mothers is for the archives now?

FRANK Well, maybe there'll be a Mothers archive recording.

CO But you're not intending to do anything with them?

FRANK No.

CO And the original nine- or ten-record set that you were going to bring out, were there unreleased items included?

FRANK Oh, it was all unreleased.

CO It was all unreleased?

FRANK Yeah. In fact, I have cassettes of some of that stuff here.

CO But that's for later times, isn't it?

FRANK Yeah, that's for a later time.

CO Do you intend to release records on a Zappa Records label? Or is that for other products?

FRANK Well, the way my contract goes is Zappa Records is for the US and Canada, and the deal with CBS states that the first three must be on a CBS label and then after that they may come out on the Zappa label if I want. It would still be distributed by CBS.

CO In Europe?

FRANK Yes.

CO And Phonogram will still take care of it in America?

FRANK Yeah.

CO You said at the press conference this afternoon that there won't be much guitar playing by you tomorrow night. I mean, not as much as we're used to.

FRANK Well, it depends on how much you want to hear, you know. The show opens up with me playing guitar—I play for eight to ten minutes, roughly. And then we start the show, I introduce the members of the band, and then we play a series of songs. And about the fifth song I'll play a short solo, and then there'll be one more vocal, and then on the next song there is a medium-length solo. And there's two or three more vocals and then there's a little longer solo, and that's it.

CO And the other guitar playing is done by the other members of the group?

FRANK Yeah.

CO How many guitarists do you have? Three?

FRANK Three besides me, yeah, total of four. Sometimes I play a solo at the end of the show—it just depends on what the audience wants.

CO Yeah, I think they'll want.

FRANK You think they'll want?

CO Yeah. You said that to the guy that asked you about your guitar playing, you said, 'Do you think there's any demand for me playing guitar?' and he said, 'Well . . . ' And you said there's a demand for hearing what's on the record.

FRANK Mm-hmm.

CO I very much doubt that. I think there *is* a big demand for you playing guitar, even if it's something not on the record. I mean, if you saw the reaction of the people with the response last year when you played 'Yo Mama' for the first time in Europe, I mean in Holland—

FRANK Well, I couldn't tell. I mean, I can't—

CO That they were quite hilarious about that. So do you really believe there's not a demand?

FRANK I don't think that there's a same kind of demand. I think that maybe you like it, and maybe *you* like it, and maybe ten other people like it, but most of the people in the audience are there for something else. They want a show. They don't have the patience to sit there and figure out what I'm doing. You know? And I'm not gonna jump around and do all the rest of the stupid stuff that other guitar players do. If I play, I just want to play my notes and get it over with.

CO Yeah, that's important, of course.

FRANK Yeah, but see, if the show isn't like a show then a lot of people get bored with it. The largest percentage of the audience—

[Jos offers a Marlboro]

FRANK No thanks ... I'll have this American swill here. The largest percentage of the audience would rather see something that was more like amusement, you know? I mean, I like to play the guitar, I really enjoy doing it. But I don't want to play the guitar and bore people with it. Because most of them spent a lot of money to buy a ticket and they want to have a good time.

CO So you also include quite a vast number of recognizable things in your shows?

FRANK Well yeah, play a lot of stuff, especially in *this* show, there is a lot of songs that they'll recognize.

CO The critics I read on the Knebworth festival, but again that is an English reaction, is that they were quite surprised when you had an encore that was a new song. Because they said, 'Well, all the old groups played their old favorites and there came Zappa on stage and he played a new song.' I believe it was 'Bamboozled By Love' you played as an encore. And they were quite shocked at that, because you didn't play 'Muffin Man' or 'Camarillo Brillo' or anything—

FRANK We're trying not to do those songs anymore, you know? I'm tired of doing 'em. I mean, if we're playing in a place for the first time and somebody requests it, maybe I'll do it. Just because it's the first time the people in the city have seen the group, and so if they want to hear it, OK. But all the cities that we've come back to year after year, I mean, we've been playing 'Camarillo' and 'Muffin Man' and all that stuff for, what, three or four years over here? So we have some different songs for encores now.

CO The first thing the members of the group have to play when they are first in your band, is that 'Peaches En Regalia' for an audition or anything?

FRANK No, the first thing that they play, the auditions that we held this year, the first thing they had to play was this little vamp figure in 21. 21/8.

And if they could play that then they got on to the next step, which was I show 'em a piece of music and see if they can read. And if they can read, then they go on to the next step, which is to see whether or not they can sing. And then they go to the next step, which is to see whether or not they got a sense of humor, and then the next step is to find out whether or not, if they're a rhythm section player, whether they can play a background that's comfortable for me to play a guitar solo on. And then after they pass those tests, then we try the next person and see how he does, and then we evaluate it like that. But I mean, the criteria for picking somebody to be in the band varies from tour to tour, depending on what kind of material is going to be on that tour.

CO About the Pignose [amp], you use it on 'The Torture,' isn't it?

FRANK Yeah.

CO How do you use it? With two microphones in front of it?

FRANK What I did on 'The Torture' is I took the Pignose and I put it in the echo chamber, the live echo chamber in the studio, and sent the signal through the echo 'send' directly into the Pignose, and then had two microphones in the echo chamber to pick it up.

CO It's a cool thing, the Pignose.

FRANK Yeah, I think so.

CO I think so. Can we—? Uhm, I see we're running out of tape. Before it's too late, can you give a final message to your regular listeners what they can expect, what they cannot expect and—?

FRANK Well, one thing I'm working on now that may surprise everybody is a guitar album. That's going to be available by mail order only.

CO Where?

FRANK Well, all over the world, it's called *Shut Up 'N Play Your Guitar*. And all it is is guitar solos. You know, all those tapes from all over the world?

CO Mm-hmm.

FRANK Well, I'm throwing the songs away and just keeping the guitar solos, and it's one guitar solo after another. If you wanna hear me play the guitar—

CO You're serious, what you're telling me?

FRANK Yeah!

CO Yeah?

FRANK Yeah!

CO So that's the response for the demand of your guitar playing?

FRANK Yeah.

CO Yeah?

FRANK Yeah! So you can get it through the mail.

CO That's a very good idea!

FRANK Yeah.

CO Not on a certain label.

FRANK I'll probably put it on NCP.

CO What . . .?

FRANK Stands for 'No Commercial Potential.'

[Tape ends]

Thanks to Frank, I learned long ago that there's no such thing as a coincidence. The whole time I knew him, the strangest things would keep happening. When we spoke at the Amstel Hotel, we discussed the song 'Flakes' from *Sheik Yerbouti*, in which a toilet explodes—you're not supposed to flush tampons. At precisely that moment, FZ's bodyguard interrupted us. He had Gail on the phone, Frank's wife.

A few minutes later, Frank came back into the room and announced that he was 'pissed off.' Gail had told him about of one of the toilets in their home that was blocked, and it had exploded. It had damaged some irreplaceable pieces of film downstairs. He didn't stay pissed off for long though (coffee and a cigarette helped), and he played a primitive version of 'Dupree's Paradise' for Jos and me. From a cassette, on a ghetto blaster, next to a two-liter thermos.

Our conversation was interrupted a few times by the telephone. Four times, Frank said, 'Not now, I'm talking to a friend.' Right before we left, Frank tore a page out of a notepad, wrote his initials and an address on it, and told me, 'At this address, there's always a cup of coffee waiting for you.'

What? I was invited to Frank Zappa's home? Yep!

I was walking on air as we returned to the lobby, where we met a man who appeared to be aggrieved for some reason. It turned out to be the vice president of CBS, who'd wanted to say hello to Frank. He'd called the room four times, and after two hours he finally got his turn.

1980

Working for Zappa

THE YEAR BEGAN WITH A SURPRISE. I knew that FZ would be touring with a new band, and that the tour was scheduled for the spring. VARA had even been talking to Zappa's management about recording one of the shows for radio.

One afternoon in January, I arrived home to hear the phone ringing. My father answered, and then (laconic as always) informed me, 'I have Zappa's manager on the phone for you.'

I dashed to the phone. I was in the middle of saying, 'Hello, this is Co,' when I heard a click and Zappa himself broke in with, 'Is this Co? Hey, Co—wanna see a movie?'

As is turned out, he was in Amsterdam for a press screening of *Baby Snakes* in the Movies on Haarlemmerdijk. I sat down with around thirty others and spent the next three and a half hours watching the partially animated movie. It included footage of a Halloween show from '77, with the same band as had played Ahoy in '78—with a bunch of special guests. I was honored to have been invited personally, of course, and I took the opportunity to record another short conversation with FZ, boasting a new, short hairstyle.

CO I just wrote some short things down. Would you mind speaking a bit in there, because there is very much background noise?

FRANK OK. Hello, hello, hello, hello.

CO First, about the film. I read an interview where it was in the title *Baby Snakes—Gas Masks* that there was Warner Bros. money in, is that true?

FRANK No. The only money that's in the film is *my* money.

CO No CBS—?

FRANK No. I paid for the whole thing myself.

CO I've heard that you are going to do a piece—some pieces with a big orchestra in Holland. Which one is that? And when is it happening?

FRANK There is no definite plan to do that and it's better not to talk about that until there's a contract.

CO Do you mind if I talk about *Joe's Garage*?

FRANK Sure!

CO A lot of Zappa-listening friends of mine say that the atmosphere of *Lumpy Gravy* is on the album. How do you feel about it? I mean, it's—*2* and *3* are mostly old songs on there.

FRANK No.

CO I mean, things that you have been doing—?

FRANK No, there is only two old songs on *2* and *3*. One of them is 'Token Of My Extreme' and the other is 'Stick It Out.'

CO You did that in Holland—?

FRANK Yeah.

CO There has been a radio broadcast by Carlos Hagen, the producer who broadcasted some of your pre-Mothers work. A piece called 'Opus 5.'

FRANK Yeah.

CO Do you have any plans to bring that period of your career to the attention of the listeners again?

FRANK No.

CO But there's very—I mean, how old were you when you did that 'Opus 5' concert?

FRANK About twenty, twenty-one.

CO I mean, it's hard to find, nowadays, composers who have an output like that by twenty or twenty-one, so it's very—

FRANK Yup, it's hard to find 'em, but they're around.

CO Do you still write music inspired by that period?

FRANK No.

CO I mean, it was a very hard period for you with the—

FRANK I don't write in that style anymore.

CO No chamber music?

FRANK Very little.

CO There was some in this film, I mean things you conduct—

FRANK Oh, conducting? Oh yeah. Well if you call that chamber music, sure.

CO You've talked about, in Dutch papers, about a nine- or ten-record set.

FRANK Yes.

CO Is that going to be released?

FRANK Not this year.

CO Not this year?

FRANK No.

CO Because the thing that I read is that there is such an album on sale in Australia.

FRANK No.

CO That is not genuine?

FRANK Not true.

CO It's called—the title that they gave, probably a bootleg I think, but the title that they gave to it is *The History And Collective Improvisations Of The Mothers Of Invention*. Is that the title of the nine-record set you are going to release?

FRANK Yup.

CO So that's a fake.

FRANK Yes.

CO *Record Review*, the magazine, there was a review of *Läther*. You broadcasted it on the air, somewhere in America—

FRANK Yeah.

CO I can't remember where. All the titles that were mentioned are titles that we know. Are those the same versions?

FRANK Some are the same, some are not.

CO Which ones aren't?

FRANK 'Broken Hearts Are For Assholes,' 'Trying To Grow A Chin,' that's all the different ones.

CO You made a promise last year to me.

FRANK What's that?

CO That you would play 'Suicide Chump' in Rotterdam.

FRANK [laughs] Well, I can't remember whether we did or not, did we?

CO You didn't! [laughs]

FRANK Well, sorry. [laughs]

CO You also said something about a—about a guitar album which I can't remember if it was a joke—

FRANK No, it's real.

CO It's real?

FRANK Yeah. It's called *Shut Up 'N Play Yer Guitar*.

CO I've been looking all—It's a mail-order one?

FRANK It hasn't come out yet.

CO When do you think we should look out in the papers for it?

FRANK Maybe by April.

CO And it's a mail order one?

FRANK Yup.

CO We see Bozzio in the film, very nice part. And we see him on *Joe 2* and *3*.

FRANK Yeah.

CO Do you think he will be back to be a drummer with your band again?

FRANK Probably not.

CO You still have Vinnie Colaiuta.

FRANK Yeah.

CO You said, about Colaiuta, that you have a very sensitive feeling with him playing rhythmic with you, and you understand each other very much.

FRANK Yeah.

CO Do you plan to do things with him in the studio, like you did with Bozzio, for instance *Zoot Allures*?

FRANK Yes.

CO And when can we expect the next output?

FRANK The next normal release won't be until September.

CO Have you figured out a title yet for that?

FRANK No.

CO There's a book called *No Commercial Potential.* You know it, of course—

FRANK Yes.

CO By David Walley.

FRANK Mm-hmm.

CO All the quotes in there, are they to be taken seriously? Are they genuine?

FRANK I don't know, because I'm not responsible for all the quotes in there. There are quotes from other people.

CO Yeah.

FRANK I don't know if they are genuine or not. And knowing what kind of a person David Walley is, I wouldn't trust anything in that book.

CO You don't—?

FRANK No, it's a piece of shit.

CO Because he had the Voice of Cheese and even your father was in—

FRANK Yeah sure. That's an exploitation book.

CO You advise your regular listeners not to buy it?

FRANK No, don't buy it and don't believe it.

CO Shankar's record was released.

FRANK It was released in the United States but not here.

CO Oh, I must have an import then. Why wasn't it released here? It's a great album.

FRANK It *is* a nice album. But Phonogram didn't promote it in the United States and it was a flop and they didn't release it over here.

CO There's vocals on there by Stucco Homes.

FRANK Yeah, that's me and Ike.

CO That's you and Ike together?

FRANK Mm-hmm.

CO Are you going to put that song, even though you've put it on Shankar's new album, are you going to record 'Dead Girls Of London' for your own album?

FRANK No. I have a recording of it, but I don't think I'll release it.

CO Don't you think that for people who want to enjoy your music, like *Joe's Garage*, completely and even—*especially* this film? Don't you think that they should have a very large knowledge of music, not only yours but also things that you quote musically, things that you quote in interviews?

FRANK It would help, but it's not imperative.

CO Could you give any examples to start with?

FRANK Things that you should have heard?

CO Yeah.

FRANK Bulgarian folk music, Tibetan music, music of Edgard Varèse, music of Anton Webern.

CO But what I want to know is, when does your Varèse book come out? Because you talk so specifically about—

FRANK I have no intention of writing a book on Varèse.

CO You don't think it would be good if—as publicity for his material, if you wrote a book about him?

FRANK No, I'm not qualified to do it, and I don't feel like writing a book.

CO You said that to BBC radio once. That you loved novels, described a novelist to us.

FRANK I'm not very fond of books. They are for other people, not for me.

CO Also not the books by Cage?

FRANK Well, I can read a Cage book and get some laughs out of it, but I wouldn't devote my life to reading his books, or anybody else's books.

CO Is it true that there is another *Lumpy Gravy* album on sale?

FRANK Not that I know of.

CO I've heard—I've read interviews in which you said that there's a *Lumpy Gravy* album, probably bootleg, but from studio tapes, that is longer and there's no spoken material in it.

FRANK No, no, no. I know what you're talking about. When *Lumpy Gravy* was first done it was done for Capitol Records, and there was no talking in it. And it's not longer, it's shorter.

CO Shorter?

FRANK Yeah.

CO It's not extra music?

FRANK There may be some extra pieces in there, but there's no talking in it.

CO The things you're going to do in Vienna or in Holland, is it like *Lumpy Gravy*, or like *Orchestral Favorites*, or neither?

FRANK Neither.

CO Could you give a description of—?

FRANK No.

CO What to expect?

FRANK No.

CO There's another thing. When I interviewed you last time in your hotel room in Amsterdam, your wife was on the phone—

FRANK Yeah, and the toilet just blew up in the basement, again.

CO A lot of damage?

FRANK It's fixed now.

CO It's fixed now? Some flake—?

FRANK Some film was damaged, yeah, because of a flake.

CO When is your next tour?

FRANK In April in the United States.

CO And here?

FRANK Maybe in the summer.

CO I've been trying to form a percussion ensemble that I wanted to play some of your music in our school for study material—

FRANK Yeah?

CO It seems impossible to get written material by you.

FRANK It's not impossible, but it is difficult. Because some people in Holland already have it.

CO They *have* it?

FRANK Yes.

CO Louis, for instance?

FRANK Yeah.

CO But he is, of course, not permitted to give copies of it.

FRANK If you wanna play the percussion parts ask him, I'll give you permission. Go ahead.

CO Great! That's nice. Because there's only one book called the *Frank Zappa Songbook Vol. 1*.

FRANK Yeah, and there's no percussion in it.

CO No, it's only—

FRANK Piano parts and—

CO Yeah, and some transcribed clarinet parts I once tried to play, they are nice. You said also in our last interview that you're not into phase music.

FRANK No.

CO But the interviewer failed to ask you what your musical objections were.

FRANK To phase music?

CO Yeah.

FRANK It's not an objection, it's just not my idea of fun. You know, I wouldn't listen to phase music for recreational purposes. I don't say it's bad, it's not my kind of music.

CO And that includes all the famous minimal music composers?

FRANK No. Well, my most favorite minimal composer right now is The Flying Lizards.

It was getting busy in the foyer of the Movies by that time, and it was clear to me that Frank considered his visit to be a proper 'promotional tour.' He missed playing with the band, and the sense that he was getting from many of the journalists was that the film was too long—and to an extent I agree. It truly is a film for diehard fans. While the music is amazing, Zappa's decision, as on his other audio/visual projects, not to involve a professional director leaves the film far from perfect.

Still, it was a wonderful afternoon. I'd seen *Baby Snakes* and I left with an original poster from the premiere at the Victoria Theater in New York.

This time, it would only be a matter of months before I saw him again. Zappa gave VARA Radio permission to record his upcoming concert in Ahoy, on two conditions: he wanted copies of all the multi-tracks, and he wanted me personally to mix the radio show. I was stunned! I wasn't even sure if he knew that I had connections to VARA through my father, but it didn't matter—of course I agreed, and promised to do the very best job I could with the mix.

Due to scheduling conflicts, the engineers from public broadcaster NOS couldn't record the show. This created a problem: at the time, because of union rules, they were contractually obligated to handle recordings for public radio. Fortunately, the people involved managed to find a solution: the recording truck would be provided by the Mirasound studio, but NOS would still need to supply the engineer. Eventually, the choice fell on my neighbor, Erik van Es.

Frank had given me an 'access all areas' pass for the tour, and I spent the whole afternoon watching the soundcheck. I met Tommy Mars and Ike Willis, and had another enjoyable encounter with FZ's big Baltimorean bodyguard, John Smothers. To sit in an empty Ahoy and watch this band rehearse was better than drugs!

The concert was recorded without a hitch. *Polygoon Journaal* (a Dutch news show that ran in movie theaters) did a special segment on the show, and reported that Zappa dedicated one tune to 'a Dutch girl.' Of course, the fans knew that he was referring to a blowup doll.

Before FZ started his rehearsals in Ahoy, I arranged an interview with him the next day in the Sonesta Hotel. When I told this to John Smothers, his bodyguard and, if you ask me, his friend also, he let me into FZ's room without any problems.

Frank, dressed in a purple outfit, was smoking quietly. Part of his suite was being prepared for a meeting with some people from the Holland Festival, so he told me to join him on the large bed.

I started my tape recorder.

CO I was delighted to hear all those old songs last night. But there was also a new one. I thought it was about dope, wasn't it?

FRANK Oh yeah, 'Charlie's Enormous Mouth.'

CO It was very hard for me to follow everything. I thought it was about cocaine, right?

FRANK Yes, it's about a girl whose nose rots off and then she dies from snorting too much cocaine.

CO That's one of the first on that, huh? You were more active about the subject in interviews than in songs.

FRANK Yeah, but see, it really doesn't do any good because when we play that song in the United States, as soon as we say the word 'nose,' half the people in the audience start cheering. They don't listen to the words.
CO You still feel the same about touring England? You are never very positive about touring through that country.
FRANK Well, we're only playing in London. Outside of London it's OK, I really don't care for London.
CO You're playing the same hall there?
FRANK No, we're playing Wembley. Two nights.
CO Remember the press conference in the Sonesta?
FRANK Yeah, I remember.
CO The way you say that—you didn't like it, huh?
FRANK Well, let it be known that I'm no longer doing any interviews for magazines or newspapers. I'll do television and I'll do radio but I'm not going to do any more interviews with magazines or newspapers.
CO Why?
FRANK Because I'm just tired of having people change things around that I say and use me for their own purpose. I don't wanna have anything to do with it anymore.
CO Is that a Dutch affair?
FRANK It's worldwide. I'm going to have more spare time to enjoy myself and less time to sit around at places like the Okura talking to people asking stupid questions. I have a meeting in the other room now.

I bade goodbye to Frank, Smothers, and a beautiful redhead who was there also. I left the room and passed Holland Festival director Frans de Ruiter and composer Louis Andriessen, who were patiently waiting outside.

Frank had made some comments during the interview about labor unions. In retrospect, they proved to be prophetic.

I'm still not sure whether it was deliberate, but the noise reduction system that Mirasound used, Telcom, wasn't compatible with DBX, which was one of its major competitors at the time. The upshot was that the mix needed to be done at Mirasound, and not 'exclusively' at NOS. So, a few weeks later, I traveled to Wijhe, where Mirasound had its studios. I was accompanied by VARA producer Louis Verschuur and Erik van Es, who'd done the engineering. The fact that I knew the music backwards and forwards saved us all a great deal of time.

Per Frank's orders, a few unusual instrument combinations had been recorded together on the same track, rather than as a true multitrack. I think Frank probably gave this instruction so we wouldn't have a recording that was close to 'album quality.' Louis left the heavy lifting to Erik and myself. After the recording was broadcast (including a now legendary 'Easy Meat' guitar solo), it quickly gained popularity as a bootleg. Nowadays it can be found on the Internet without much difficulty.

The issue of the labor unions led to an interesting situation. Because of the quality of the concert and its broadcasted recording, and because NOS was less than amused with how it came about (even though NOS was in fact to blame for what happened), Willem van Beusekom was forced to deliver the following message during his show *ElpeeTuin*:

> *We do not wish to disguise that we believe the following program, which is a recording of Frank Zappa's concert, was wrongfully recorded in breach of section 25 of the Dutch Broadcasting Act. Because we have no desire for any disagreement with our fellow technicians, and certainly don't wish to interfere with anyone's job security, and because we don't wish to withhold the Zappa concert from the radio public, I have the following statement to make on behalf of the technicians and engineers united in [trade union federation] FNV: The following program was realized using facilities not provided by NOS. NOS's technicians and engineers maintain that this is in breach of section 25 of the Dutch Broadcasting Act, and consider it to pose a threat to their job security. This broadcast is against the wishes of the NOS technicians and engineers.*

The entire concert was then broadcast in full: the first full broadcast of a Zappa show in the Netherlands.

Later that summer, on June 9th, I was in Düsseldorf with my German friend Bettina and with Jos Houniet. At the soundcheck (I still had my all-access pass) I ran into Frank, Smothers and, by chance, Coy Featherstone. As I recalled every detail of that evening in the Pulitzer in 1977, I started to realize that I was becoming part of the 'in' crowd.

1981

Dangerous precedents

DUTCH FANS WERE AMAZED AND DELIGHTED TO LEARN THAT ZAPPA AND HIS ORCHESTRAL MUSIC WOULD FEATURE PROMINENTLY AT THE HOLLAND FESTIVAL THAT YEAR. The finances and the programming had already been agreed, and because (to the fans who remembered) *200 Motels* was almost a Dutch production anyway, the idea that all this was actually happening was slightly surreal.

One thing that anyone knew who had any dealings with Frank: he wasn't easy. He was always honest, and above all, a deal was a deal. So, when the Holland Festival's De Ruiter and Andriessen informed him that the orchestra was demanding royalties—even though Zappa also had invested a significant amount of his own money—it seemed that the whole deal was off. And Zappa canceled the whole thing there and then. A deal was a deal.

Of course I was disappointed—every Zappa fan in the Netherlands was! To my surprise, however, not much later I received a letter, signed by Frank himself, with reference 'FZ/sr.' 'SR,' it turned out, was Frank's assistant and secretary Susan Rubio, who was to become my friend also.

Dated April 22nd, the letter read,

> *As you must know by now, the orchestral performance in Holland has been cancelled due to the greed of the musicians in the orchestra who demanded a royalty on the recordings of the concerts. No matter how much I might want to hear my music performed by an orchestra, there*

is no reason why I should set a dangerous precedent. As far as I am concerned, they can all go fuck themselves. As long as I have control over my music catalogue, none of my performances will be allowed to be performed by that particular orchestra in Holland. Anyway, see you on the next trip over. Keep up the good work.

Your friend,
Frank Zappa.

Signed by the man himself.

1982

Rubio & Vai

THROUGH FRANK, I MET TWO WONDERFUL PEOPLE WHO ARE STILL VERY CLOSE FRIENDS OF MINE. One of them is Susan Rubio, the 'SR' referenced in Frank's letter. I got a phone call from her early in the year. She told me that she was Frank's private secretary, and that she was going on her first European vacation in the spring. Frank thought it would be a good idea if she hung out with me for a few days to acclimate. It was some years before I told her that Frank had phoned in person, asking me to keep an eye out for her, as she was traveling for the first time. She stayed with me in May 1982, and soon became close with my family. I took her to the ten-yearly flower show Floriade in Amsterdam, and we visited other tourist destinations and became firm friends. In May, Frank was performing in Ahoy again, and I met Steve Vai for the first time. This other 'lifelong friendship' had a tremendous impact on me also, although it didn't make itself felt for some years yet.

It was becoming clear to me gradually that my relationship with Frank would be peppered with what I can best describe as 'anecdotes'—I'd already abandoned the word 'coincidences.' In 1982, Frank played a few covers, and one of them was 'Mary Lou,' a 1950 release by Young Jessie. Frank had sent me a cassette of live recordings by the new band, including that piece. I made another radio-special specially for Willem van Beusekom at VARA, as a promotion for Frank's concert in Ahoy.

I was doing a bit of production work at that time too. The label Turning Point Records gave me my first opportunity to become a *real* record producer, working for acts like Dutch jazz singer Soesja Citroen. Turning Point was run by two colorful guys—an organizational specialist named Bart Baayens, and his buddy Jasing B. Chu, who was also a hotelier.

Mr. Chu's hotel De Waterwolf, in Loosdrecht, was a hotspot for weirdos and creative types. One sunny day in May, I'd arranged to meet with him to talk about a new project. It was only ten minutes away from my place by bike, and I got there early. Mr. Chu was still in a meeting, but his assistant told me to grab a beer in the bar, and he'd be back shortly to collect me for my meeting. I sat, drank my beer, and listened to the cassette Frank had sent of the new band. My Walkman was on full blast, and I didn't realize when an older, well-dressed, very Black gentleman sat down next to me with a beer of his own. When the encores had finished playing, the last being 'Mary Lou,' I took off my headphones and noticed my new neighbor for the first time. I nodded in greeting.

'I could hear that song leaking from your headphones,' he said.

'It was the new Frank Zappa band,' I replied.

'You like that last song?'

'I do!'

'I'm glad, because I wrote it!'

I was sitting next to Obie Jessie, known at the time as Young Jessie. He was in the middle of a short tour with jazz pianist René van Helsdingen. He told me how moved he'd been, sitting in on Zappa's rehearsals in Los Angeles and hearing what Frank had done with 'Mary Lou.' He also told me he'd heard Zappa's version on the radio in a taxi the week before. He'd also heard the show I'd made for Willem. When I told Frank all this in 1984, he said, 'I'm not surprised, that's just a Co thing.'

That year, Frank stayed at the Sonesta Hotel in Amsterdam, and I recorded another conversation for radio the day after the show.

CO Were you excited when you played your solo on 'Zomby Woof' last night?

FRANK No.

CO You weren't?

FRANK Well, it's not that I'm bored, but that just isn't my favorite style to play in. Because the rhythm is so strict. If I have to choose between a song where the rhythm is very stiff or where the rhythm is free, I'll take the free rhythm. I'd rather play on 'Zoot Allures' than on 'Zomby Woof.'

CO Were you surprised by the reaction to the *Guitar* box?

FRANK In some countries, yes, some countries no. I was surprised it did well in France, and uhm—you know, I think it did well anyplace.

CO Did it sell better than *You Are What You Is*?

FRANK Oh yeah! That album didn't sell many copies at all.

CO It's a great album.

FRANK Yes, but you have to remember that *Hot Rats* didn't sell well either in the USA. It came into the charts at number 90 for one week then disappeared.

CO I read on the inside cover of the *Guitar* album that there is gonna be a book with sheet music.

FRANK They're working on it right now. The guitar solos from *Shut Up 'N Play Yer Guitar* are all written down and there is gonna be a book about two hundred pages of that music—I don't know how we are gonna distribute it yet.

CO What happened to the film *Baby Snakes*?

FRANK It's gonna be a while before it comes out. Probably it won't come out in theatres in Europe. I made two television shows out of it. They are being offered for sale now.

CO So in the USA it's in the cinemas?

FRANK No, not yet, because I have no more money to work on it.

CO I thought the version I saw was the final version?

FRANK Yes, but there is one problem in the USA. If you make a film and somebody in a scene whistles a tune and it is not your song, you have to pay money to the person who wrote that song. In *Baby Snakes* there are thirty songs by other people—maybe two *seconds* each of somebody whistling or humming it. You have to pay each of those composers, which I did—except for this one guy who wrote one song that is in *one* scene, who refuses to give permission to have it used. A song called 'Smoke Gets In Your Eyes,' an old song . . . and the copyright owner demands that it will be removed from the film, otherwise he'll sue me . . . but in order to take that one song out of the film which lasts about three *seconds* it will cost me fifty thousand to a hundred thousand dollars to chop the movie up. So that's a problem in the USA.

CO You sent me this letter about the Holland Festival—

FRANK The reason why the people from that particular orchestra give out wrong information about it is because they don't wanna let people know how fucked they are, and that they have to cover it up to let it look like something other than what it was. It was a case of pure union greed, just like in the USA or in any country where unions think they're fantastic . . . *Fuck unions* is what I got to say. Ultimately what all unions do is tend to cheapen and make boring the . . . uh . . . life and the quality of the community. The way it works is that whenever somebody in a union says, 'We are going on a strike and get more money'—they think that when they win the strike they have succeeded. But they never do, because the person they are getting the money from turns around and charges even more money to the consumers of the goods. In the USA, where the automobile workers go on strike to get more money—'OK, fine, we'll give you more money.' But then the guy who owns the factory raises the price of the car even more! *And* makes a profit off the strike. The person who loses is the consumer, and the union members themselves are consumers. It's a fantasy—union members listening to union leaders who will say, 'We go on strike and make more money' are just fucking themselves in the *nose* and they don't even know it. . . . The guy who already got all the money is still gonna have the money . . . you don't change that overnight . . . if you are a laborer and you wanna join a union, OK. Maybe you need to stick together so you can get a fair pay for digging the ditch, but if you're in the business of making *music*, I think the *music* should come first.

SMOTHERS The press conference is ready.
CO May I join you?
FRANK Sure!

So I went to another room in the hotel, where the journalists had gathered together, and Frank was giving interviews.

Later that year, I discovered that Frank had edited the famous 1981 Halloween show at Palladium (with the band with Steve Vai in it) into shorter TV specials, and wanted to bring it to the attention of the Dutch broadcasters. Frank promised to send me the tapes, but I heard nothing for some time. On October 7th, a letter arrived, with 'Glotzer Management' on the letterhead:

> *Dear Co,*
>
> *I can't apologize enough for the immense delay in your receiving this material. At this time I am only able to send you 'The Torture Never Stops' on American line system videotape, but Bennett assures me it shouldn't be too much of a problem for you to see it in this format. I HOPE THIS IS THE CASE. I am trying to get Swedish Television to send you 'YOU ARE WHAT YOU IS' as that is already converted to PAL 625. ('YOU ARE WHAT YOU IS' is the one-hour version of the same performance.)*
>
> *Thank you so much for your patience,*
> *Camilla de Crespigny*

And on October 28th:

> *Dear Co,*
>
> *It was good to talk to you yesterday. Thank you so much for all your efforts on Frank Zappa's behalf. Enclosed is the one-hour show*

'YOU ARE WHAT YOU IS.' I hope you enjoy it as much as 'THE TORTURE NEVER STOPS.'

Thank you again.

Very best regards,
Camilla de Crespigny

1983

TV Glotzer

ZAPPA AND MANAGERS—IT WAS ALWAYS AN INTERESTING COMBINATION. I learned from the letter that Bennett Glotzer, his manager at the time, had tried to sell the tapes of the '81 show on the European market. Bennett had wrangled some financial deals for Nina Hagen involving huge sums, and this meant that he was in Europe quite frequently. If he'd marketed anything on the Dutch market, I hadn't heard about it. I asked Frank if I could give it a try, and a few weeks later a bundle of U-Matic, NTSC-formatted videotapes arrived: 'The Torture Never Stops' and a shorter version, *You Are What You Is*. Using my father's contacts, I organized a viewing at VARA, and Han van Essen, who was in charge of broadcasting there at that time, was immediately keen to show it. So VARA was eager for the broadcast, and a deal was quickly made. When Frank expressed his surprise that I'd gotten it done so quickly, I replied that I couldn't take all the credit, I'd been lucky also.

Under the umbrella of a special music programming for VARA in June, we assembled an interesting broadcast for the 17th: from 8:28pm until 10:05pm, Emmerich Kálmán's *Die Csardasfürstin*, and from 8:45pm until 11:50pm. *You Are What You Is*, an hour-long show of Zappa performing in Palladium. Steve Vai was in the band, and the broadcast included some riotous attempts at subtitles by the VARA team.

1984

It can't happen here

JANUARY 8TH. Even though he was already busy with Pierre Boulez and the Ensemble InterContemporain, Frank took time out to play host to me and Elise (my girlfriend at the time) in his hotel suite in Paris. It was one of the most expensive hotels I'd ever visited, called the Nova Star I believe. Frank's suite consisted of several floors, linked by a spiral staircase right in the center of the room.

I got to see firsthand how charming Frank was with women. He'd already met Elise, but considering how many people Frank saw every day, I thought it might be polite to introduce her again. I opened with, 'You may remember Elise . . .,' but he looked her straight in the eye and said, 'Sure! A handshake I'll never forget.'

I'd brought a gift for Frank. The mother of a friend of mine had recently passed away, and she'd owned a large collection of old American books. One of them, by Sinclair Lewis, was called *It Can't Happen Here*—which was also the title of one of the tracks on Frank's first album. My immediate thought was, 'So *that's* where he got it!' I was allowed to have the book, and I wrote a personal message for Frank on the inside cover page and giftwrapped it. I couldn't wait to see how he'd react to the fact that someone had cracked the code. He unwrapped the parcel, and was astonished—he'd never even heard of the book! Even so, I was pleased that he now had a copy.

He played us a cassette recording of his new album. It included a wonderful version of 'Sharleena,' with a long guitar solo. This was at a time when religious types in the US were warning everyone about hidden messages in pop songs—especially if you played the recordings backwards. Why would anyone do that, anyway? Frank's response was the track 'Ya Hozna.' I immediately recognized Duke and Brock's voices, and said, 'Nice, Napi and George in "Sofa #2," but backwards.' Frank's eyes went wide; it felt good to surprise Frank twice in one conversation. He offered us each a beer, and I started my recording.

CO I'm sorry I didn't have the tape on, but before I get to my questions I wrote on a piece of paper—before that, maybe you can tell us—I might use this when the album comes out—there are two backward songs on there, why's that? In short.

FRANK Because in the United States right now there are people who are from fundamentalist Christian organizations who are trying to pass a law in Congress that makes it illegal to have any information on a record which is backwards. Because they claim that messages favoring the devil have been transmitted to the youth of America by that media. And so, in order to keep America pure, they were trying to pass this law in Congress that no one may put backwards things on a record. So I put two complete backwards songs on mine.

CO As a gesture—?

FRANK Yeah, defiance. That's right, this time the Christians have gone too far.

CO Right.

FRANK And, as you know, throughout the ages, most of the biggest problems that have confronted mankind have been the result of Christian activities. If it's not the Christians it's the Muslims. They just take turns causing trouble.

CO We're talking now, here in Paris, because you are going to do a concert tomorrow. There is a concert of Pierre Boulez's ensemble. And he's going to play three pieces by you. 'Perfect Stranger,' 'Dupree's Paradise'—I remember that, when I was talking to you one time in Amsterdam, you played me a tape by your—I think it was the band from '74—

FRANK Yeah.

CO There was a song there called 'Dupree's Paradise.'

FRANK Yeah, this is the melody from that song done into an arrangement that that band could never play.

CO How did this all come to a concert with Boulez?

FRANK This started years ago, when I sent him some orchestral music and I asked him whether he was interested in conducting it and he said that he couldn't. He didn't have the facilities to do it. But he invited me to write for his ensemble. So I did and they programmed it. But it took about four years for the whole thing to happen.

CO You have a lot of problems getting your orchestral stuff played, in the Netherlands we should know that.

FRANK Yes, you should know it very well.

CO But the thing that I would like to ask you is, you did the *London Symphony Orchestra* record in London, now you're having three of your big instrumental pieces played in Paris. How does America treat its composers?

FRANK Well, next year in the United States 'The Perfect Stranger,' which is one of the pieces that Boulez—it's actually the piece that he commissioned—will be performed in Ohio, at a convention of university composers at which I'm speaking. The orchestra there is going to play this piece along with 'The Black Page' and some other things. And then in San Francisco in May, the San Francisco Contemporary Music Ensemble will play 'Dupree's Paradise.' And then three days later the Berklee Symphony and the Oakland Ballet will give premieres, with dancers and scenery and full orchestra, of a number of compositions, including the world premiere of 'Sinister Footwear,' which is a very large and difficult score for a special orchestra that includes seven saxophones along with seven of each other type of woodwind instrument. And there have been invitations from different other ensembles in the United States to provide them with music where they have performances. I can't remember the name of group in Pittsburgh, but they have a contemporary music ensemble that asked for some stuff. And there's a percussion ensemble in Los Angeles that is going to perform the composition 'While You Were Out,' which is one of the tunes from the *Guitar* album, at a series they call the Monday Evening Concerts in Los Angeles. Monday Evening Concerts is where they play all their contemporary music at the museum in Los Angeles. So there's a lot of other performances of this stuff in the United States this year.

CO That's funny, this year. I mean, in the past—

FRANK In the past, nothing. But this year a lot.

CO Is there an explanation for that? Or is it coincidental?

FRANK Just coincidental. I've also been invited to participate in a festival in Florence in June called the Omaggio Musicale. Luciano Berio asked if I would come there and conduct or participate in some way with that. But I don't know if I'm—whether I'm gonna do that yet. We haven't worked out all the arrangements on it.

CO I'm gonna play some of—in the program—some of the things from the *London Symphony Orchestra*.

FRANK Mm-hmm.

CO Um, you made recordings *after* the concert, three days after the concert.

FRANK Yes.

CO Why was that? Why didn't you just record the concert?

FRANK Because during concerts people cough and move their feet.

CO And was there also a, let's say, a business reason for doing the concert? Why didn't you just record it?

FRANK Well, in order for a person to make a recording and have rehearsals for the recording, union regulations specify that there is no scale payment for rehearsing for a recording. There is a scale payment for rehearsing for a live concert—so the concert is something that is inflicted on you if you want to make a recording.

CO It says *Vol. I*.

FRANK Yes, there's more stuff. There's not quite enough for a whole record—There's about another thirty minutes of music.

CO But we can expect a *Vol. 2* of the orchestral material?

FRANK Yes.

CO Is that maybe something you can combine with the Boulez stuff?

FRANK No, with the Boulez stuff I'm gonna combine things that I'm doing on the computer.

CO Personal question: did you also record 'Strictly Genteel' with the orchestra?

FRANK Yes, and 'Bogus Pomp.' The version of 'Bogus Pomp' that was recorded is the twenty-seven-minute large concert version.

CO Large version, different than the *Orchestral Favorites* album?

FRANK Yes.

CO I just received a record called *Barking Pumpkin Goes Digital.*

FRANK Right.

CO With, as you put it, 'retweezed songs on it.'

FRANK Mm-hmm.

CO Can you give a little information on what changes that might have? On the type of recordings done by you?

FRANK Well, because of the new digital equipment that I bought for the studio, it enables me to do certain things that were not possible with analogue technique before. And provides an increase in quality of the sound for all the records.

CO Does that mean that your albums will also be available on compact discs?

FRANK Not necessarily—because compact discs are controlled by Sony and by Philips. And in order to have a release on compact, you have to do it through them, and there's quite a bit of politics involved in the selection of *what* goes on a compact disc. Because at present their manufacturing capacity is so small that not everyone is allowed to make a compact disc. They only record important things like the *Loggins & Messina Greatest Hits*, or *The Planets*, or things that they are convinced that the public really wants.

CO Or David Bowie albums from the '60s, stuff like that?

FRANK Right, that's what they put on there. So I've contacted them but they weren't interested in putting out any of the things that I did.

CO Mm-hmm. But you see that development as something that might improve some of the—?

FRANK I think compact disc sounds great, it's just the material that is offered on it is not that exciting. But those are decisions that are made by record company executives, and not by the audience.

CO Mm-hmm. You've been pretty active from video areas. As you might know, I talked one of our stations into doing the *You Are What You Is* show, and can we expect more in that field?

FRANK Probably not. Because they're too expensive for me to do—unless I had some outside financing. That's not something that I want to invest any money in.

CO I believe that you told me once that you altered your film *Baby Snakes* into two video shows.

FRANK Well actually, there's one version of it that is suitable for like . . . HBO. You know what that is? Home Box Office, which is the largest cable television system in the US. It's a version that's suitable for that. And there's enough left over from that to make another completely separate show, but in order to finish these things off it costs so much money I can't do it.

CO Oh, they weren't done yet? I mean—

FRANK The first one, the one for HBO, that's done. It's available.

CO For any station to—?

FRANK Right. That's ninety minutes.

CO And I've read that at The Ritz in New York you showed something called *The Dub Room Special*?

FRANK Yes.

CO Can you tell us what that is?

FRANK That's also ninety minutes. It combines concert footage of the band with George Duke and Ruth Underwood, and concert footage of the most recent band that I brought to Europe on the last tour, intercut with each other, so you can see differences between the performance style and the material. And this is held together by a situation which takes place in a room at the video editing facility, which is called Compact Video. And there's a little room down there that's called the dub room, which is where they make tape copies. And one day, when I went in there to make tape copies, I happened to ask the engineer whether or not it was possible to plug a camera directly into one of the machines. And he said, 'Well I don't know, I'll have to call somebody else.' And when he called, the other guy says, 'Oh yeah, it's theoretically possible.' I said, 'Great!' So I called Thomas Nordegg and told him to bring his camera down there, we're gonna make a TV special in that room. So we were in that room for thirteen hours, and we were doing impossible things there, like shooting and editing in the tape copy room, and I was interviewing people who worked at the Compact Video. It's kind of an interesting thing, the way it's put together.

CO Mm-hmm. And that is also an item available for broadcast?

FRANK That's right.

CO Great! Good to know. What about the plan to reissue all the old material in boxes?

FRANK That's still moving along. It's quite a complex procedure to re-prepare the old albums because a lot of the master tapes, especially for the Verve albums, were damaged in storage. And they have to be remixed and a lot of work done to 'em just so I can put 'em out again. So far, I've done the basic work on *Ruben & The Jets*, *Lumpy Gravy* and *We're Only In It For The Money*. Those are the ones that seem to need the most repair.

CO In what terms?

FRANK Well, to give you an example, the 2-track master tapes of mixes of those albums were stored in such a way the tape closest to the center of the hub of the reel was deteriorated so you could see through it. Like the oxide had fallen off. So you couldn't use the original mixes anymore, you had to go back to fundamental material and reassemble that. And you know how complicated *We're Only In It For The Money* is, that's made out of many little pieces of tape. And I had to go through the whole process of putting that back together again.

CO Which gave you an opportunity to remix it?

FRANK Yeah, so I've got a chance to do things to it to clear up the sound. First of all, we added brand new digitally recorded drums and bass to it so that it improves the presence of the recording and some of the . . . since it was made on primitive material, primitive equipment in the early '60s—a lot of that equipment had noise in it. And so, with modern appliances, we were able to suppress that noise and make the recordings more fun to listen to. So perhaps it was a blessing in disguise, but it's a lot of work and it takes a lot of time.

CO But it's not something that is canceled?

FRANK Oh no, still happening!

CO I read that there would also be material included that hadn't come out, is that true?

FRANK That's right, because for each album there were always things that had been left out of the album for space reasons, or one thing or another.

CO Mm-hmm. And is there some sort of overall name for it? Or is it going to be a—?

FRANK No, it'll just be in boxes according to era. Should be, like, five boxes with seven records each, maybe release one per year over the next five years.

CO And is it everything up to, let's say, *Sheik Yerbouti*?

FRANK Yes, it's got all the—everything, the entire catalogue.

CO Right. You're working on a musical called *Thing-Fish*.

FRANK Right.

CO The musical, is it going to be something for record purposes?

FRANK There will be an album of it, yeah. It was designed for the stage but so far I haven't raised enough money to put it on the stage yet. So at least all the music for it has been recorded . . . and I'll probably make that available by mail order, with some notice in the next album, because it's most likely going to be a three-record box. And it's not of interest for everyone because there is a lot of dialogue in it . . . it's like all the—the whole story from the show. And the dialogue is difficult to understand if you don't speak American idioms. So I don't expect that *that* particular thing will be of very much interest to any European audience.

CO But sometimes your mellower things sell bigger, sometimes your mail-order things sell bigger numbers of records than some of your regular releases.

FRANK Yeah, but see, to be perfectly honest with you, I wouldn't want to disappoint a European consumer about that particular thing, because although it does have songs and music in it that they might enjoy, so much of it is based on language that there is no way to translate and there's no way to supply lyrics, that they might not be happy with the thing.

CO Mm-hmm.

FRANK Because it is fairly expensive and it's—unless you can really understand what's on it, I wouldn't advise getting it.

CO I've heard rumors, maybe you can tell me if it's true or not, that there will be some sort of, let's say, office or merchandising company that could supply T-shirts, posters, stuff like that—cassettes. Is that true?

FRANK Yeah, I have a mail order business in the United States called Barfko-Swill. And through this mail order you can get T-shirts, you can get posters, you can get printed music, you can get video cassettes—All that stuff is available. And information for that will be inside the next album.

CO It also includes cassettes?

FRANK Audio cassettes? No, the cassettes referred to in there are digital audio cassettes—that if you happen to be one of the few people that have a system called F1, it's possible that I could make F1 cassettes of certain things. But this is a very specialized type of merchandising. It's not like Columbia Record Club or anything like that, it's real specialized.

CO And it will be probably an American matter whether those will be within the reach of European audience?

FRANK The problem with selling things mail order in Europe has to do with customs restrictions and methods of payment. It's very complicated to have an American mail order business, and to get through all the crap that you have to fight with the customs and stuff, I don't know what to do with that.

CO Mm-hmm?

FRANK I know that a lot of the people who want this stuff do not live in the United States, they live other places. But, in order to accommodate them, I'm faced with a lot of international regulations that are different from country to country, and it makes matters very complicated.

CO Mm-hmm. What was the American response to *The Man From Utopia* album in the United States?

FRANK Nothing, it was a flop.

CO Which is funny, because your previous album was, for instance, in the *Billboard* charts for quite some time.

FRANK Yeah.

CO But there's no way of getting into that audience again, or was it something that might be accredited to the 'Valley Girl' song?

FRANK Well, the main—the success of the *Drowning Witch* album was solely a result of the 'Valley Girl' song. It had nothing to do with the other stuff that was on the album.

CO Mm-hmm. My personal taste was that the interior editing and buildup of the *Utopia* album was much heavier than the *Drowning Witch* album.

FRANK Mm-hmm.

CO Do you think that it might be, for instance, you put three songs on there that I can imagine a 'Valley Girl' buyer—

FRANK Would hate.

CO Well, that's your words but, I mean—

FRANK But the fact of the matter is that I never set out to cultivate a 'Valley Girl' buyer audience. The way in which 'Valley Girl' was perceived and consumed was totally out of phase with its intent. 'Valley Girl' was a parody of certain types of stupid behavior. And just to prove how dumb Americans really can be, the same people I was making fun of thought the song was terrific! So it's like the ultimate proof that what I'm saying is true, you know. People *want* to be dumb.

CO Mm-hmm.

FRANK And so they identified with that. So if *The Man From Utopia* comes along and there's a song on it called 'The Jazz Discharge Party Hats,' which a lot of people who even worked at the office *really* hated—they hated *that*, they hated 'The Radio Is Broken,' they hated 'Dangerous Kitchen' … you know? These things drove them wild, they begged me to take these things off the album, you know? But who are they to say? I happen to like those things. I happen to think that 'The Radio Is Broken' is a wonderful song—I like all three of those. But anybody who makes a record, they not only have the *right*, but have to accept the *responsibility* for what goes into the record. And if I just made records that had only things that other people wanted to listen to in there, then that makes me a slave to their desires. And that's not—

CO You wouldn't be in this business then.

FRANK Yeah, I don't wanna do that.

CO Mm-hmm.

FRANK That doesn't mean that everybody who buys a record has to like what they hear on it.

CO You're very busy now as a composer, you've always been—But you just played me some tapes with a lot of Steve Vai wonderment and also amazing Dweezil technique.

FRANK Mm-hmm.

CO How is your life as a guitar player nowadays?

FRANK I very seldom touch the instrument. I think that I've probably played everything good that I'm ever gonna play, so I've stopped.

CO Stopped?

FRANK Yeah. There's still plenty of other tapes that haven't come out that have nice things on them, but I've basically . . . stopped.

CO Mm-hmm. Talk to me about the word 'stopped.' I heard you say that word a few times in your most recent tour here.

FRANK What?

CO When things were thrown on the stage you said that.

FRANK Yeah.

CO Was it two? Or a lot of incidents? Seemed like there were more incidents than on other tours.

FRANK What, the last tour in Europe?

CO Yeah.

FRANK Not *that* much more. Let's put it this way . . . if I go someplace to play music, that's what my job is, to play music. Not to stand there and be a target for people who wish to throw things on the stage, for whatever their reasons, whether they're good or bad. I have no desire to stand there and be a target and I don't think that any member of the band should be a target. And when I see things being thrown on the stage I have no desire to come back and play at that place ever again. So, consequently, there won't *be* any more European tours, that's it. That was the last one.

CO Definitely?

FRANK Definitely.

CO Because those are the rumors since you left last June.

FRANK It's not a rumor, it's true. And if I ever play on stage again, with a rock'n'roll band, it may be an isolated concert in the United States. But I have no intention of ever bringing a band back to Europe.

CO So it's going to be airplane tickets for European fans?

FRANK [laughs] Nah, stay home, it's not worth the trip.

CO Well, maybe that's a little cynical to say. But I mean, you plan to do more stuff like you're doing now? Have your music played by other people, I mean?

FRANK Well I've *always* had my music played by other people.

CO Yeah, but it was also very nice to have you here to take some solos, for instance.

FRANK Mm-hmm. The world doesn't need to hear my solos, they're interested in rhythm tracks that are exactly uniform with Simmons electric drums playing fake handclaps in the back. There's no longer a market for extended guitar solos in the contemporary musical scene. It's like, you know, one of the—probably the lowest priority on any listener's list is a long guitar solo. And nothing could be less fashionable or interesting to a modern record buyer. So there's no sense in even *doing* them, just forget it. The only thing you need for musical success today is to make sure that the handclaps are turned up very loud in the mix.

CO But, if I may, I will remind you of a statement that you made in an interview that I did with you about the *Guitar* album and you said, 'Well maybe you will buy it, and maybe he will buy it . . . and that's it.'

FRANK Mm-hmm.

CO But still on the inside cover of *Drowning Witch* you said, 'It's amazing what these albums have done.' Is that contradicting your statement now?

FRANK Well, no. Because that's a reference to a certain album with certain content and that was sold during a certain period of time.

CO Mm-hmm. Unexpectedly well.

FRANK Well, you have to understand what 'unexpectedly well' would mean. The thing that's unusual is the record was a three-record box, the price was high compared to any other type of pop music that a person could buy, and the sales figures were high compared to how expensive it was and how different it was from the rest of the product that was available. But still, nothing that would cause a major upheaval in modern record merchandising. The total number of sales of that box worldwide probably did not exceed one hundred thousand units. Which is—I would call that a respectable sale for an unusual item, but we're not talking about a hit record. And the thing is that, when the album was released, the sale expectancy for it from all the professionals involved, you know, at the record company and so forth—they thought maybe you could sell five thousand copies. So it was a surprise for them, but still.

CO Do you think there will be a second project like that?

FRANK *Guitar* album? I've got enough stuff to do it, yes. But I don't know—

CO Not immediately.

FRANK No, I'm not working on it now, but there's plenty more tapes to make one.

CO To ask you a real personal question—Isn't that frustrating, to have piles of, I mean, in our previous talks you let me hear tapes, and I thought, 'That's absolutely gonna be on the next album—'

FRANK Mm-hmm.

CO How do you think you'll get that to your, let's say, heavy consumers, like myself? I mean, how do you get it to people who can't get enough of that kind of material?

FRANK I don't know. Because, you have to understand, before I can make it available I have to invest a considerable amount of money to manufacture it. The way my business works is I'm self-financed, and just like any other small business you can only do so much with the capital that you have to do the projects. So if, for example, if *The Man From Utopia* album would have sold twice as much as it had sold, I would be doing completely different things now. But if an album does not sell well it limits what you can do in the future.

We took a break so I could turn the tape over. Frank grabbed a coffee and another cigarette, and told us to get whatever wanted out of the minibar. Then we continued:

FRANK First of all, I don't know if you heard me tell them that the Boulez recordings are going to be on EMI. And EMI has also made a deal to distribute the *Orchestral* record. But as far as the next rock'n'roll album, we have no European distribution for it yet. It's going to be out in the US. within about six weeks. But I don't know if it's coming out in Europe, or how or when, because I have another lawsuit against CBS International because of the royalties on all the records they had before. And so we don't have anyone to distribute product outside of the US now.

CO I mean, that should be . . . a distribution, like that should be European-wide. It should be—

FRANK Well, it should cover all territories outside the US.

CO Wow—!

FRANK And so far we have not found sufficient interest from any record companies who have distribution that is worthwhile outside the US to take on such a product.

CO Mm-hmm?

FRANK I mean, sometimes they are interested in distributing it, but they don't want to pay, and if they don't pay they don't get it.

CO But the album that is coming in the US then is called *Them Or Us*?

FRANK *Them Or Us*, yeah.

CO Is it like, for instance, *The Man From Utopia*? Material from different periods with different people playing—I mean, three bass players and four different lead vocalists? Or—?

FRANK Well, I have a number of different lead vocalists on it. But most of the stuff is from the same period.

CO Mm-hmm. With your most recent band, that is?

FRANK Yes.

CO And I saw you're tape-recording all the concerts here in Europe?

FRANK Right.

CO What happened to that material? Are you using—?

FRANK Some of those are basic tracks that are on the next album.

CO Mm-hmm?

FRANK And some of the things will be released in a live album from that tour.

CO When can we expect that?

FRANK Oh, that's a year or two off.

CO Because if you finished touring Europe, do you think that touring such a vast amount of cities is really contributing to selling those albums? Do you think it will have a serious effect on your sales there?

FRANK I don't think that the touring had a serious effect on the sales when I did it. And I don't think that *lack* of touring will have a serious effect on the sales. The sales will be what they are, whatever it's gonna be, that's what it's gonna be.

CO Are the sales from your albums always approximately the same?

FRANK Mm-hmm. Yeah, approximately.

CO So it's a—?

FRANK The only ones that were outstanding sellers were *Hot Rats* and *Sheik Yerbouti*. But each country has its own thing that's sold extremely well, and they're very strange. Like for instance, Thailand—*Chunga's Revenge* was a big hit in Thailand. It was also a big hit in Italy. *The Grand Wazoo* was a hit in Finland, but no place else on the planet. *Hot Rats* was a Top 10 album in England, and I think it did very well in Holland.

CO Yeah.

FRANK But in the United States it went to number 90 on the charts in one week and then disappeared. And *Sheik Yerbouti* sold well over a million units worldwide, but mainly outside of the United States because of the success of the single 'Bobby Brown.' Which was a thing that made people pay attention to the album, whereas they could never play 'Bobby Brown' on the air in the United States.

CO And 'Dancin' Fool'?

FRANK 'Dancin' Fool' a little bit. That though wasn't really a hit. Nothing like the response to 'Bobby Brown' in Scandinavia and Germany, because it was a very big hit. In Scandinavia, that single was the largest selling single in CBS's history in that territory, and it took everybody by complete surprise. It was to the point where, in Norway for instance, college students were mounting speakers on top of their cars and driving through the city playing 'Bobby Brown.' It was totally ridiculous. It was as stupid as 'Valley Girl.'

CO [laughs] Yeah! And I believe that your two live albums with Flo & Eddie were big successes in Australia and New Zealand?

FRANK I got a gold record for *Just Another Band From L.A.* and the *Fillmore* album from Australia. I also got a gold record for *Joe's Garage* from Canada.

CO You mean the second or the first one?

FRANK First.

CO The land that banned 'Torture' and—!

FRANK Yeah, well they seemed to like 'Catholic Girls' and 'Crew Slut.'

CO Yeah, yeah. Will you tour these countries in the future?

FRANK No.

CO Would it be also in the United States on a very limited basis?

FRANK Well, the only reason I would not say I'm not touring any place ever again is because I could see a couple of different types of situations where some kind of a live performance would occur in the United States, but not necessarily in conjunction with a tour. Like, maybe some special concert in New York, or some special concert in Los Angeles, but not to go out and tour like I used to do. As a matter of fact, I've sold all my lights, I'm in the process of trying to sell my PA system, and the recording truck itself is for sale. . . . So, I'm done with that.

CO You've toured immense numbers of times and concerts.

FRANK About twenty years, and why should I do this for the benefit of bootleggers? Those little pootheads that sit out there with their cassette machines and then make albums out of it that sound shitty. Ya know? *Fuck* those people!

CO I was at a little meeting which took a day, in the south of Holland, and because I have contact with you, I stay away from fan mags. And sometimes I publish the warnings against bootlegs, or really kill them with criticism.

FRANK Mm-hmm.

CO So I stay away from bootleggers and stuff like that. Some friends of mine from Belgium send me tapes and send me lists. And I was really surprised when I got down there, because they were playing some videos that I never saw, made in Scandinavia, with Ruth and Jean-Luc Ponty, that tour.

FRANK OK, that's got to be from a performance that took place at the Zoo.

CO Yeah, it's open air. And, by the way, I don't want to be rude to you, but sometimes you confuse me with your answers. I'm not all that old, and the very first concert that I saw by you was in '73, in the Concertgebouw in Amsterdam—

FRANK Yeah.

CO And one of the things that made the biggest impressions on me was 'Brown Shoes Don't Make It.'

FRANK Mm-hmm?

CO Because that was a pretty instrumental performance. So the vocals were—recognizing some stuff that I knew from the two albums I had at that time—

FRANK Mm-hmm.

CO And you told me you never played 'Brown Shoes' with that band.

FRANK I don't think we did.

CO You did.

FRANK I don't recall ever doing it, and I have tapes of most of those tours. The two groups—When? In '73? '73, that was the band with Vinnie.

CO '73 with Vinnie?

FRANK No no no, that's not Vinnie.

CO No no, it was with Ralph Humphrey, Jean-Luc Ponty—

FRANK And we were doing 'Brown Shoes'?

CO Jean-Luc Ponty, Ian Underwood, George Duke. Ian was sitting on the stage still playing those keyboards, and you did it as an encore.

FRANK Hmmm!

CO You don't recall that?

FRANK No.

CO Because I dug up some old reviews—

FRANK No, I don't recall that.

CO Oh.

FRANK The original Mothers, when we came to Europe in '68, that was one tune that we played sometimes on that tour, but that band never played it very well. I think that we were playing it much better when we had the band with Vinnie.

CO And Warren—?

FRANK Yeah.

CO Yeah, the version that is on *Tinseltown.*

FRANK Yeah.

CO If you have tapes of that at home, I don't know if you have—?

FRANK Of that show at the Concertgebouw? No, we weren't recording then.

CO The funny thing was you, you were—I don't know if you had a cold or something, or if you weren't feeling well, because you did two shows that day. So it was at the end of the second one, and all the time you went, when it comes to the 'hecka-plecka' stuff—you said, 'I can't do it now but it goes something like this.'

FRANK [laughs]

CO Stuff like that, and it was all because you did all the vocals yourself.

FRANK Mm-hmm.

CO It was a pretty hilarious version of that tune, and—

FRANK Well, I don't remember doing it.

CO But you've been in Holland so many times.

FRANK Yeah, actually we've probably toured Europe more frequently than any other American band, because we first started coming over to Europe in '67, that was the first time. And just about every year since then. Sometimes we'd miss a year, sometimes we'd do *two* tours in a year.

CO Yeah, but that is for the archives now.

FRANK Yeah.

CO It's done with?

FRANK Mm-hmm.

CO What do you think about people who trade, on a non-commercial basis—who let their friends hear cassettes that they have of all kinds of tunes? Not just concerts but things that have been on the radio and—?

FRANK Mm-hmm. Well, I don't like it, but it doesn't bother me as much as the people who do it commercially.

CO Mm-hmm. If you'll allow me, I would like to finish with three questions that have been on my mind, besides the radio stuff.

FRANK Mm-hmm.

CO I talked to Captain Beefheart and told him about—he was talking about bootlegs also, because there are some grand bootlegs out by him.

FRANK Mm-hmm.

CO And we talked about a thing called 'I Was A Teenage Maltshop.'

FRANK Mm-hmm?

CO And there's a guy on there saying, 'I'm Captain Beefheart,' and 'This is a tiny rock opera,' and stuff like that.

FRANK Mm-hmm.

CO And he said that *no way* it could have been him.

FRANK It is him.

CO It is him? Well, he was pretty—

FRANK No, it's him. He goes, 'I was a teenage maltshop!'

CO [laughs]

FRANK It's him.

CO And another thing I would like to ask you. Do you know a bootleg called *The Ark*?

FRANK Uhm, no. But the Ark has to be the name a place in Boston that we worked at in 1968.

CO That's right. Because right now, I saw it at the convention, they make labels by Bizarre. They made an album with pictures similar to the *Uncle Meat* thing.

FRANK Mm-hmm?

CO And they have pretty good artwork, I must say, on it. And it is a concert that you did there in '68. The sound of it is really good.

FRANK I know, because the tapes were made on a 4-track machine, and they've been stolen from me. So that's the worst kind of bootleg. Those tapes—those were actual master tapes then.

CO Right, and they presented it like a normal album.

FRANK Mm-hmm?

CO And just to show you what kind of people you're dealing with, on the back it had the band, but they left out a picture of you.

FRANK Mm-hmm?

CO And it said, 'Not in the picture, FZ.'

FRANK Mm-hmm.

CO So it's uh—but when I heard it, a friend of mine made a tape of it, I heard it—I thought, 'How did they do it?' Because it really sounds like—

FRANK I even know the name of the engineer. His name is Steve Waldman.

CO Yeah?

FRANK And the tapes were originally taken to a recording studio called TTG, in Los Angeles.

CO Mm-hmm?

FRANK And some rough mixes were made there, and I took those rough mixes home. I still have some of those 2-track rough mixes, but the master tapes disappeared. That means that they vanished out of the vault at TTG.

CO Yeah. The nice thing is to hear your conceptual continuity that is in this piece called 'Some Ballet Music'—

FRANK Mm-hmm?

CO You hear some things that are later found on *200 Motels*—

FRANK Yeah, and 'Greggery Peccary.'

CO And 'Greggery Peccary.'

FRANK And also I think that it will probably contain a performance of 'The Orange County Lumber Truck.'

CO Is that on the—?

FRANK Yeah well, that's one of the pieces that we played there.

CO Well, I mean, if you mean the soloing part from 'My Guitar,' that's what it is.

FRANK No, I'm just thinking of the repertoire that we played at that time. That was one of the pieces that we used to do. 'Orange County Lumber Truck'—And because I remember announcing that to the audience and having a discussion with somebody in the audience about it.

CO Mm-hmm?

FRANK Then there's another thing where I was talking to this guy about eating the label. Is that on there?

CO It's on something else. I've seen it.

FRANK That's from that same show.

CO One of the things that I like very much, because it was a real buildup of how you look at, let's say, doo-wop material, it's a very clear version of 'Status Back Baby.'

FRANK Mm-hmm.

CO Which has really rough vocals on. I had the impression it was a cynical 'put down' of that music, even though you like it.

FRANK 'Status Back Baby' is not a doo-wop vocal. That's got a—

CO Well the end, it has some sort of fade out at the end.

FRANK Yeah but 'Status Back Baby' was *never* a . . . that's a complete misinterpretation of the song, 'Status Back Baby' was never intended to have anything to do with doo-wop vocalism. As a matter of fact, If you want an idea of how I feel about doo-wop vocalism, you'll hear a song on the new album called 'The Closer You Are,' which is a—

CO The Channels—?

FRANK An old, yeah, Channels record. And our version of it is very, very good.

CO Yeah, I heard you do it on the last tour. 'Doo-wop' was the wrong—maybe I should have used the word 'teenage' song.

FRANK Yeah well, that style, 'Status Back Baby' style, was a parody of Liberty Records style. Which is like very 'white-person' music. Like, stupid white person youth music. That's what it is, it's not doo-wop. Doo-wop is something else.

CO By the way, that is one of the songs that I also played in the first hour of that special, 'The Closer You Are.'

FRANK Oh yeah? That's a great song.

CO Yeah. The original version of it by The Channels.

FRANK Mm-hmm.

CO I have a feeling that when I heard the first seconds of it, it implies a completely different harmony feeling.

FRANK Mm-hmm.

CO And then suddenly it goes into the song, and I had to listen to it again. Because—I don't know what his name is, the thing that he was doing was so [singing] 'The . . .,' and he really falls into the harmonics which are really different in those first seconds.

FRANK The interesting thing about that song is, I—in the process of raising money for the Broadway show, I met some guys from Wall Street. And there's a man who is the vice president of a company called Canter Fitzgerald Securities, which has an office on the 105th floor of the World Trade Center in New York City. And Mr. Canter owns the world's largest private collection of Rodin sculptures, including the statue of *The Thinker*, you know—the guy like that?
CO Yeah, yeah.
FRANK And it's in the lobby of this place. I mean, it's a real Wall Street brokerage house.
CO Yeah.
FRANK This man, Skip Nell, who was the vice president—

[Buzzer]

FRANK It's unusual that a person in that line of business has this guy's background. First of all, he used to sing baritone in a doo-wop group called The Passions, that made a record called 'Gloria' in the '50s. And then—
CO Which you also did.
FRANK Huh?
CO Which you also did one time.
FRANK No.
CO Wasn't it another 'Gloria'—?
FRANK Oh, the 'Gloria' you're talking about is the one that was recorded by Them. 'G-L-O-R-I-A.' This is not the same song. And then he was a lieutenant in the Marines in Vietnam, and he is in the stock brokerage business on Wall Street. And he's such a misfit for that thing, you know? And when I brought him the cassette of the *Thing-Fish* show, there's one song on there that has some doo-wop kind of flavor to it, and he immediately got excited about that. And a few weeks ago he happened to be in Los Angeles, and he came to my studio and I played him the digital recording of 'The Closer You Are,' and he was almost crying over it. Because it's 'exactly like the original' . . . you know? And he really liked it.

CO Yeah?

FRANK There's a few people out there who *really* like that kind of music. Just like there are a few people who *really* like Webern.

CO [laughs]

FRANK Or a few people who *really* like Bulgarian music, or whatever. It's a specialized taste.

CO Or your instrumental music?

FRANK Yeah.

CO Last year I was in a bar near my hometown, I had an appointment there with somebody, and I knew that I had to wait a long time. So I brought over that thing that you sent me, a tape of a show you did the night before in Brussels.

FRANK Mm-hmm? Oh, about the grandma and the waffles?

CO Yeah!

FRANK Oh, Grandma! 'Grandma, Grandma goes to Belgium.' [laughs]

CO Yeah. I was playing the encores. Because I've lived, lately, on *Strictly Genteel*.

FRANK Mm-hmm.

CO And you went through *The Man From Utopia*, and then you went and did the 'Mary Lou' part—

FRANK Mm-hmm.

CO And I was sitting next to this really huge Black man, and when you got to the encores I just had *Strictly Genteel*, so I turned up the volume and just went into those other encores.

FRANK Mm-hmm?

CO And when I finished I took my headphones off, and he said, 'Did you like that last song?' I said, 'Yeah, I *love* it. And especially the way it's done because it's all medleys.' He said, 'I'm glad you like that song, because—'

BOTH 'I wrote it!'

CO And it was Obie Jessie!

FRANK I know! I met Obie Jessie, he came to the rehearsal, and one of the few rehearsals we had before we came to Europe. Most of the other guys in the band had never heard of him before, ya know?

CO Yeah?

FRANK And I brought him to the rehearsal and said, 'C'mon, sing your song!' You know? It was great!

CO He told me!

FRANK Yeah, he's a nice guy.

CO But shall I tell you something that you won't believe?

FRANK What?

CO He was touring Holland with some sort of—

FRANK Jazz group.

CO Perverted jazz group.

FRANK Yeah, he plays piano a little bit.

CO And he sings a bit.

FRANK Yeah, I didn't know he was singing with—

CO Yeah, yeah! He sang 'Angel Eyes' ... and sang 'Love For Sale' and stuff like that.

FRANK Oh! 'Angel Eyes,' yeah!

CO Must be real depressing for him.

FRANK It is.

CO It must be, because he was playing in the drinking hall. What you used to sing about, and write about. He did this matinee and they had to get him a cab—this was on Tuesday night—and at half past eight he got into his cab, which had pop radio on, and he heard 'Mary Lou.' His song that he wrote ages ago, how long ago would it be—?

FRANK About thirty years ago.

CO Thirty years, and he couldn't believe it. And there was this three-and-a-half song show that I played, and that was one of the songs. Because I wrote down everything you did—not by you—that you did during that show, and got it out of some other library and played it.

FRANK Mm-hmm?

CO And he got in there and he heard his song. And he had this strange—he just did all this crap in this little place. Two weeks later he's drinking at his hotel, in the bar, and he meets me and he tells me this funny story. I said, 'I'm at the show.' He said, 'Well, there must be something going on ...'

FRANK Yeah, yeah, yeah!

CO And he was *so* delighted!

FRANK Yeah.

CO So I had him hear it, and he said it was just like that during rehearsal.

FRANK Yeah, he's a hell of a guy, I appreciate him. He told me this story that somebody else recorded it, I think it was Ronnie Hawkins.

CO Mm-hmm, yeah.

FRANK And recorded it and didn't pay him—no no, his name was Steve Miller.

CO I know the version of 'Mary Lou'—

FRANK There was a recent recording and somebody claimed—no, Ronnie Hawkins recorded it a long time ago. And then when Steve Miller re-recorded it, he gave the credit to Ronnie Hawkins. And so there was some kind of lawsuit about that and he had some trouble to collect his money.

CO Yeah. And he said there were two reasons they wanted to do it at that time. Because first of all, when he was fourteen, he had the voice of somebody who was almost forty or forty-five.

FRANK Mm-hmm.

CO And the other reason was that, even though the words are so obvious, not very many people understood that it was about a hooker. So he said it was just a funny experience. And I don't think that he ever did anything again that made it big.

FRANK Well, I have his other records. He has another real good song called 'Shuffle In The Gravel.'

CO Mm-hmm?

FRANK You ever heard that?

CO Yeah, I have heard it.

FRANK That's on *ATCO*. And the thing that I really liked, and it stumped him, because when he came to the rehearsal, I said, 'All these years I've been trying to figure out *one line* on the B-side of "Mary Lou."' And have you ever seen the original record of 'Mary Lou'?

CO No, I am not a collector.

FRANK Well, the B-side of it is a song called 'Don't Think I Will,' and it starts off, '*Should I hit him in the head with a bottle of beer / Or should I hit him in his ear so that he can't hear / Don't think I will, don't think I will / He's a pretty big fella and this time I might get killed.*' And each verse is what he thinks he might do to this guy who's messing with his girlfriend. Who's bigger than him.

CO Yeah?

FRANK And it's really a funny song. And there was one line that I never could understand what it was. And he couldn't remember either, and he called me up a few weeks later and told me what the line was, and I laughed so hard! And now I can't remember what it was. It was a great fucking line! And I know he must have some more songs like that around someplace, but who's going to record 'em? You know? Who's going to release that kind of stuff anymore? Everybody's too serious.

CO Yeah! Because, for instance, that's the same with the words in 'No No Cherry.'

FRANK That's a great old song.

CO Right?

FRANK The original version of that, by this group called The Turbans, it's terrific! The nerve of anybody thirty years ago making a song like that, it's almost as absurd as recording 'Jazz Discharge Party Hats,' because you know people are gonna go, 'We can't play this!'

CO Yeah!

FRANK That's really some sensational shit, and nobody knows where these guys are now.

CO Right, and the thing is, it's so amusing, it's entertainment on a certain level.

FRANK Mm-hmm.

CO I mean, if you look what's happening right now, but only in the musical buildup, those are the words that have to be connected to a certain way of life. Which doesn't leave very much space for any humor, for instance.

FRANK Well look, it's like this. In order for it to be *good* today it must not be amusing, because if you laugh at something it can't be worthwhile. And it must not really *mean* anything, because if you say something someone could be offended. So all of the lyrics to the most successful songs are vague or they're in a general direction of things having to do with a love situation, or a hate situation, or a rejection situation, or something against some sort of authority, or some formula. It all falls into the formula packages. And certain types of orchestration *must be there*! The handclaps must be loud in the track, in other words, and it has to have a synthesizer bass repeating the same notes over and over again, and stupid stuff. You know? Where everybody wants to make their stuff the same as the next guy, but just a little bit different. And the main way of consuming it is you don't listen to it—you dress up to it. The music reinforces your wardrobe. And so, by the music being like this, it gives people the chance to act out this fantasy of how modern they think they are.

CO They come to see and not to hear?

FRANK Yeah! *But* if that is what they want, then they should have a lot of it. They should have as much of it as they can stand, because that is good for them.

CO Yeah.

FRANK Because that's what they want, they should not be denied access to that type of entertainment.

CO Mm-hmm. You're working with—Roy Estrada is coming up again. We had Jimmy Carl Black on *You Are What You Is*, and I believe Jim Sherwood was there?

FRANK Yeah.

CO Roy Estrada is the one that—?

FRANK I see him more frequently than the other guys. Because he calls me up, he says, 'You got anything for me to do? Any songs to sing?' You know, sometimes I do and sometimes I don't, and he comes over and he sings.

CO The *Rare Meat* album. There's you playing on it and something that you wrote on there also.

FRANK Yeah, there's some songs I wrote.

CO Does it have anything to do with you?

FRANK No, it hasn't. These were masters that were recorded in Cucamonga, then leased to another company, then those masters were purchased by Rhino.

CO So it's a legal album?

FRANK It's legal.

CO Because right now there are stories that—?

FRANK I did have to call Rhino. And I've had some very bad relations with Rhino. It's also the distributor of The Grandmothers' material. I wouldn't call it a very fine operation, they basically have a bootleg mentality.

CO Yeah, they took that little fragment from the *Over-Nite* cover, I heard they took that out now?

FRANK Yeah.

CO You warned them?

FRANK Oh yeah, I got my lawyers on 'em.

CO Because there is a lot of material there. I mean, if you listen—I don't want to be nasty about people you work with or you might still be friends with—but what they did to your tunes—especially on the live album they put out. I can imagine that the first one might have, for some freaks, some sort of value as a very weak nostalgia album. Let's put it that way.

FRANK Mm-hmm.

CO But when they start playing those tunes. For instance, 'Peaches,' which is for a lot of people a sacred composition. The recording was bad, they played it weird. I mean, how big is one's control over one's catalogue?

FRANK Once a record has been released, a person might want to record the same song, all they have to do is get a mechanical license. As far as I know, they never even asked for a mechanical license for that. And I didn't know that they had recorded 'Peaches.'

CO Mm-hmm. You heard the version?

FRANK No, never heard it. I didn't know that they—I didn't think that they could play it. Because from what I knew of the instrumental makeup of that band, if they attempted to play songs that I had written, I had doubts whether they could play them correctly.

CO They played 'Uncle Meat.'

FRANK Yeah? Well, they never played it right when they were *in* the band, so I can't imagine how they were doing it with their own band.

CO Mm-hmm.

FRANK Now, basically the concept of The Grandmothers was a way in which these guys, who are no longer employed by me, could use my name and my material to make money for themselves. And they thought that they had the right to do that, and we have a disagreement on that point. I think that anybody has a right to form a band and go out and play, but when you start playing my music, you either play it right or don't play it at all. They don't *care* about my music, and they were only using it as a device to make money for themselves. So I have no respect for them for doing that. Especially for Don Preston, because he was the ringleader of the thing.

CO Yeah, I mean, he has some things in there that were—I mean, I see this as a privilege that I can discuss this with you, but when I knew they were coming I went down to the concert and talked to—the only guy I wanted to talk to was Jimmy. Because I'm fond of his singing, and I knew that he had recorded the 'Husband' song. So, what I asked him is that I thought it was a good idea for him to form a new band, because I enjoy his singing. 'But why such a nostalgic name? And was it meant to be a nostalgic band?' I asked before the concert. And he said, 'No no, this has nothing to do with Frank. We play some of his songs but it has nothing to do with Frank.' And they opened up with 'You Didn't Try To Call Me.'

FRANK Mm-hmm.

CO Which Jimmy sung well, and which had his—

[Tape cuts out]

I put a new cassette in my recorder, and Frank said we could get a cold beer from the minibar. I pressed 'Record' and we continued.

I'd mentioned The Grandmothers to Frank because I'd helped out with the recording of their 1981 Paradiso show for VARA Radio. For me, at that moment in time, it was weird to be in a tiny dressing room with some of the people who'd featured on albums I literally grew up with. Especially Jimmy Carl Black exhibited a peculiar blend of love and disappointment when we talked about the old days. He was very friendly to me though.

Bunk Gardner was less friendly, Tom Fowler just sat plucking at his bass, and Don Preston was definitely not in the mood to talk. I later went on to work with Jimmy in our Siësta Studio, a nice session with The Muffin Men from Liverpool, and in 2006 we worked together on a special on *Freak Out*. I told Frank I owned the album *Welcome Back, Geronimo Black*.

FRANK Mm-hmm. Is it on Rhino? Or is it a bootleg?

CO It's all on Rhino.

FRANK Oh . . .

CO There is one collector's talking album out, but there are two albums out that are in import shops all over the place. The first one is called *The Grandmothers*, or something. And the other one is called *Looking Up Granny's Dress*, or something. And it has you playing on drums on one track. And the only thing that I liked was, but didn't have anything to do with The Grandmothers, a song called 'Mayonnaise Mountain.'

FRANK Mm-hmm, that's Ray Collins.

CO Yeah. Because I like his voice. He still has something that he had then.

FRANK Mm-hmm.

CO But he wasn't in the band.

FRANK If you saw him today you wouldn't recognize him.

CO How come?

FRANK He's very, very thin and he's got two or three teeth missing in the front. And he's trying to make an album of ballads. You know, like a nightclub singer type album?

CO Mm-hmm, chemical amusement aids?

FRANK I think so.

CO Yeah. But when we talk about these bootleggers—the catalogue put out by the German guy—don't you have any plans of doing that yourself? Because by itself it's an interesting matter when we look at your catalogue, to have something like that.

FRANK Well, I can't afford to. See, they can afford to do it because there's no quality in the things, you know. Cassette tape transferred to a disc? Any cover, 'Put it out.' And then foolish people buy it.
CO Yeah.
FRANK But I don't make records that way. If I'm gonna do it, it's going to be mixed right, and that takes hours and hours, and it's too expensive to do.
CO Mm-hmm. And books of lyrics, or something?
FRANK You see? The net result of hearing all this stuff just reinforces my belief that I dislike people intensely, this'll make me hate people more. It also reinforces the fact that if I hated them in the first place I was right to do so, because they are so scummy.
CO Just for instance, this band is not doing anything right now in Europe. How is the situation in the US?
FRANK I don't know. I don't keep track of it. I mean—but it's the very idea, the reasons for doing it and the ignorance of the public that would consume it. And the whole attitude of these people toward using a dummy and stuff on stage. I mean it's so small and so dumb, so mindless!
CO But I think that problem will be solved when you put out these boxes, because—
FRANK Probably not. That problem will never be solved, because there's always going to be a guy someplace who will find some little piece of shit that he can stick on a box and, you know—
CO It's incredible what is put out.
FRANK Yeah, but at least they won't be able to bootleg any new concerts.
CO That's for sure. OK, well I think I can mix and match things out of—and uh, try to get some orchestral things on a pop station. Do you think there will be any use for that?
FRANK I don't think so, because I think the net result will be that they'll turn the pop station off. I think that pop stations should be pop music, and that people who like to hear pop music should hear it, and other things that are not pop should not interfere with their lifestyle, or their wardrobe. And to inflict it on them in a subversive way like that probably will not make them happy, will not make their life more beautiful in any way, so

it probably should not be done. I think that it's enough to say that if the orchestral stuff is available, for people who want to hear that—it's available, and it shouldn't be crammed down anybody's throat, you know? It's not something that should be administered like some bad medicine, where you hold their nose and then pour it in like that. It's not designed for that. It's prepared as specialized entertainment for people who like that kind of entertainment. And those are the ones who should consume it, and the ones who like other things should listen to other things.

CO They should get the chance to consume it.

FRANK They should have the chance to consume it, but to inflict it on them in a pop format might be the wrong thing to do. I don't know.

CO Well, we also have space on more specialized networks—

FRANK Well, the fact of the matter is that it doesn't belong on a classical station either.

CO No no no! I mean, not classical, but we have some stuff that is done by—well, people that might be on the same line as you, stuff that we can play. I mean, I didn't play the *Guitar* boxes on that pop station either, I did that on the—

FRANK On the other—

[Tape cuts out]

CO As a matter of fact, I played 'Envelopes' also on our more specialized channel—

FRANK Mm-hmm.

CO And, for instance, also a piece like 'The Radio Is Broken.'

FRANK Yeah.

CO And we got some pretty good—I do these kind of things more regularly with other composers also. And you see that if you do it at a certain time with a certain type of announcement—

FRANK Yeah, then it works good. I think that's the way it should be done, because the people who like that sort of thing know where to get it.

CO Yeah.

FRANK Rather than somebody who wants to hear The Scorpions should be able to be offended by it.

CO Mm-hmm. Is it correct, for a more free question—because I ordered the album already—is it correct that you play on an album by a band called Flint?

FRANK Yes.

CO That is genuine?

FRANK Yes. Flint is the remaining members of Grand Funk Railroad.

CO Oh, I see!

FRANK They called me up and—Flint is the name of a town in Michigan, that is where some of them are from, and they called me up and asked if I would help them out and play on this thing, so I did.

CO Mm-hmm. And is it also correct, because I purchased that one too, that you played with Duke as Obdewl' X?

FRANK Yes.

CO That's also you?

FRANK That's very old, that's about twelve years old.

CO Yeah, all these things are becoming rare.

FRANK Mm-hmm.

CO As a matter of fact, all your participations with other people are getting rarer and rarer. Even the Grand Funk Railroad record that you produced.

FRANK There are some songs on there that I really like. I like 'I Miss My Baby' and—oh, what was that other one that's on there? Something about Sunday. I don't know, do you have that album?

CO Yeah, yeah.

FRANK I like it.

CO You play one solo on it.

FRANK Yeah, that was against my will, but it was something that was done out of necessity, because when the album was being finished—I don't know quite what—It was just a bunch of inner politics between members of the group. But I had to do it, because there was a hole in this one song and the guitar player had already gone back to Michigan, and the album was being finished in Los Angeles so I had to do it.

CO It wasn't one of the things that you would say—

FRANK No, 'Go listen to this album cut.' It was just something that had to be done to get the album done.

CO Mm-hmm. By the way, do you intend to produce any other artists in the near future?

FRANK God, I hope not! I really don't—I don't enjoy doing it.

CO So that means that the Utility Muffin Research Kitchen is closed for other bands, for instance?

FRANK Yes, it's never *been* open to other bands.

CO No, no—

FRANK It's the kind of a place where—you know what a zoning restriction is?

CO Zoning restriction?

FRANK In a city, each part of the city is divided into zones which can be used for various purposes—residential zones, commercial zones, industrial zones. This is a recording studio in a residential zone, it is not zoned for rental to other people. So it's only for my own use, it's in my home and it's totally private. There was never any intention of using it like a normal Hollywood recording studio.

CO Do you have any plans for the release of the material that's going to be recorded this week with Boulez?

FRANK Do I have plans for release of it?

CO No, dates.

FRANK Oh, dates?

CO I mean, I take it you're gonna release it?

FRANK Yeah, it's going to be released, but I can't say when, because I have to take it back to Los Angeles to mix it and edit it, finish off the computer music for the other side, package it, and it's going to be a few months before it's out.

CO Yeah yeah! But let's say in the near future?

FRANK It'll be this year, it's not something for next year. Probably by the summertime at least.

CO OK, and you also have European through EMI—

FRANK Right, that's already worked out. They'll have it in the United States too, they have it worldwide.

CO Did you get any response, negative or positive, to the *LSO* album?

FRANK Mostly positive, and the sales on it have not been too bad. As a matter of fact, the only problem with it is making a European distribution deal. I mean, it took a long time to make a deal for it because CBS wasn't interested in it. So it took a while to get it to EMI to get them to put it out over here. But it's not the kind of the thing that anybody is going to be jumping through a hoop of real fire in order to obtain it, because there's no chance of getting on the radio. There's no video to play on Electron, no five-minute clips... so how are they going to merchandise it?

CO Yeah.

FRANK There is nobody on it with blue hair or a dagger through their face, you know? There's no interesting clothing, there's no attitudes, there's no pouting, it's exactly out of phase with merchandising realities. So it's not an easy thing to get somebody excited about. But the people who like it really like it, so I'm glad. That's for them.

CO But don't you have any space on American radio for stuff like this? Because we didn't.

FRANK Well, college stations have played it. As a matter of fact, for several weeks one of the top request items on the Georgia Tech—you know that university called Georgia Tech? They have a college radio station in Atlanta, and 'Sad Jane' was the top request item on that radio station, and getting a lot of play there, but normal classical stations and rock stations didn't play it at all.

CO I mean, because that is completely out of—your normal albums are hard for them to swallow.

FRANK Yeah, I mean, I didn't even bother mailing it out to the normal stations.

CO I like your comment on—I think it was the back of the promotional of 'Valley Girl.' That piece of paper that you have, with the logo from the *Drowning Witch* album, with yellow, and you wrote what should happen with disc jockeys and which ones should be promoted.

FRANK Yeah.

CO But the result is that as soon as it was shipped here, CBS started selling them to collectors instead of going to the radio. I had your wife on the phone, when you were in London, and told her what the prices were for that item.

FRANK Hmm.

CO Another item in the shops is 'You Are What You Is' combined with 'Valley Girl.'

FRANK As a split single?

CO As a 12-inch single, one side is 'Valley Girl,' the other side is 'You Are What You Is.'

FRANK Hmm. Well, they don't have permission to do *that* either.

CO Lyrics printed on it.

FRANK Mm-hmm.

CO That's not official either?

FRANK No. I mean, as far as I understand, my contract with CBS, for those materials, they do not have the right to repackage or re-couple.

CO Well, they took those two—

FRANK Yeah, I had a big argument with CBS in London, because they decided to take just a few pieces and make a sampler out of *that* and sell it.

CO That was the one including 'Drowning Witch'?

FRANK Yeah.

CO Yeah, the EP with 'Drowning Witch.'

FRANK Yeah, I had a *big* argument with them about that.

CO Also, prices are going up immediately because it was only done in England.

FRANK Well, collectors are strange people.

CO Yeah, but record companies also. They put out things that are not authorized . . . it's, uh, pretty funny. Dweezil's single never got here either.

FRANK There was never a European distribution deal made for it. There's no interest in it.

CO Was there—let's say, the people that knew that Moon had put out a single—was there a request from that group of people for Dweezil's material?

FRANK We still sell that single mail order in the US.

CO There's also a 12-inch I have of that, it's a pretty good single. Is he planning to do any more things in the—?

FRANK He's started working on some other material, but it's not done. It's gonna be a long time before he's ready to make an album. It's one thing to be able to play a guitar, it's something else to be able to make an album, and he's not quite ready to do that yet.

CO Well, I hope that we get as much as we can then!

FRANK Well, you got it.

CO So, albums and sheet music. I love the *Guitar* book, it's done, uh... even though there are some versions of well-known solos that were not on that record... I think that Steve—for instance, 'Yo Mama' was not the version that's on *Sheik Yerbouti*.

FRANK No, it's not. It's called 'Mo Mama.'

CO Yeah, I don't know if that is coincidental, but I laughed my head off when I saw it. For a strange job also I used to work for a classical promotion department at Phonogram Records.

FRANK Mm-hmm?

CO One time, I forced them to reissue a Decca Varèse album by getting a lot of airplay for it. They said, 'Why are you promoting an album that's not in our catalogue?' Done by your good friend Zubin Mehta, I think you know the album?

FRANK No, I don't.

CO You don't?

FRANK I didn't know he recorded that, no.

CO He recorded 'Arcana.' 'Intégrales.' 'Ionisation.'

FRANK How is the version of 'Arcana'? Is it good?

CO Well, it has a lot of tension in it, it's very—

FRANK Is it rhythmically good?

CO No. It's messy, some parts real messy. I have a version on a bad-quality tape which is really good, done by the orchestra from the Concertgebouw with a conductor named Bernard Haitink, I don't know if you know him?

FRANK I know him, yeah. The best version I heard is from the Chicago Symphony.

[Tape cuts out]

FRANK No, Jean Martinon. It's on RCA.
CO RCA?
FRANK It's older, it's about twelve years old. It's real good.
CO I have some French records with 'Amériques' and coupled with—
FRANK 'Déserts.'
CO Yeah, that's pretty good. And a very strange album with the Reihe Ensemble on Vox. It also has 'Density' on it.
FRANK Yeah, but see, that's an easy piece to perform. It's a flute solo, and it takes up so many minutes on the record, you know, that's why it's always included.
CO Yeah.
FRANK I don't think there really has been a definitive version of that recorded yet.
CO I hear a lot of influence of Varèse in your tape compositions from the early records. I mean, sometimes there are some really high, squeaking notes in there that I think, 'That is about the same pitch as the one on "Nasal"—
FRANK Oh yeah, 'Nasal' yeah, but it's done in a different way though. And for a different reason, and produced by a different device. But I suppose when it comes down to the last analysis, any high, squeaky noise equals any other high, squeaky noise that's coming from a piece of tape. One tape that you'd probably enjoy and that's a tape of me conducting 'Ionisation' and... what was the other piece? 'Intégrales.'
CO Yeah, I've read about it, you did it in San Francisco.
FRANK Yeah.
CO I've read a lot about it.
FRANK The performances were great! Those tapes, if you really wanna hear the rhythm in those pieces, I got it. I got 'em. And it was a great ensemble to work with.

CO What is the way to hear that?

FRANK I would have to—there's only one little cassette, and it's someplace in a pile of other cassettes in Los Angeles.

CO Mm-hmm?

FRANK And if I think of it, maybe I can duplicate it and send it to you.

CO Oh, that would be great! I mean, it's absolutely safe here as you know.

FRANK Yeah, but you'll really be surprised when you hear it.

CO Yeah?

FRANK Because it was hard for me to conduct. 'Ionisation' was easy to conduct, the other one was very difficult. And I had to sit at home with the score, working out all the beat patterns, and mark it up and because I only had two rehearsals with them before the show, they had already sent music and everything, and then I went to San Francisco and had two rehearsals—

CO Which orchestra was that?

FRANK It's called the San Francisco Contemporary Music Ensemble, and it's conducted by a man named Jean Louis LaRue.

CO Mm-hmm?

FRANK And they're going to be playing 'Dupree's Paradise.'

CO How is your relationship, artistically, with Kent Nagano? Who is famous for his contemporary—

FRANK Oh, he's a great guy. He comes to the house and visits, I talk to him every once in a while on the phone.

CO Yeah?

FRANK He's conducting the ballets in May.

CO Oh, great! Because I have a tape of the orchestra which I think—I think you'll agree, because you put it out that they did a pretty good effort of performing the music that has to sound the way it has to sound. Even though your comment on the cover that, of course, some mistakes get in there because of the length of time. But I heard on the tape that they were *really* getting tired when the trumpets in the encore had to go high in 'Strictly Genteel.'

FRANK Oh yeah, their cheeks red and out like this and their eyes closed, it was pure pain. But see, they all drink so much! At the Barbican they have a bar backstage which is bigger than the bar for the audience. And when they go offstage the whole orchestra is *drunk*! And I commented about it the next day at the recording session, they didn't like it. We're not talking about a few beers, we're talking about hitting the whiskey in between, and I was appalled. Because I was sitting in the audience and I heard them making mistakes that were just totally inexcusable because they had to be drunk. If they weren't drunk then they were totally incompetent, you know. At least that—

CO It's probably the first.

FRANK Huh?

CO It's probably the first matter, that they were drunk.

FRANK Yeah, yeah! I mean, I would hate to think that they had been trained to play that way. But still, it's inexcusable for an orchestra to give a performance of anybody's music in that condition. Period.

CO True. Did you conduct 'Strictly Genteel' yourself?

FRANK Yes.

CO It's amazing. I don't know, probably, what is with the problems at CBS that it's so hard to have any public attention for you doing a relatively *big* project for anybody. I mean, who would hire an orchestra?

FRANK Mm-hmm.

CO There is absolutely no way—and I don't believe I *know* that there is space for information like that. But there is absolutely no way of getting such an event to people that might want to hear that, and might want to *know* that.

FRANK Well, maybe EMI will do something about it now that they're distributing outside the US. But you know, the concert tomorrow is being broadcast.

CO Oh, is it?

FRANK Yes, I made a deal, I think it's going to be all over Europe.

CO Later? Or direct?

FRANK I don't know. I heard them talking at the IRCAM about the arrangement they made with French radio to broadcast it.

CO You gave permission for that?

FRANK No, they did it without my permission, but I wasn't gonna stop 'em because they're very poor, they really don't have enough money to do anything, and I didn't want to make life miserable for them.

CO Well, I hope EMI can do it. By the way, I wrote a letter, probably after you left for Europe, all the things I want to get to you I sent to Susan's address.

FRANK Yeah.

CO Because I figured that's the best way.

FRANK Mm-hmm.

CO There is some room—I know that there is some room, especially in the areas that I work in, to do more things than are being done. Because I recently stopped—when I heard that the *Orchestra* album wouldn't be done by CBS—I stopped because all these record companies are near my house. I live in the center of Holland, and I know all these people from my former jobs. And moreover they try to promote *their* classical and pop stuff in *my* programs.

FRANK Mm-hmm.

CO And since I'm a freelancer, I have the opportunity to get my stuff elsewhere, and when they come with ten albums, I'm not like the other people who say, 'Give all ten to me, I'll play some of them.' I just say, 'Give me that *one*...' And they're always amazed. And it's not my job, but I've had really tough discussions with people from CBS in France, in Belgium, and in Holland. It all started when they called me up and said, 'We have something amazing for you to see.' I got into my car and drove to them, and they showed me the *You Are What You Is* promo clip. Just three minutes ten, or something.

FRANK Yeah.

CO I liked it very much, I read about it in *Billboard*, with a photo of you and Scott.

FRANK Mm-hmm?

CO And I really loved it, and knew people who were interested in it. And I just waited to see what would happen, and it hasn't been played once. One time in Belgium and it *never* got on the air in Holland.

FRANK That's amazing, because they paid for it.

CO They *paid* for the copy?

FRANK They paid to make that.

CO Who did?

FRANK CBS. I never would have made it if they wouldn't have put up the money for it. They requested it, and they paid for it. And then they didn't do anything with it.

CO Was it on the air frequently in America?

FRANK Very seldom, as a matter of fact, this year they just started playing it. When it was made *nobody* played it, nobody. Because at the time Reagan had just been elected, the whole country was very, very conservative. Nobody could make fun of Ronald Reagan—you can't show Ronald Reagan getting the electric chair, it's not going to be any good. And now today, every once in a while, some places that show videos will show it.

CO It must have cost an enormous amount of money.

FRANK It was about sixty thousand dollars. It's a lot of money, but still far less than what most video clips cost today. Some of them are a hundred and twenty, three hundred thousand dollars for four minutes. And the new Michael Jackson—

CO Was a million dollars.

FRANK Yeah, a million dollars. It's ridiculous! For what? One minute of that clip is nothing but a synthesizer bass and a handclap track, you know? And with people doing the same steps that he uses in all the rest of the videos.

CO No effects. Hardly.

FRANK Well, you know, the face and all that stuff.

CO Well, we knew that from a lot of motion pictures. But I mean, the amount of effects in 'You Are What You Is'—But anyway, I told them, I said, 'You have this material, you know where to play it.' And the stupid thing to do was they knew that [Dutch broadcasting station] Veronica once had done something with you, an interview or something.

FRANK Yeah.

CO And they said Veronica will show it, which is the most conservative company. And they liked it, they liked the first twenty-five seconds, then

Reagan came in and they just put it off. So I said, 'Next time you get something, call me and I will give you free advice on who to contact, because it can be done.'

FRANK Mm-hmm.

CO So when I saw this Halloween announcement in Billboard, even before you did the show I called up Susan. I'd never met Susan at that time, but I talked to her a lot, and I said, 'Listen, I copied this and sent it to some people, and told them if they want to do something with it they'd have to be quick.' So one of the people I work with a lot told me that he might be interested, and they said contact CBS. And he wrote about four or five letters to CBS—

FRANK But CBS had nothing to do with that.

CO No, but I mean, it can't be bad for them to promote an artist that they have so much material of.

FRANK Yeah, but see, they don't think that way, because at that point CBS was deeply involved in Boy George-ism. And it's a case of 'go for what you know.' If you have any one artist who shows the slightest hint of selling large quantities of material, they put *all* the weight behind that, and everything else falls along because—you want some of this?

[Frank holds up a huge Toblerone bar]

CO Yes please!

FRANK Want some?

ELISE Yes please!

FRANK But that's the way it generally works in the record business, they follow the path of least resistance. If it looks like the public already wants something, then they sell them more than they need.

CO We have ratings in Holland, going from 0 to 10. And we ask them for two things. First of all, the amount of people that watch. Second, how they like it—appreciation rating. The *You Are What You Is* show was broadcasted after a news program, and normally after that they have a cheap movie. It's primetime though, it's a pretty good time—it's half past ten. Their normal ratings are 6/5, but when I showed them the one-hour version I supplied them with photo material. I supplied them with information about the band, I supplied them with all kinds of information about your last tour. Their press unit sent that to newspapers and music magazines. And it was the only information that I had supplied them with, because it was really specific to that show. The normal 6/5 went to 7/8 that time after the news show. There was a switch from channels, we only have four channels, and it was really an obvious switch to channels. So I said to CBS, and to a lot of other people, especially the people who told me that your three-minute clip was too much—I said, 'He hasn't been on Dutch television for more than ten years.' Roelof Kiers was the last one to do anything on television with you, so I said, 'This is preposterous, because he comes here every year.' So I just proved to these people that it can be done with a high appreciation and quantity rating. So I wrote a letter, but I think that she had made some costs that were probably high or not really workable for you, because she had sent me this U-Matic tape of the show, and I drove over to these people and showed it to a couple that I had on a special list, and then they got in contact with Bennett Glotzer and made all the arrangements, which I hope went OK So I told Susan that if you have some people here who know what can be done, and with who, why send expensive promo 12-inches of Moon or expensive video clips—which they pay for themselves in this way—why send it to people who just put it in a closet? And she said, 'Well, even though it's fake,' meaning the relationship, I said, 'What can I do? Because I know all these people and I have the time to do it.' So she said the only thing that would make any sense is to draw up a letter and say, in a few words, what you think and what you want to do. Which I did, but for some reason the original of that letter never arrived. We had a mail strike here, so maybe that's why it never got to you.

FRANK I never saw it.

CO And I addressed it, it is kind of—how would you say it?

FRANK Formal?

CO Formal, I tried not to be formal and I left some typo mistakes in because it was just a letter, and I addressed it—for formality's sake—to you, to Susan, Bennett, and to Gail, who also told me I should do something like that. I only talked to your wife through the phone once, in London. So what I did is, I think it was just before Christmas, I sent a bunch of cards to the office, to the people that I phone regularly to—to wish them a Happy New Year, and I included to Susan a copy of the letter and sent it to Vose Street. She said it would be better to send it to Vose Street. So probably on your return you will see it and I don't want to—

FRANK Do you have my home address?

CO No.

This was a strange thing to say, because I'd had his actual address since 1979. I can't imagine now why I said it.

FRANK Well, I'll give you my home address and you can send it direct to the house because Susan works there. Her office is in my house, and she works there, like, eight hours a day during the day. And if you've ever talked to her on the phone, that's probably where you are talking to her, there in the office in my house.

CO When I call, I first get probably Jane at 9115, which is Glotzer Management.

FRANK Janet, not Jane.

CO Janet?

FRANK Janet.

CO Janet.

FRANK Jane is the PR lady, and she's in New York.

CO Is that of the Wartoke concern?

FRANK Yeah. I'll give you the home address and send the stuff directly there.

CO And I'm glad that I have the opportunity now to tell you that this letter is not some sort of pompous way of—you know what it's about. Because I know it can be done and, I mean, I have a part-time job as a producer for radio programs and stuff like that, a lot of music recordings—moreover, I studied music and in my free time I do this. But it would be better to coordinate it, I think.

The tape stops here. This moment proved to be a key moment in developing my professional relationship with Frank.

The whole time during this interview, some strange noises—soft shuffling and similar sounds—were coming from the upper floor of the suite, where the sleeping quarters were. After about three hours, Frank asked us to leave so he could prepare for a dinner with the heads of EMI. We took off, calling, 'See you tomorrow at the show!' and went out to the elevator.

When we arrived in the lobby downstairs, Elise realized that she'd left her umbrella in Frank's suite, so I went back to get it.

I knocked on the door, and a familiar—and audibly annoyed—voice demanded, 'What? Who's there?'

'Hey Frank, it's me, Co. Elise forgot her umbrella.'

After a moment or two, the door opened a crack, and out came an arm holding the umbrella. I caught a glimpse of my idol standing there, wearing nothing but black boxer shorts. Suddenly realizing what all the noises had been, I said, 'Enjoy your EMI dinner!' As I turned to leave, he flashed me a huge grin. Nothing further was said of the incident until years later, in Los Angeles.

During the interview, we'd spoken of a new video production, which I offered to pitch to Dutch TV On May 14th, a letter arrived, with 'Frank Zappa's Music' on the letterhead:

> *Dear Co,*
>
> *It was a pleasure speaking to you on the phone last Friday. I spoke to Frank and relayed your thanks for the cassette and your question about the DUB ROOM SPECIAL. There is indeed an official one-hour version of the tape which would be used if it were to be broadcast on television. If you have any further questions, please contact me.*
>
> *Regards,*
> *Carol Farley*

The 1982 tour ended in Palermo, where with the performance went horribly wrong, and Frank announced that he was done with touring, to focus all his energy on classical music. He was, first and foremost, a composer. Most of the time I talked with him in 1983, this shift is what we discussed. News reached me from San Francisco that they were organizing a big Zappa concert featuring his classical music, but before I could call Frank to ask whether I could have copies of the recordings, he suddenly announced that he *was* going to tour again after all. Even better, he was coming to Europe in the fall, *and* he was releasing a few new albums. One of them was *Them Or Us*, the album he'd played for me in Paris.

I called him on the phone.

FRANK Hello?

CO Frank?

FRANK Co, how you're doing?

CO You must be very busy now.

FRANK Oh yeah!

CO Your decision to tour again messed up a part of the interview I did with you in Paris, as you can understand! How did you come to the decision to tour again?

FRANK I spent the last two years in the serious music world, and I found it to be in the United States probably a hundred times more corrupt and pathetic than rock'n'roll. The fact of the matter is that it's not the world for me, I don't belong in that. I just get away from it as fast as I can.

CO I will broadcast this little conversation when you send me the new album. Could you tell us something about the additional record? Because when you played the tape for me it was a one-record set.

FRANK You wanna know what else is in there? I have added in a rock'n'roll version of 'Sinister Footwear Second Movement,' and 'Truck Driver Divorce,' 'Marque-son's Chicken,' and one new song called 'Be In My Video.'

CO I've heard that you played some material on a radio station, including some of the orchestral things that were performed recently. Is that correct?

FRANK The radio station in Berkeley, KPFA, did a live broadcast of the show with the puppets.
CO Is there any material available for, let's say, a European broadcast of it?
FRANK It's possible. You would have to contact KPFA. They broadcasted and taped the whole show, it's about two hours.
CO So maybe something could be worked out in conjunction with you?
FRANK Yes. They're supposed to send me a tape of it this week, I have no idea what the quality of their recording is. They made a digital recording of it.
CO Maybe Bennett [Glotzer] or your new secretary could fill me in on that?
FRANK I'll tell her to send off the new version of *Them Or Us*. You have *Thing-Fish*?
CO I have nothing.
FRANK OK, I will have her send *Thing-Fish* and *Them Or Us*. Let me buzz her and you can give her all the mailing instructions and I'll send the tapes today. Hold on.

One rule that I learned from Zappa was this: a deal is a deal. So a short while later I received a parcel containing three cassette tapes and a letter from Barking Pumpkin Records:

> *26 June 1984*
> *Dear Mr. De Kloet,*
>
> *Enclosed please find three cassettes: 'Thing-Fish.' 'Francesco Zappa' and 'Them Or Us.' Mr. Zappa has asked me to forward these tapes to you per your conversation this morning.*
>
> *Sincerely,*
> *Susan M. Fottrell*
> *Enc. 3 cassettes FZ/sf*

The fan in me was over the moon. I sat down and listened to all three in a row—three brand new Zappa albums that no one else had ever heard!

Now I had something to look forward to: September, and the new band! The first European show was scheduled to take place in Brussels, on September 7th. Frank visibly wanted the band to offer something that he didn't find in the world of classical music. The vibe was totally different from what it had been with the '82 band: looser, with more vocals and humor. I spoke with Frank after the soundcheck, and asked if I could interview him in a few weeks, before his Rotterdam show—this time for prominent Dutch music magazine *OOR*. He agreed, and on September 15th I made my way over to the Amsterdam Marriott, where everyone was staying. The fact that everyone was staying at the same hotel spoke volumes of Frank's attitude toward the tour: usually he stayed in better, more expensive hotels than the band and crew. This time he was looking for the feeling of a band on tour together.

I sat drinking a Coke while FZ's bodyguard John Smothers devoured an enormous plate of spaghetti bolognaise. After a while, Frank came into the lobby with a lady—curly red hair, dressed in a tracksuit with Mickey Mouse printed all over it. He told me that he'd be ready for me in half an hour, and when I arrived upstairs Ernest Potters, the photographer, was busy taking portraits of Frank. This was proving difficult, as the room's primary light source was a single ceiling lamp.

Ernest told me that he'd been allowed early access to the room to set up, and while he was doing that Frank was giving an interview to another journalist (I believe from *Panorama* magazine), which should have lasted half an hour. His first question had been about why Frank's solos were so long and tedious, and Frank kicked him out after just two minutes.

Ernest and I got down to business, and I asked Ernest to take a photo of Frank and me together. Frank grumbled, but he laughed when I said I only planned to sell the picture to the magazine I'd set up myself, *Big Nose International*—the joke being that I've got an enormous honker also. My argument worked, and Frank let himself be persuaded.

While writing this book, I asked Ernest if it was OK for me to use some of his pictures in it. He very kindly agreed, and a few days later I received an email from him, in which he recalled the story of our collaboration that day.

> *It started at the editorial board of OOR, when Editor-in-Chief Jan Maarten de Winter called me over. 'Hey Ernest,' he asked, 'you like Frank Zappa, don't you?' I replied that yes, I did, and he told me, 'Then the day after tomorrow you can join Co de Kloet at the Marriott Hotel in Amsterdam.' It was in the hotel lobby that I met Co for the first time. There was also another journalist, and John Oomkes, esteemed music writer for the Haarlemse Courant/GPD newspaper. John was someone I worked with regularly, especially in the jazz scene. As usual, the dynamic part of a journalist's life consisted of waiting: waiting for the star to be ready to talk to the journalists. I was lucky. I discovered that Co wasn't just any journalist, who'd get to ask Zappa a few questions in the ten minutes allotted to us, with time for a quick picture, and then out. No, as it turned out, De Kloet was a highly knowledgeable music producer who'd known Zappa for years, and regularly corresponded with him. Zappa's management gave us the final slot of the day, which offered the opportunity for the interview to run a little longer. Then even more time was freed up for John Oomkes, Co, and me (as the only photographer to be admitted). The unknown journalist I'd seen in the lobby, who said that he worked for Panorama, had said the wrong thing to Zappa. He'd told us downstairs that he considered Zappa to be a very colorful pop artist, and he could appreciate his music but, he asked us, didn't we also hate those long and depressing guitar solos? The first question that he'd ask Zappa, he said, would be what the reason was for that guitar violence. The rest of us looked at each other in stunned amazement, but told him to go ahead. To our delight, he went in first. The door closed behind him, only to open again a few minutes later, and we gathered that he'd led with his burning question. 'And . . .?' we asked. He replied, 'Sure, I got something!' John was allowed more time, and later we did as well. To my delight, in the terrible ambiance of that terribly dull brown hotel, Frank agreed to let me take a picture that was used to illustrate the*

feature on Zappa and religion in OOR's Christmas issue. It became one of my best portraits ever.

One of the many advantages about working for the classical division of Dutch public broadcaster KRO was that I had access to their extensive international network. I knew that programmer and festival organizer Charles Amirkanian had played an important role in organizing the San Francisco project. Digging out his contact info from KRO's files, I wrote to him explaining that we wanted to broadcast his *Speaking Of Music* recordings from May 20th, and another show, called *A Zappa Affair*, from June 15th. He'd interviewed Frank that May, in front of an audience at the Exploratorium, and joined him in performing some music also. On June 15th, the Berkeley Symphony Orchestra performed Zappa's music under the baton of Kent Nagano, who'd also conducted the *London Symphony Orchestra* project. All of this was at the Zellerbach Auditorium. The budget for the performance spiraled wildly out of control, but the music was phenomenal.

I received a reply from Charles at the end of July. He was enthusiastic about my plans to broadcast the projects. At the time, he was working for KPFA, a listener-sponsored radio station since 1949. Even though the project had cost hundreds of thousands of dollars, he'd let me have copies of the tapes for 250 bucks. All that was left was to get Frank's approval, which I received later that year, in the form of a letter in which Frank wrote in red marker, 'Charles, this is okay with me. FZ.' That was how Frank did business: straight-up and to the point.

Charles sent me the tapes, and the labels read:

Speaking Of Music At The Exploratorium.
An Evening With Frank Zappa.
Radio production by: Russ Jennings.
Recorded by: Tony Ferro & Jim Bennett.
Live event produced and hosted by: Charles Amirkhanian.
Partial funding: The Exploratorium.
Recorded 5/20/1984, San Francisco, Ca.

Back at the Marriott, Frank took another look at the KPFA letter, and we started talking.

CO Last time I talked to you on the phone, you told me that you were going back on the road. You told me that one of the reasons was that you found out that the classical music was even more corrupt than the rock'n'roll scene.

FRANK Classical music world in the United States, yeah. More depressing too.

CO How did you meet with that? I mean, you take everything in your own hands, for instance the LSO project, the way that you organize it, what kind of corruption can you meet in that situation?

FRANK No, I'm talking about what I experienced doing business with the Berkeley situation. It was really unbelievable. It took years to put that together, and what finally happened in the end was, the man who made the puppets was so enthusiastic about the project that he invested eleven thousand dollars of his own money to make sure that everything was right, you know? Went over budget and he put it in there and everybody was working real hard to make it happen, and then after it was all over they didn't pay me, they never payed me for the, uh . . . they were supposed to pay me six thousand dollars for a mass of paper, music on paper, which cost me about a hundred and fifty thousand dollars—for salaries for other people to copy the parts, copy the scores, the mechanical reproduction of the scores, about a hundred and fifty thousand dollars. OK, they never paid me. Then, against my wishes, they made a bootleg videotape of the second one. And then, after it was all over, and the man who made the puppets found out that he had lost his eleven thousand dollars and the Berkeley people were not going to reimburse him for that, he found out that his homosexual lover and bookkeeper at the place had AIDS, he found out that night, all this stuff sort of happens. He has a shop that is maybe three times larger than this room and the puppets are very large and they completely fill his shop. He can't take another job in his shop, he has no way to store the puppets. The puppets are jointly owned by him and the

Berkeley orchestra, he can't sell the puppets. And he can't take the puppets apart because they own 50% of it, and they don't know what to do with it. And here is this man, he earns his living by making these things and he is stuck! OK, it's really sad and then—let's see, the dancers didn't get paid. It was horrible.

CO It's a shame! You were so enthusiastic when you told me in January in Paris.

FRANK Yeah, well it was a lovely event. I mean, to see it on stage it was great and when you hear the tapes of the performance, you'll hear that the people are laughing and having a good time, it really worked out nice, but the business side of it was controlled by people who are just, you know—no sensitivity whatsoever. If I'm going to have to deal with assholes, I'll deal with rock'n'roll assholes.

CO Yes, because I thought also when I saw you last week, there must be a difference for you having your music played by other people and being such a part of it, it must be a very special thrill. I mean, to be frank with you, I hope you don't feel offended, but comparing you last week in Brussels with Rotterdam in '82, it was like another Frank Zappa to me.

FRANK Oh, but it is! But it's a different band too. And that's one of the reasons I changed the band. I'm having a lot of fun on this tour because I love this band. This band has amazing potential. This band is the antidote to the '80s, because they actually go out on stage and deliver something that nobody else is delivering right now. The show tomorrow night will be totally different than the one in Brussels.

CO Still very vocal-orientated, of course?

FRANK Well, there will be vocals, but the names of the songs will be different and all the solos will be different, and who knows what the joke of the night will be here. For the last two nights it has been the word 'spoo,' which is very hard to explain to you. And a few nights before that it was the word 'malamute.' But these things have a tendency to liven the show up. I'll have to find out what tomorrow's mystery word will be.

CO It's gonna be hard in a place like Rotterdam.

FRANK Oh, everything is hard in a place like Rotterdam!
CO Is that the negative side of your profession, that you are forced to spend time in the Ahoy every once in a while?
FRANK Well, I wouldn't say that the Ahoy is one of the worst places we worked at. I hate the Drammenhallen in Drammen, which is near Oslo, I always hate working there. There's another building in Lyon that I dread, we played two outdoor shows right after the concert in Brussels, freezing cold and it snowed at one of them. In Ahlen it snowed just as we were finishing the set, and the next night in Lorelei rain was pouring down, went out there and did two great shows. I figure if the audience will stand there in the rain why shouldn't we just go out there and, you know, give it to them?
CO Sure!
FRANK But in general, when you work in Europe you are playing in the worst halls in the world. They have terrible halls for rock music over here.
CO Makes you remember the days that you were in Amsterdam, in the Concertgebouw, because those were always—acoustically speaking—great events.
FRANK Yeah, the Concertgebouw is OK.
CO What problems do you face with your specialized entertainment?
FRANK Well, I face a lot of problems but I would rather not discuss the problems, I'd rather say that on this tour we're having people come up to us and say, 'I will never forget this concert for the rest of my life,' which is something that I haven't heard people say about the shows for a number of years. I'm happy that in the United States, for example, the general acceptance of the band was like—the audience gave the impression that they were very grateful that there was somebody still doing 'that.' Because most of the other groups, the really big hit groups, you know, with the diagonal zippers and the fancy hairdo and all that stuff, some of them are going on stage and have their shows on tape, it's on a Revox in the back, they're not even playing. They're just out their posing, and they are doing their hits, and they're pretending to do their video, and then they take your money and go away. We actually go out there and do something! We play

music and we play it for that particular audience, and if the audience gives us a little bit of energy we're gonna give it back to them in a special way.

CO Your unique position in that is that I think that this band is—as we discussed before—very, very different.

FRANK Yes.

CO If I may put it like this: your former bands had a certain appeal, and it seems that you have a lot of those bands in this group, if you know what I mean.

FRANK Yeah. Well, this group has more scope, has more possible varieties of types of music that they can play convincingly.

CO And it is good to see Ike Willis again!

FRANK Yeah, I'm happy for that too.

CO He is one of the leading roles in *Thing-Fish.*

FRANK Yeah, he is Thing-Fish.

CO What are the chances of having that released, and in which countries?

FRANK It's coming out everywhere.

CO Do you think that it will be hard to get it across here?

FRANK It will be difficult, but I think the challenge is worth it. It's gonna have a book in it that has all the lyrics and all the stage instructions, so that you know what you're seeing while the story is going on, and if you can read English the thing will make you laugh a lot.

CO It's extremely funny!

FRANK Yeah!

CO You use some of the *Hustler* material in that booklet too?

FRANK Nothing that you saw in *Hustler* will be in the book.

CO Because that was worth a couple of laughs also.

FRANK Oh yeah! But I don't own the rights to those photographs and there is no way I can use it.

CO On the *Them Or Us* album, the 'Ya Hozna' song. Which is—

FRANK Backwards.

CO Backwards 'Sofa.'

FRANK There's something else backwards too. There is an exercise rap that Moon is doing, that's in there. And there is a few bars of 'Lonely Little Girl.'

CO You sent me a tape of the *Francesco Zappa* stuff on the Synclavier. A cooperation of two Zappas—

FRANK I produced his album! I did the same thing for him as Quincy Jones did for Michael Jackson. I helped him with his arrangements a little bit. Except that I didn't ask him to wear a glove or get his nose made smaller.

CO And when is the first *Francesco* video coming up?

FRANK [laughs] That is a good question! Nobody has thought about that yet, but it would make a fabulous video.

[Tape ends]

As mentioned in Ernest Potter's email that's quoted above, one of the photos that he took in Amsterdam (with the cheapo ceiling lamp) actually turned out amazing, with the lamp forming a halo that frames Frank. It fit perfectly with the piece I wrote for the Christmas issue of *OOR*, which I gave the title 'Zappa & The Christ Biz.' It focused on Frank's fascination with awful TV preachers.

Also that year, for the October 6th issue of *OOR*, I wrote the piece called 'The Zappa Affaire,' which I closed with Zappa's line, 'If I have to deal with assholes, I will deal with rock & roll assholes.' That piece also was accompanied by Ernest's wonderful work.

At the show the next day, Frank seemed to have shaken off his frustration with his classical adventures, and his 'boogie band' was in top form. One small disappointment for me, though, was this: just like in Brussels, the band no longer included Napoleon Murphy Brock.

1985

Old master

IN THE SUMMER OF 1985, I WAS WORKING FOR KRO AT THE WORLD MUSIC COMPETITION IN THE SOUTH OF THE COUNTRY, AND I SPENT A WEEK AT A BEAUTIFUL FAMILY HOTEL IN MAASTRICHT. When I returned home to Kortenhoef, I found a large package waiting for me: a press copy of the first of *The Old Masters*, a beautiful repressing of some of Frank's old LP work. The large, silver-colored box was illustrated by Donald Roller Wilson, who'd already designed art for Frank in the past. The box contained an extra LP with odds and ends, and a full-color booklet. Included with the beautiful gift was a packing invoice from ICA—Intercontinental Absurdities, Frank's company.

> *Pro Forma Invoice 7-2-85*
> *1 box weighing 6 pounds containing:*
> *1 seven record box set total value $100.00*
> *UNSOLICITED GIFT*
> *Country of Origin: USA*

It was a time of upheaval in the American music world. Lobbying groups such as the PMRC—the Parents Music Resource Center, a hobby project of Al Gore's wife Tipper and some other senators' wives—were threatening First Amendment rights by demanding that album covers should carry 'Explicit Content' warning stickers. In September, Gail sent me a package, the 'Z- Pac,' with a letter that began, 'Dear person who has NOT been fooled by the Wives of Big Brother . . .' Included in the package was a transcript of Frank's full testimony before the US Senate on September 19th, 1985. It also contained a copy of the letter Frank had sent to Ronald Reagan on August 29th, with the incredible opening line, 'Mr. President, even though I disagree strongly with many administration policies, I have never doubted that your personal views on basic Constitutional issues are sincere.'

I shared Frank's hatred of censorship, and when he sent me the videotapes of his Senate testimony, I felt a sense of shared responsibility, as an ambassador. Gail called and asked if I could help to generate traction for the issue in the Netherlands, and asked for a list of DJs who were likely to play Zappa on the radio.

In October, I received another letter from Gail, along with a package containing videotapes of the testimony, stickers, and photos:

> *Dear Co,*
>
> *Thanks for all your assistance . . .*
>
> *This is to remind you that I am quite anxious for the hot radio list—particularly stations (and the names of the DJs if possible) that play FZ's music. Also, please copy me with names you collect so we can add them to our mail list. Enclosed are some items we put together for you.*
>
> *Best regards,*
> *Gail Zappa*

1986

Partners

WITH MENNO KALMANN, MY PARTNER IN CRIME, I MADE A BUSINESS TRIP TO NEW YORK AND LOS ANGELES, TO TAKE CARE OF SOME ARRANGEMENTS. The first meeting we had was at Zappa's house, at 4pm on June 6th. Frank was downstairs in his studio. We chatted to Gail for a while and took some photos, and we explained to her that Menno and I wanted to import *The Old Masters* to Holland, through our production company Siësta Productions. The deal was simple: we'd buy the albums at a reduced price, paying in advance, and we'd hold the right to sell them in the Netherlands. Gail went down to fetch Frank, and we asked if she'd mind if we took a few pictures of the 'Dangerous Kitchen.' She told us to go ahead.

When Gail returned with Frank, it was clear that she'd already told him of our plans. Frank walked in, grasped my hand with his famously firm handshake, and exclaimed, 'So, we're partners now!' That's how quickly these things can be done.

That same day, June 6th, Steve Vai turned twenty-six and threw a birthday party for himself. After a few coffees in the kitchen, Frank led Menno and me downstairs to the studio, to listen to some of the music he was working on. Gail walked in, and announced that she was on her way to Steve's party. Frank replied that he was too busy to go, but he'd sign the book that Gail had chosen as a birthday gift. He put me in the role of a living music stand, to hold the book for him to sign. I obliged, and noticed that it was an illustrated children's book by Maurice Sendak, *Where The Wild Things Are*.

Years later, Steve went on to make a CD, LP, and DVD with the same title. We were already good friends by then, and while we sat in my living room in Kortenhoef he played his new album for me. I remarked how sweet it was that he'd used the title of that birthday gift from Frank and Gail. His jaw dropped, and he asked how I knew. I told him the story of that day, and we agreed that everything happens for a reason—coincidences don't exist. I'll leave it to Steve to share the exact dedication with the world, should he ever choose to, but I'll say here that Frank's professional and personal admiration of Steve, as well as his love for him, shine through in the words he wrote.

Our 'kitchen session' included some moments that are too personal to share here, but I'll make exception for one. As Gail was busy pouring coffee and grapefruit juice, and Frank was hunting around for a pack of smokes, I happened to mention the Boulez days in Paris, and that amazing hotel suite. Frank surreptitiously slid around behind Gail, caught my eye, and silently put a finger to his lips: what happens in Paris stays in Paris. So there stood my hero, acting like a child caught with his hand in the cookie jar.

The following month, I got a phone call from Jan Douwe Kroeske, a highly respected promotor at VARA. At the time, he was doing a show called *Tracks*, and he asked if I'd be up for making a Zappa special. He knew that I'd been to L.A., and that I had both the Berkeley tapes and the PMRC material. I prepared my material at home, and we recorded a live special in the Hilversum 3 radio studios. As it turned out, it was exactly twenty years after the release of *Freak Out*. I played 'Mo 'N' Herb's Vacation' on a pop station—from the maxi single *Barking Pumpkin Goes Digital*. Our special included long discussions on 'Porn Wars' and the vinyl pressing of *Frank Zappa Meets The Mothers Of Prevention*. 'Porn Wars' contains a steady stream of snippets from the PMRC hearings before the US Senate. I played a few clips of Zappa's testimony, and of course 'Porn Wars' itself. I also played a few selections from *The Old Masters* box Menno and I had just made a distribution deal for.

The icing on the cake was a phone call late in the broadcast. While our final musical fragment was playing, I called Gail and asked if Frank would like to join us on the air and say a few words. She told me she'd have to pull him out of a meeting, but she thought it might work—and it did!

FRANK Sorry it took so long, I was in the middle of a meeting.

CO Oh, I'll be short, all right?

FRANK OK.

CO First of all, I would like to ask you—we just played part of the *Prevention* album—could you tell us in short what your procedure was when putting together the 'Porn Wars' piece?

FRANK First, you have to gather all the dialogue pieces, and they were stored as digital samples into a machine called the Synclavier, and then things called patches were made. The patches, a list of samples determining which sample lives under which key on the keyboard. In other words, middle C might be Senator Hollings saying, 'Well,' and C sharp might be Paula Hawkins saying, 'Burn, burn, burn,' and so on and so forth. All the different lines are located underneath keys on the keyboard, and then when you just play the keyboard, instead of musical notes coming out, different parts of speech would come out.

CO Great! Did you get any reaction on it so far?

FRANK What? From the people in the Senate?

CO For instance.

FRANK Well, most of them say, 'No comment,' and the only actual comment that we got was from an aide to Senator Paula Hawkins, who said, 'Oh, that's funny!'

CO Hey Frank, we heard that you are working on the new *Old Masters* box. Is it definite already what's gonna be in it?

FRANK Yes, everything between *Uncle Meat* and *Just Another Band From L.A.*, so *Uncle Meat, Hot Rats, Burnt Weeny Sandwich, Weasels Ripped My Flesh, Fillmore East, Chunga's Revenge*, and *Just Another Band From L.A.*, plus a mystery disc.

CO A mystery disc also? That's great!

FRANK That means I think there is either one or two more records in this box than the other one, because *Uncle Meat* is a double.

CO Did you also add extra instrumental parts like you did for instance on *Cruisin' With Ruben & The Jets*?

FRANK No, it's all the original tapes, they just have been digitally remastered.

CO I see. When I was over, you played me some material from 1968 and 1974 that were wonderfully remixed. Do you have any plans for that?

FRANK Oh yeah! I'm working on another CD package now for Rykodisc, called *You Can't Do That On Stage Anymore*. And a lot of the things will be included in that package.

CO So there's a lot more new stuff coming up?

FRANK Yeah, as a matter of fact I just have been rushing through my vault and looking for really odd little pieces of tape that I can transfer to digital, and that's what I have been doing for the last week: finding original 7.5 IPS tapes that were recorded on this Uher that I used to carry around with me, and those have been transferred over and I have found some amazing things. A whole concert from the original Mothers Of Invention, recorded in a little nightclub in the Bronx called the Factory, and just odd stuff like that. I mean, I couldn't even believe that I still had some of these things, and I have been transferring them to digital and then they'll be edited and put together into stuff.

CO So you're diving for treasures in your own dungeon?

FRANK Yeah, I'm working in a sequin mine.
CO Another thing that will interest a lot of fans is simply one word, which is 'touring.'
FRANK Well, right now the answer is no, because the main thing that I am working on right now, besides these tapes, is to try and do a television show. I had a meeting last week with the head of nighttime programming for ABC Network, I had a meeting today with the programming guy from Fox Network, and on Thursday at four o'clock I have a meeting at Disney, and what I'm trying to do is put on a one-hour, five nights a week with a live band, which I hope I'll be able to send to Europe via satellite.
CO That would be great! Like Elvis!
FRANK No, it's not like Elvis, you know, it's like the show is not just musical performance, it's a combination of music and politics and interviews. I want to get videos from Europe and, if there are any, from the Middle East or Japan. Just to have different kinds of things from all over the world in the show for the American audience, and also it makes a little bit more interesting if it goes out to other countries.
CO So it's going to be an immense TV extravaganza?
FRANK Well, within the budget that they allow you for doing this, so I don't know how extravagant.
CO There is a revival going on here in Holland—
FRANK Huh? Say that again, Co?
CO You hear me now?
FRANK Yeah!
CO There's a revival going on here in Holland, with a lot of guitar bands, '60s-orientated. Is the same thing happening over in Los Angeles, and what is your response to it?
FRANK I don't know whether it's happening here or not, because I don't pay any kind of attention to that kind of stuff.
CO Do you think that if it was there, it might go parallel with for instance the interest for *The Old Masters*?
FRANK I would say that is only a remote possibility, because usually what happens with revival bands is it's people who don't know anything about

the original doing a real pale copy of what the original was. There are some groups in England right now who are trying to play bogus psychedelic music and, you know, it's a lot of costuming, but really that's what's being revived is the costuming, rather than the musical style.

CO Do you have any plans on releasing Synclavier music like you did on *Francesco* or the *Boulez* album?

FRANK There's a contract sitting on my desk right now with Angel Records. They want three classical computer albums, and I'm not sure whether I am going to do the deal with them, but they have offered a deal for three of those kind of albums.

CO We'll keep an eye out for that. There are two more things I have on my list here. You played me some stuff from your *Guitar* box. Can you give any information on that?

FRANK From the new *Guitar* box?

CO Yeah, I mean the new one.

FRANK I'm still working on it. For example, last night I found a piece of tape that was recorded in Tokyo, which I believe is the earliest recorded version of 'Zoot Allures,' which is real slow, and it's really an interesting version. And I think before I put this next *Guitar* box out I'm gonna do some more digging in the archives, because there are things that might be interesting in there.

CO Would that be a version from around '75, '76?

FRANK That was approximately '76, because we were only in Japan once.

CO We talked about a lot of big projects, very interesting projects. What about a new LP, like a rock LP?

FRANK We're mixing it now.

CO Is there already a working title?

FRANK Well, I'd rather not say, because probably if I would make this deal for the television show the album will have the same title as the show.

CO The last thing I have here is *Having A Bad Day*.

FRANK Oh, Dweezil's new album! We're just about ready to ship it.

CO How did it turn out?

FRANK It turned out great.

CO Did you produce it?

FRANK Me and Bob Stone.

CO Do you also play on it, or is it Dweezil on guitar all the way?

FRANK No, it's all Dweezil. I am not performing on it in any way.

CO There's a friend here, and he's asking, 'How does he find time to do all this?'

FRANK Well, I slept three hours last night.

CO OK! We're gonna play 'He's So Gay' now, so we want to thank you very much and we'll be in touch again!

FRANK OK, see you, Co!

CO Bye-bye!

FRANK Bye-bye!

During the remainder of the year, I did a few odd jobs for Frank, wrote some articles, did a little radio. My next direct encounter with the world of Zappa would be another one of those magical coincidences.

1987

Maestro Nagano

ONE SUNNY DAY IN OCTOBER I WAS SITTING IN MY GARDEN IN KORTENHOEF, DRINKING COFFEE AND MUSING ON ALL THINGS MUSICAL. I was teaching saxophone at the time, as well as working part-time as a music producer for KRO, a broadcaster that (back then at least) boasted a bustling and colorful music department.

Kortenhoef is a tiny town. My house is situated by a small dike, and opposite is a lovely restaurant. At the time, a few small apartments stood behind the restaurant, which were rented out as hotel rooms. One morning, late in what was proving to be a lovely Indian summer, I saw a slim Asian man enjoying a stroll along my dike. He glanced into my garden, and our eyes met. Stunned, I recognized him as Kent Nagano, the conductor.

'Good morning, Mr. Nagano!' I called, and now it was his turn to be stunned. There he was, long before he became world famous, out for a walk in a small town he'd never heard of before, and the first local he encounters knows who he is! I invited him into my garden and explained that I knew him thanks to my friendship with Frank Zappa, and that I really admired his work on the *London Symphony Orchestra* album. As it turned out, he was friends with Susan Rubio also, and we remarked on what a small world it can be—something that has been true my whole life.

By another coincidence, Nagano was in Holland to work on a project with a colleague of mine at KRO.

Because I was frequently promoting Zappa on the radio, I asked Nagano if I could interview him. He agreed. We went back to his apartment, and I recorded the following conversation:

CO Mr. Nagano, you are here in Holland to conduct music by Stravinsky, and I think you are going to do the *Sacre du printemps* tomorrow?

KENT Yes, *Sacre du printemps* and Szymanovsky's *Harnasie*.

CO Yeah. The reason that we are talking now is that you are actually the first director, first conductor, that made a real profound, real intensive recording of the orchestral music by Frank Zappa. Could you please tell us—I believe that you grew up in California—when was the first time that you heard about his material?

KENT Well, Frank Zappa's music was very popular during the 1960s, and I was young at this time, but my interests weren't really in rock music very much. So even though I had heard his name, and I had seen his pictures in magazines or on the cover of record jackets that my friends had, I didn't really personally know his music at all at this time. I only knew him as a rock phenomenon. So when I came to know Frank Zappa's rock music was many, many years later, in 1983, just before we made the recording with the London Symphony. As part of my preparation, I thought it would be best to educate myself. And so I went out and purchased the complete library of his rock music and listened to all of it, and to my surprise I found it very, very interesting! Far above the quality of the normal rock music which, I felt, was being written at the time, and this period being the late 1970s, early 1980s, to me had almost no interest in terms of popular music. Now it's a different story, I feel. There have been over the past couple of years sort of a re-emergence of creativity within the rock popular medium. Led by groups like The Police or the vocalist Kate Bush, or the independent enterprises of Sting, formerly from The Police. There are some really interesting avenues that are being explored, but in the period of the late 1970s, for me personally, there was nothing really particularly fascinating about the rock music. So, when I listened to Frank's albums, it was very refreshing, and in a way encouraging that someone was actually writing music which young people, or all ages of people, were enjoying that was still of a popular genre.

CO Frank had worked with orchestras before that. For instance, with the movie *200 Motels*—he also did the recordings and performances with Zubin Mehta, has always shown a great interest in the classical repertoire. Even in his rock band he made quotes—literally real quotes—by different classical composers. Somehow he never managed to do a recording—before you came along with the *LSO*—never made a proper recording of this music. I think maybe that has something to do with the role of a contemporary composer in the United States. Do you, as a conductor, have any views on how, for instance, a Californian audience treats its contemporary composers?

KENT Well, yes. It all depends on how good the composer is. So many times people just think of music as contemporary music and is it performed or is it not performed. And the point is that of all the contemporary music, perhaps less than one percent of that music, in my opinion, is worth performing. Now, I do a lot of contemporary work—twentieth century work. So you imagine how many scores I look at, and how many scores I really discard as something I personally don't care for. So whether a performer, whether a composer, is played by orchestras really depends first of all on how good of a composer he is, and secondly on how good of a musician he is. Now, you have to be your own judge in terms of how good of a composer Frank Zappa is. But I can say honestly, as a musician,

I have never worked with anyone of a finer caliber of musicality and just plain technique than Frank Zappa has. And that's everyone. He is a superb musician with fantastic hearing capability. He's very, very sensitive, he cares a lot about how music is put together and about the orchestra, because when you take into account that Frank Zappa is such a superb musician—like all musicians, it implies a certain amount of versatility and a certain amount of just basic literary skills. And by that I mean Frank is learned: he's studied music history, he's studied composition, worked with Varèse, worked with Berio, he's very, very much in tune with contemporary American society, and with contemporary American society come prevailing trends in art and prevailing trends in music. He is truly an artist by the strict definition of the word. Educated with a sense of history, and writing with his own equipment in his own time. Now, he does make a distinction between the types of music that he writes. Some music he calls 'money-making music' or just plain rock'n'roll music, other music he calls more 'fancy music.' But I think it's fair to say that what he hears in his mind definitely stretches what the normal limitations of rock music would be, certainly, because he needs more instruments to make the sounds that he hears in his mind. And those forces are much more similar to those forces that we deal with on an everyday basis within the symphony world, or within the computer world, than is available with a couple guitars with a rhythm section. Which is pretty unsophisticated in terms of the basic music-generating elements. So, in answer to your question, I guess what I'm saying is that, as a composer, the audiences have to decide, and historians have to decide, how good someone is. But as a skilled musician I can say that I think of Frank Zappa very much as a close friend and as a colleague, one that has equal capabilities.

CO One thing that Frank probably has in his favor is that he has a name for himself—also has a career for himself, which can provide—well, let me put it differently. Let's say you are a twenty-one-year-old composer in California, it's not very likely that you'll buy tickets, go to London, and hire an orchestra. Do you think that within—I think you are the best judge of this—within the American systems there is, on a musical level, music by new composers? If it has the quality that you think it should have, is there a possibility for it to be performed?

KENT Yes, there's always a possibility. All it really takes is enough money, you can buy your own orchestra and have a piece performed. And oftentimes that's how composers will get their works heard. They'll find sponsorship, or they'll find somebody to help sponsor them as an individual, or they'll find some government underwriting—this is speaking of the United States—to help them get their music exposed. I have personal opinions about that, because it's been on very rare occasions that I've found that someone who is that profound of a business person, who is able to coerce or otherwise get people to agree to support them monetarily, that so much energy is put forward to tracking down the finances, that oftentimes the artistic product itself becomes almost secondary—

CO Yeah.

KENT And it's very rarely that I've come to find a good piece that's come out of a big government commission, for example. But when I find a young composer, and there are *many* young composers now who are just unbelievably skilled, we seem to be—I was talking with some of my colleagues just last year, how bright the future looks with some of the composers who are on the horizon now. People like Michael Torke, or George Benjamin, Aaron Kernis. These gentlemen are between twenty-three years old and twenty-seven years old, and they're writing very, very sophisticated, mature music already, which is reminiscent of the big glorious writing boom that came out of the early part of the century. So it's looking very, very positive. And when I feel I'm fortunate enough to come in contact with some of *this* kind of music, of this caliber, superb caliber, by someone who is obviously at the beginning of their career—People like myself, and I'm not alone, other people like Maestro Ozawa or Maestro Boulez, Maestro Previn, lots of people—even Zubin Mehta, with an organization as large as the New York Philharmonic, will oftentimes step out of their way to encourage young composers by simply programming one of their pieces. No sponsorship or anything, just program it to let it be heard, so that the composer can learn and grow, and so that audiences can become familiar with the name. I would say that I would have to honestly believe that if the composer is really, really strong, and good with his artwork, and is determined enough to at least let the people *hear* the music, that in time he will get some performances. Now you were saying, in a way, Frank Zappa has it lucky because he has a name already, so of course, yes. I mean, he also has a name which is very easy to ridicule. I know that this has been very difficult for him. People don't take his music that seriously, they just maybe laugh and say, 'Oh well, here's a rock fellow trying to do something in the classical field.' I mean, fame has its price too. It may be easy to get a performance, perhaps it's very difficult to be taken seriously.

CO Yes, for instance at the beginning of the '70s the concert in the Royal Albert Hall was canceled because they dug some old albums out of the closet and said, 'Well, once you made a song which went like *this*, so now we are going to ban your orchestral concerts.' So I understand what you mean.

KENT I don't know that story at all but—but, you know it's never very easy to be a composer. This in a way is a curse, because if you are a composer you *have* to write, because that's what your soul and heart is telling you to do. But it's very, very difficult to have people judge your creativity.

CO You mentioned Varèse, which interests me, being Frank's idol when he was in his teens, so to speak. Frank was desperate to get in contact with him, which unfortunately was a telephone call only. The comparison between the music of Varèse and Frank's music, how do you see that? Because some tone colors, some orchestrations—especially the use of percussion—do you think that Varèse has been a teacher in a way to him?

KENT Well, it's not so much a matter of what I think. If you quote Frank Zappa, then yes, Varèse has definitely been a teacher and an influence on him. I personally don't see that as such a strong connection, other than the very use of percussion and the strong role that percussion takes in the music. More, one has to recall that Frank Zappa is very, very much an American. He calls himself an American, he's immersed within American popular culture, and he's immersed with an American lifestyle. And all of these sociological facts display themselves in little snatches of Americana melodies that you can hear. And he sews together these melodies in various collages that come with a very striking effect sometimes. And even though the music sounds nothing like it at all, and there's no real comparison in terms of writing technique, some of the other composers who have done that same sort of tradition with Americana melodies, if you will, where composers like Charles Ives and early parts of Aaron Copland—just by the fact that they will take existing melodies, even folk melodies, and then sew them together and come up with a symphonic form—in a very, very loose way I'd say that *that* is more of the tradition that Frank Zappa follows. Taking existing culture and then putting that together in a large form, rather than the strict rhythmic development of a Varèseian student.

CO The question that interests me is, how does a conductor work? How does the conductor talk to the orchestra, work with the orchestra, when the composer is sitting beside him on the rehearsal stage? I saw you do it in London, on video, and I was wondering, is that a very different style of working? Because you have the source talking next to you and you can discuss things. How does it *feel* when you do it? You did it with Messiaen last year. What's the difference with conducting something that was written by somebody you've never met?

KENT Well, I always enjoy working with the composer right there. Especially if it's a piece that I happen to respect a lot. In general, I'd say it's a wonderful, wonderful thing, because you can impose your interpretation, but at the same time you can always have the feed-in, or the input, from the composer, whether or not this is in the right direction. Now, this implies that the composer is mature, and that the composer is a good musician, and that the composer understands the compositional process. Which is that once the piece has been written you have to let it go, and let it go through the creation process. In other words, let it be performed. When I worked with Messiaen, when I worked with Benjamin, anybody, it's always a very, very big delight, because there's a sense of spontaneity and creativity that can be generated. A conductor can feel like you can take—you can try many, many more risks that perhaps otherwise you might be a little shy to turn it away from what the composer really had in mind. You can just ask the composer right then and there, 'How about if we do this? Or how about if we do that?' And sometimes you can deviate, to a degree, from what is written on the score. But it's not always a nice experience, particularly if the composer is a bad musician and you realize, much to your disappointment, that you know the score much better than the composer knows. Which happens, believe it or not, much more than the other way around. I'd say, in my experience, almost two thirds of the time the composer doesn't really know what the score sounds like, which is terribly discouraging as a performer. And *that* is always a terrible collaboration. Or there are other times when the composer can be extremely arrogant, to the point where it doesn't matter what's on the page, it becomes more of a computer programming exercise. Just simply to realize what's on the paper, without any blood or love, or breathing or any living kind of qualities. Then it's always a horrible collaboration too. So it's not always a rewarding thing to do, but I feel fortunate that many times it has been.

CO My last question is, do you see it as an opportunity—you mentioned some names that frankly I must say I don't know—*yet*, I hope—about these new American composers. You are a conductor, you are becoming more and more famous, you conduct good orchestras, talk to a lot of people, most importantly you travel around the world. Do you think that it might be part of your—to put it bluntly, your job to bring those people from the United States, their music, with you? Maybe introduce it in different countries? You are doing it now in an interview, but do you see other ways that you can be some sort of promoter of the music that might otherwise not be heard here?

KENT In a sense, as a musician, it's really your job to share as much as possible, and I *do* do that. Last month I brought George Benjamin from London, he's a British composer, to a festival—the George Benjamin Festival that I created and that I sponsored, just simply so America could hear some of his music. Later on this month, when I go to the New York Philharmonic, I will also take scores of George Benjamin, different scores, with me so they can be heard. Likewise, I've asked the Ensemble InterContemporain, and they've approved, to bring the young Michael Torke and Aaron Kernis over from New York to have their works premiered in Paris. I've taken music from Japan and brought it to Paris with the ensemble as well. With the Opéra National de Lyon, where I work, we've commissioned Japanese composers, American composers, French composers. People whom I've met—I've come into contact with, who are very, very important and need to be encouraged and need to have a platform to have their music heard. Yes, of course, this is all part of our responsibility. Particularly right now, when there is so much economic pressure, for some reason which escapes me actually, because it's illogical. In the interests of economics, people oftentimes program what they feel are sure-fire box office draws, which usually translates into only the most staid, recognized warhorses of the traditional repertoire. Which is a trend that's alarming, because—in the United States anyway—it's resulted in first of all a horrible reactionary climate that's taking place, followed by several orchestras going bankrupt and closing their doors. I mean, you can never actually live without going forward. The moment you start going backwards, by definition you're going to die. And it's a very important period right now for us as musicians, and us as performers, to keep the fresh water coming in, otherwise our very medium could change drastically in the next ten years or so.

CO I think that is a great line on which to end. Thank you very much.

KENT You're welcome, thank you.

1988

Genius with horns

THE NEW BAND HAD ARRIVED—AND WHAT A BAND IT WAS! Alongside a few veterans, it featured some new names and a five-piece horn section. Word from America told of a massive setlist, tons of new material, and some interesting covers. Expectations were high when I arrived in Ghent, in Belgium, on April 10th, for the first European show. Zappa was in a great mood, and the soundcheck was almost a concert in its own right. One of the new guys was multi-instrumentalist Mike Keneally, who could sing also—his Terry Bozzio imitation on 'Titties 'N' Beer' had Frank grinning from ear to ear. It was also great to see Ike Willis again, and I'd heard rumors that Flo & Eddie would be joining the band. Unfortunately, rumors were all they were.

Backstage at the Sportpaleis venue—programming, according to Frank, their very first rock show—we talked about an upcoming Honker home video production on Bruce Bickford and his Claymations. Frank asked for my help with a film festival in The Hague, which had expressed an interest in the film. He told me he'd be OK with me making the arrangements for the film's showing at the festival, but that the tape couldn't be copied because the official release date hadn't been pinned down. I was glad to help, of course. Frank thanked me and said that Gail would be in touch.

The Ghent show was phenomenal, and I couldn't wait for the two shows in Ahoy that were scheduled for May.

In the meantime, I was still in touch with Jan Douwe Kroeske, who was preparing for an interview with Frank, for his TV show *Kippenvel* on VARA. He asked if I'd help coming up with questions and if I'd accompany him to the taping at the Amstel Hotel. On May 2nd, I was sitting in the lobby, thinking back on that night in 1979. I arrived far too early, long before the TV crew got there. I was reading a newspaper when I heard a voice calling out behind me. 'Hey, Co!' It was Frank, with his new bodyguard, Dave—they were checking in. Dave was a short guy (compared with John Smothers, at least) from England who'd lived in Spain for a time. What he lacked in height, he made up for in muscle and a steely stare: Don't fuck with Dave. Frank sent Dave to arrange for a piano to be put in his room, and half an hour later I saw several of the hotel's people carrying it up a staircase. I met Dave again later when he was with Dweezil, and again at the Yellow Shark in 1992.

Jan Douwe's tapings were influenced a little by the fact that he was completely starstruck. Zappa remained charming throughout, and they clearly connected, but the conversation never really got rolling. Still, all things considered, it was a nice piece for *Kippenvel.*

Just before the Ahoy show, I was in Frank's dressing room when he asked if I'd like to read some new lyrics to a song he'd worked up for that night's show. Would I? Of course I would! They were the lyrics to 'Elvis Has Just Left The Building,' jotted down on Amstel Hotel stationary. 'You think they will like this?' he asked. Yeah, they'll like it! The song was to become a great showcase for Keneally's vocal talents.

Frank got ready to perform, and I walked down into Ahoy's backstage area, where I ran into Mike Keneally. We chatted for a while, and he handed me a cassette of his own music. Not much later, I played his piece 'Airport' on Dutch radio. It was the beginning of a long personal and professional relationship.

Frank heard that the second show, on May 4th, hadn't sold out. In the Netherlands, May 4th is a day of remembrance for all Dutch civilians and armed forces killed since the beginning of World War II—perhaps that was the reason? During the first show, he read aloud the setlist for the second show, making sure to add, 'You see? No repeats.' The band could easily have filled *three* shows without playing the same song twice. Was it not Jeff Simmons who said, 'You have your armies, you have your rock bands . . .'?

At any rate, the second show sold out quickly after that, and the two shows were so good that Zappa later used the multi-tracks from those two nights in various releases. I saw no signs of any growing tensions within the group, nor that Frank was becoming sicker and sicker. The story of the '88 tour is documented in the book *Zappa The Hard Way* by Zappa historian Andrew Greenaway.

During the first show, a fax arrived at my home:

May 3, 1988

Dear Co De,

Frank has agreed to allow the amazing Mr. Bickford to be screened at the third annual Image and Sound Festival which is being done through the Film Foundation of The Hague. They are planning to show the video Thursday, June 2nd at 21:30 and 23:00. The circumstances under which Frank has agreed to allow this viewing are that you will be solely responsible for the video at all times, that it will not leave your hands except to go into the projector, and that you will return it to us immediately. We need to make sure no copies are made as we do not have a scheduled release date. If you can assist us and agree to take care of this, please confirm by return fax or telex. Then I would ask you to contact Marc Thelosen at: Film Foundation of The Hague.

Kindest personal regards,
Gail Zappa
For HONKER HOME VIDEO
GZ/bh

I never learned who exactly the secretary 'BH' was, but Gail later told me that she gave her a good talking-to about my first name being 'Co' and not 'Co De.'

On May 6th, two days after Zappa's very last Dutch concert, I sent a return fax confirming that I'd take care of everything.

I spent the rest of that year happily going about my 'business' of airing Zappa's music on the radio. Among other things, I put together a months-long series for my show *4FM*, in which I played every single official Zappa release in chronological order. Why not?

1989

By the way

AT THE BEGINNING OF MARCH, I SENT FZ A FEW CDS OF MY RADIO SHOW. On the 29th, I received a fax from Gail, sent from their mail-order company, Barfko-Swill:

> *Dear Co,*
>
> *Thank you as always for your continuing interest. We did receive the cd & note—FZ is in Spain via Russia at the moment. FZ will receive on return, thanks. Broadway will be released May or June in Europe via Music For Nations. You may want to contact Steve Mason in London. We are currently working on Moon and Dweezil's TV pilot for CBS which will be filmed mid-April. Best wishes and good health to you also. I am sure we will speak soon.*
>
> *Gail.*

Frank was scheduled to deliver the keynote speech at the International Music and Media Conference in Amsterdam that May. I was looking forward to seeing him, and so it was disappointing to hear that he'd been forced to cancel his appearance. It was no secret that he wasn't feeling well, and the first serious rumors of health problems were beginning to emerge.

We spoke on the phone that summer: not an interview, no questions and answers, Frank just called me. We talked about his last tour, about Dutch orchestras, and a variety of other topics. Unfortunately I didn't record this rambling conversation, but I'll never forget how, as it wound to an end, he calmly said, 'Oh, by the way, I got cancer.'

For a moment I was speechless. Then I asked whether it was treatable, and Frank answered, 'We will see,' and that he actually felt all right, considering.

From that point onward, Frank's life became shrouded in mystery, and understandably remains undocumented—it was obviously a disorienting period for him.

1990

Supplement

ON JUNE 29TH, I RECEIVED A FAX FROM ZAPPA'S PRESS AGENT, JIM NAGLE. Menno and I had enjoyed a hilarious lunch with Jim at the Sunset Marquee back in 1986. The fax read as follows:

> *ICA*
> *Dear Co:*
>
> *Anthos will publish the Dutch translation of The Real Frank Zappa Book in September. Gail was wondering if you might be interested in reading the galleys to confirm that it is a good translation. Please let me know.*
>
> *Regards,*
> *Jim Nagle*
> *Cc: Gail*

More homework for me, then.

Frank was turning fifty on December 21st of that year. Even though he wasn't in the greatest of health (to put it mildly), I was eager to celebrate it with a Frank Zappa special. NOS had a weekly four-hour program on Dutch Radio 4 called *Supplement*. This, I felt, would be the perfect length of time, *and* the perfect opportunity, for a birthday special. I called Frank in the summer, and told him that I wanted to do the recording in his studio, the Utility Muffin Research Kitchen (UMRK for short). I promised that I'd be quick and efficient about it, given the circumstances. My plan was to spend two days recording at Frank's, then bring in my colleague, radio presenter Vincent van Engelen, to help me edit everything into large blocks for *Supplement*. On Frank's birthday, I'd provide continuity between the blocks.

Frank and Gail agreed, and extended an official invitation so that I could submit a request to NOS and get the production ball rolling. I got a budget together and contacted Mark Volman and Howard Kaylan (widely known as Flo & Eddie), who had their own show at the time on K-Rock—I wanted to interview them as special guests for the broadcast. They were keen, and my budget was approved by (again) Willem van Beusekom, who by that time was Director of Radio at NOS. I collected my buddy Menno Kalmann and we left for the USA. NOS wanted to verify that we were in fact welcome, so Gail sent me the following fax:

> *To: Co de Kloet*
> *Siesta productions*
> *From: Gail Zappa*
> *Re: FZ interviews/schedule*
> *Date: 10-8-90*
>
> *Dear Co,*
>
> *This is to confirm that you will be in Los Angeles to conduct interviews with Frank Zappa on the 26th and 27th of October. We look forward to seeing you.*
>
> *Kindest personal regards,*
> *Gail*

And we did indeed receive a warm welcome. We were staying at the Hyatt ('The Riot House') on Sunset, and our schedule was laidback, partially because of Frank's routine—he was suffering from pockets of severe exhaustion. He was friendly and cooperative throughout, but the cancer was clearly taking its toll. We recorded a few cassettes of material, and Frank gave me a DAT tape that he'd labeled 'Interview Music.' It held unreleased material, including the Synclavier version of 'Outrage At Valdez.' He asked if I'd share my interview tapes with his friends from the Eastern Bloc, and of course I agreed.

Menno and I watched as Frank worked on assembling *Civilization Phaze III*. One of my favorite memories is of him spending hours to perfect a sample of a wine glass. 'Buffalo Voice' features the sound of a metal bar hitting an empty wine glass. The sample was slightly distorted, and Frank was convinced that the piece would work better if it could be cleaned up. One of his studio compatriots, a whiz kid by the name of Todd Yvega, was growing increasingly frustrated with his inability to fix the problem, and he was further put out, perhaps, by Frank's own growing frustration. Todd tried to weasel his way out of it by suggesting that the sample sounded good as it was.

Frank looked at Menno, then at me and Bob Stone, the engineer, and replied, 'That's because you've been working with these fuckin' avant-garde composers for such a long time!' We made another pot of coffee, and Todd returned to his work. He nailed it eventually, and the wine glass indeed features prominently on 'Buffalo Voice.'

Because Stone needed to work in the control room, Frank decided that we should go sit in the studio's live room. I sat down with my back to the drum booth, and to the imposing Bösendorfer grand piano with its extra sixth on the bass side. The wall was decorated with several guitars (including the infamous Hendrix Strat) and various posters from the *Freak Out* era. Menno sat down behind me with the recording equipment. The first part of the interview began when I presented Frank with a copy of an old advertisement. Frank had a fondness for monster movies, especially a film called *It Conquered The World*, as documented on *Roxy & Elsewhere*, in the song 'Cheepnis.' The movie features this cheesy monster, and one of the big brains at the movie studio had come up with the idea of selling dolls of the monster to children. I handed Frank the advertisement, hoping that he'd never seen it. Just as I had that time in Paris, with the book *It Can't Happen Here*, I got lucky.

Selections from the first conversation:

CO Have you ever seen this?
FRANK [laughs] No! That is fabulous! Oh Jesus, isn't that the greatest? Oh no—
CO [to Menno] That's the title of a movie Frank talks about on the *Roxy & Elsewhere* album.
FRANK Yeah! Well, I describe this monster. It looks like a little inverted ice cream cone with teeth around the bottom. What a stupid fucking monster. It's so stupid!
CO We're sitting in the UMRK. I believe that *You Are What You Is* was the first music to be recorded in this studio?
FRANK Yeah.
CO Before that it was your workplace?
FRANK No, before that it didn't exist. It was actually a—we had a Collie then, and there were some fruit trees here and the Collie used to play in the—it was like a little yard.
CO And then around 1979 you started talking about the studio?
FRANK Yeah. Well, it took a couple of years to build it. Maybe not two years but like eighteen months, something like that. It was real slow building it.
CO But it is a quite unique situation for somebody in the L.A. area to have this. For more than the L.A. area, I would suspect.
FRANK No, in Los Angeles actually a lot of people have home studios, but not very many of them have fully equipped home studios. Most of them just have, like, one room with synthesizers in it or something like that. Very few people have a setup where you can do vocals or other instruments.
CO Yes, this studio has a lot of parts. If I look over there, there is a more acoustic—
FRANK That's the vocal booth. This is the drum booth, and that's a live part of the room back there where the piano is. And this is medium dead in here.
CO And when you record here, when you did recordings with, like, band stuff, overdubbing live tapes and so on and so forth, in the beginning you didn't work digital?

FRANK It hadn't been invented yet.

CO And then you changed it around? So then the problem came up that probably a lot of the stuff you had, had to be transferred.

FRANK Yes. Not a hundred percent of the catalogue has been transferred, but maybe fifty percent.

CO Right now there are people working in there, on a new piece. You've had the Synclavier for a couple of years and you talk about it a lot. This is your ideal situation—how many musicians can you get in there?

FRANK In that box? As many as I want. And they are all virtuosos. And they all like each other. And they never threaten to quit in the middle of the tour because they hate the bass player.

CO About that particular tour [1988]—you did something I think was a first in live music situations, in the US. You had the voter-registration thing.

FRANK Yeah.

CO That turned out to be quite a success, didn't it?

FRANK Yes, it was pretty good. We managed to register eleven thousand voters in two months, in spite of local authorities trying to keep us from doing it.

CO Would that also be a type of multi-phase censorship?

FRANK Well, it's a type of political censorship, sure, because if you come into an area like, for example, Philadelphia, where we had one of the problems, the guy who was in control of the forms that you needed to fill out in order to register to vote told our people that they already had enough registered voters, they didn't want any more. And the reason he would say that is, because if you put those forms out on a table you don't know what party people are going to register under. And what they try to do is maintain a political majority in each one of those sections, and that happened to be a Republican area. And he wanted to keep a Republican majority, and he was afraid that the kids who came to my concert would register for the other party and that would then change the balance of power in his district. So it's not a small thing to do voter registration. You do it the right way, you can actually change the balance of power in a town. And some places they made it very difficult for us to do it. The other place where it was difficult was Washington D.C., and also Detroit, they had some very strange rules there that made it impossible for us to do it, even though we were sitting in the same theatre for three days and we could have registered a lot of people. They made it impossible.

CO And the impact was so big. I remember hearing a tape of you with, I hope I'm pronouncing his name right, Daniel Schorr—I think that was somewhere in the Washington area—

FRANK Yeah, Washington D.C.

CO And he sang a couple of songs with you, and he was very enthusiastic about the whole thing.

FRANK Well, I think that anybody who takes politics seriously has to realize that, unless you have people registered so that they can participate in the political process, you don't really have democracy. When some party official tries to keep people from registering to vote, I think it's a sad commentary on the state of democracy in this country. They really don't wanna have total participation of all the people. They only want to keep their position. There were a couple of other people who did it because I called them and asked them to do it. John Cougar Mellencamp did it a few concerts, Earth Wind & Fire said they would, but I don't think they ever did, and there may have been a couple of others in heavy metal that tried it but nobody stuck with it. In order to do it right you have to have somebody who is a member of the touring ensemble, a road manager or an assistant or something like that, who sets up the procedure every day of the tour. It's, like, extra work, a lot of extra work, because you have to coordinate it with the local authorities, you have to get the volunteers to come to the hall, you have to get permission from the promoter, you have to get the tables and the forms and the signs and all the rest of that stuff, and you have to set it up and take it seriously and do it, day after day after day. You can't just do it one time at one concert and say that you did it. And we did it every day. Unless somebody stopped us from doing it.

CO And almost constantly putting it on albums, starting from the *Fillmore East* album—

FRANK Prior to the *Fillmore East* album in 1971, people below the age of eighteen didn't have the right to vote in this country. And they passed the 22nd Amendment in that year, which gave kids of draft age the ability to vote. And I thought it was important that if the government can send you off to fight in a war, and you can be killed, you ought at least be able to vote to say whether or not you want to have a war, or even have a draft. So you can imagine that, during the Vietnam War, what kind of pressure was put against the 22nd Amendment. They didn't want to have eighteen-year-olds to be able to vote in this country, because everybody was afraid that all of a sudden all the protesters who had been in the street complaining about the war would suddenly register to vote, and they would vote everybody out of office. But human nature took its course and not very many of those kids actually did vote or register. They actually had a chance to make a big difference in a big hurry right around that time. As soon as they got the right to vote they could have really done something, but they didn't.

CO Maybe that also takes time, you know? A certain barrier that has to be overcome.

FRANK Well, I think that if you never had the right to vote and suddenly somebody gives it to you, maybe you don't know what it's worth when the ability to vote is handed to you. And maybe you don't take it seriously enough.

CO And probably the people who didn't want it to happen in the first place have had years and years of experience of keeping their attention from it.

FRANK Of course! You know, the easiest way is just to draft them and send them off to some other country and have them blown up. Americans are good at that.

CO Something that is starting to become a grim kind of actuality right now [during the Gulf War].

FRANK Yeah, it's unfortunate.

CO What are your personal feelings about that whole situation?

FRANK My feeling is that basically it's an Arab problem—it should be settled by Arabs. I don't think that every time there is a problem any place in the world that the United States should suddenly jump up and send hundreds of thousands of soldiers over there to fix it. And I believe that when the US government says that we are sending soldiers there to fight for a principle, they are being somewhat dishonest. Because the only thing they are really concerned about is the oil. They're not going there to protect democracy, because Kuwait was not a democracy and neither is Saudi Arabia. Both of these countries have very, very strict regimes, and to listen to speeches about people giving any other reason to this force in the Gulf other than protecting US oil interests is totally fake. And I think that it's even more absurd that you have a lot of US soldiers going over there to protect the interests of the oil company, meanwhile the oil companies have screwed the US consumer by raising the price of gasoline. And if you look at the price of oil per barrel, day by day in the news, you see it's going up and down, but the gas price doesn't go up and down. It just went up and stayed there. So I think that if they actually do start shooting over there, not only are they going to wind up killing a lot of US soldiers, but they're going to have some protest on their hands, at least as strong as during the Vietnam era, and maybe even more so. Because I think that the casualties will be higher. During the Vietnam War they were having casualties like two hundred men a week; they could have two hundred men per hour—that's what was on CNN last night, they could have two hundred guys an hour dying in the desert. And nobody really wants to admit that the machinery that they have sent over there to fight this imaginary war is not really suited to the task. It was all designed to fight a war in Europe, at much lower temperatures and without the worry of sand.

CO On highways.

FRANK On highways, that's right. Tanks made to go fast on autobahns.

CO Well, that's what they were designed for anyway, so—

FRANK Yeah, well, the main tank, our special tank that we have over there, with all the laser-sighting weapons and the rest of that stuff, it requires five gallons per mile to run that tank, and I can't imagine how they expect to keep enough fuel in these vehicles to keep them going in the middle of a desert that goes on and on and on. There's no gas station out there.

CO Well, maybe the guy who came up with the idea said, 'Hey, this is Kuwait, there must be a lot of gas stations there!'
FRANK Yeah, maybe he did! Except that he probably thought, 'Well, if we're gonna roll these things on the autobahn in Europe they certainly have some gas stations there.'
CO About the things you are doing now, besides working on a lot of new stuff, you are putting your whole catalogue out on CD. I was wondering, you have always been known for working extremely intensely on all the products that you have put out over the last twenty-five years—how did it feel when you picked up those see-through master tapes and decided to look for the old masters and started remixing all that and adding things? I mean, there you were again mixing *Freak Out*!
FRANK Well, it is just more work. Just work. There was no romance to it, I can tell you that, it was just more work.
CO When you say romance, I was wondering, did it—?
FRANK There's no nostalgia for me for that stuff, I mean, that band had as many evil things wrong with it as the one in 1988. I don't have any fond memories of that particular period, it's just dealing with another set of personalities. Just a whole other set of personality problems, that's all.
CO There were some very nice things about that last tour, some links forward and backward. We talked about the Daniel Schorr thing. When you were in Rotterdam, you passed me a note that you had written at the Amstel Hotel, and you said, 'Read this!' And it was the text to 'Elvis Has Just Left The Building.' To my big surprise that was fixed and done on the *Broadway The Hard Way* album. How did that happen?
FRANK I don't know why I decided to write that song. It seemed like a stupid thing to do, and we kept working on it bit by bit at the soundchecks in the afternoon, and at the point where I thought that it was playable we put it into the show, and I think there was only five takes of it. We only played it five times during the tour, and then the performance that's on *Broadway The Hard Way* was edited together out of several different cities.
CO This household has a special relation with Elvis.
FRANK Why?

CO Doesn't it?

FRANK No, why?

CO Well, let me ask you this, then: what would, for instance, Dweezil think about this song?

FRANK I don't know. I never asked him! [laughs]

CO And he never told you himself?

FRANK No.

CO It didn't give an extra insight for his visit to Graceland?

FRANK [laughs] Well, let's just say that this house is not filled with Elvis fans, you know. But Dweezil, being a curious type, did have to go to Graceland and take a look for himself.

We decided to take a short coffee break. Frank wandered over to the pantry by the control room and brewed a fresh pot.

CO We get a lot of news coverage in Holland about the case of the 2 Live Crew stuff, and the record merchandiser being arrested for selling an album. And then the court statement mentioned 'filthy thoughts.'

FRANK That's right! This sets a precedent in US law, that if this decision is allowed to stand, it's the first time that the content of a person's thoughts will be the thing which is the crime. Or the thing that generates the crime. And because of the way US law works, that particular theory can be extracted from that case and applied in other instances, do you understand? Because if it's true that when a person makes a record, that record could induce another person to have filthy thoughts. And if that is a crime, then a person who designs an ad for an automobile which has a girl standing next to the car could also be accused of the same thing. Or a person who designed a greeting card which had a funny thing on it which induced a filthy thought, or—you know? The list goes on and on and on. If filthy thoughts are going to be against the law in America, my question is: who is going to go around and enforce this filthy thought law? It takes us right back to 'Who Are The Brain Police?' from the first album.

CO That's what I was thinking! And it's so abstract.

FRANK It's very abstract. And it's one of those kinds of things that a certain segment of the US population would think that it was a fascinating topic to debate, and they tie up the courts with it for years.
CO Does it make you wonder if all the stuff that has been going on with people speaking for a certain liberation of different aspects of life? Doesn't it give you the feeling that the circle is round and we have to start all over again?
FRANK I don't understand the question.
CO I mean, you made a recording in '66, a song called 'Who Are The Brain Police?' and after that a lot of people followed and have spoken out against certain movements. I mean, if you hear something like this, if you didn't know better, you might think that never happened. That those forces have never been around.
FRANK Well, you might think that unless you knew better. I mean, fact is, that sort of evil tendency has been a fact of life in America since the Puritans first landed here. The whole idea of a filthy thought is a religious concept, not really a legal concept. The idea of that sort of filth connected with thoughts of sex is something that is derived from a special type of religious orientation. And my basic argument with it is that the US Constitution says that there should be no mingling of religious thought and the law, because the minute you start mixing the two together you wind up with a situation like you have in Iran, it's called a theocracy. And it would be the worst of all possible scenarios to see the United States be controlled by Christian thought, because the Christians who are the most involved in politics right now are Christian extremists who believe in this, uh—the imminent approach of Armageddon, the end of the world. And in their theology, in order for Jesus to return, we must have another very big war because only after this war can their Savior return. So, with that in mind, to think that these people are connected with the Defense Department or any other aspect of the US government endangers the rest of the world. Their religious beliefs should be something that they can cherish all by themselves in private. They should never be in a position where they could speed up the process of having their Savior return by pushing a red

button to blow the world up. And that's the real danger about letting those kinds of Christians have a strong influence on US government policy, and we saw them make a lot of progress in that direction during the Reagan administration, because they helped—that whole section of the born-again Christian community helped to put Reagan in office, and he paid them back by giving them appointed jobs in the government. In other words, they were in positions of power but you couldn't vote to get them out because they were appointed, they weren't elected. And the whole Reagan administration was populated by these religious mutants. And Bush has kept a few of them on. His administration has a few of these silly guys in positions of power too.

CO On the other hand, we are seeing a certain slowdown, as we can see it from our standpoint, that the whole dust that was stirred up with the whole TV evangelist stuff. I mean, we talked about this way back when, when you told me about that guy who played records on TV—

FRANK Pastor Gary! You remember that, right? Did you see CNN, about four days ago, the comment by a guy who was an assistant to Senator Clayborn Pell, who issued a memo on the senator's stationary indicating that he believed that Bush's speeches regarding the Middle East had a secret backwards word in them? You didn't see that story? CNN ran it two days in a row. This guy said that there are secret codewords backwards in George Bush's speeches regarding the Middle East. Now, this guy is in the government! And he's still there. You know, he got a little slap on the wrist, and the main complaint was not that his premise was absurd, but that he used the senator's stationary to issue the memo.

CO That was what was emphasized?

FRANK That was the bad thing, yeah. And the senator who employed this guy didn't deny it. I mean, he didn't say, 'The guy is out of his mind and I am sending him to a mental institution and he should never have anything to do with government again.' The guy is still working for him. In fact, his position with Senator Pell is advisor on parapsychological matters, and he makes a fifty thousand dollars a year salary.

CO Did he say what the words were?

FRANK Oh . . . yeah, they said what it was—it was I think some kind of a woman's name, I can't remember what it was. It was just something stupid and he actually played part of Bush's speech backwards. You couldn't hear anything in there. It's like the time that this minister in Indiana claimed that the theme song for *Mr. Ed*, that old television show about the talking horse—if you played the *Mr. Ed* theme song backwards, it said 'Satan is the source.' CNN ran that story too.

CO You sing 'Jesus will think you're a jerk,' and he will think I am a jerk and it might be true. What do you think that a guy like that is thinking about what's happening right now?

FRANK You mean, what does Jesus think about what's going on right now? Well, it depends on what kind of Jesus you would like to imagine. I think, if you think of Jesus as a guy who probably had some good ideas, who died a few thousand years ago, he isn't thinking about anything. But if on the other hand you think of this all-powerful figure who squats in the cloud above your head and is waiting for you to be dead so you can come up there and sit next to him, I think that a guy like that obviously has a very perverse sense of humor. Because if he made everything, heaven and hell and all that business, he also made the situation in the Persian Gulf, he made that guy who works for Clayborn Pell hearing the backwards words in Bush's speeches—this guy has got a hell of a sense of humor. But he's dangerous. Seems like the thing that he gets the most enjoyment out of is seeing people being mutilated, which appears to be most of what is going on today in the world. Most of the world is endangered today—there is only certain places where people have comfortable lives. And everyplace else there's nothing but imminent danger and death and destruction and pestilence, and just horrible stuff going on. Well, who can we blame for that? Because if you blame the devil then you have to think that the devil is more powerful than that guy on the cloud. If the guy on the cloud is the boss, he's the boss, he is making it happen. So, what does he think? I don't know. If he likes what he has created, as it is said at one point, he was satisfied with what he built, then I am sure he is delighted. He is probably doing a little breakdancing up there.

CO And he can do it to tunes written about him, no matter by who—

FRANK Of course!

CO I wanna put two things from your recent activities into perspective. You've been to Eastern Europe quite a few times, and we saw some footage of that. You looked as if you were constantly absorbing impressions up there.

FRANK [laughs] You bet! I mean, it was actually really exciting to be there, because when I was in Prague in January, I got the impression it was a very special place that had a lot of very special people, who had managed to do something that everybody else in the world believed was impossible. To get rid of a very cruel form of government without having a bloody revolution. People are still scratching their head and saying, 'How did you do that?' And Gorbachev didn't help them. They did it themselves. And they're proud of that. So I was definitely impressed to be there, it was quite an experience. And Vaclav Havel is an amazing individual. What I can do for you, for your show is, uhm—I can give you a transfer of the audio track of this video that I edited about my trip to Czechoslovakia, that has my conversation with Havel. I had two meetings with him, one in their Oval Office and another one at lunch. So there is some things that you can put in there.

CO Great! That would probably be different than what was broadcast up there, because that had only the Oval Office stuff in it.

FRANK Yeah. I mean, there is not a lot of the lunchtime thing, because he wanted the cameras turned off, but there is a couple of good lines.

CO I saw the bottle standing in the editing room that you were drinking—

FRANK That was a gift from Olga Havel. It's a bottle of Czech liqueur called *bechorovka.*

CO Sounds like cookies to me.

FRANK Well, it's actual kind of nice-tasting. It's liqueur that you can have with lunch.

CO You being there all the time and seeing all these things changing, and then you get back to the States and I hear you doing an interview about which I, if I'm quoting you correctly, you were talking about—I was thinking of 'Concentration Moon' then—a concentration camp in Louisiana?

FRANK Yeah! The story of this concentration camp was run on the ABC Network show Nightline, I guess it was '87, whenever I was editing on *Uncle Meat* at the Pacific Video, because that's where I saw it. It had an interview with the mayor of this town in Louisiana, where they've built a concentration camp to round up Arabs. And he said he wished they would round them up soon, because it would help the economy of his city. And this place is not far from Jimmy Swaggart's place by the way. It's near Baton Rouge, Louisiana. And it was further reported that the concentration camp was built as part of Oliver North's plan to suspend the US Constitution.

CO To suspend it?!

FRANK That's right! And this show ran at 11:30, I think it was on a Wednesday night, and the next day there wasn't one piece of news coverage follow-up to this story at all. It never went anywhere else. It vanished.

CO But if CNN puts something out like that—I mean, they should follow it up in the first place.

FRANK But CNN didn't put it out, ABC put it out.

CO Oh, excuse me. But *they* should be following it up then.

FRANK They should but they didn't, and I'm sure the reason they didn't is because in 1980, when Reagan took office, he created a new branch of the US government, I believe it's called the 'Department of Domestic Diplomacy.' He hired the man from the CIA who had been responsible, for the last twenty or thirty years, for all the propaganda all over the world, and made him the head of this agency, and the task of the agency was to control US public opinion. Basically, this agency calls broadcasters and tells them what stories to drop. *Newsweek* reported this. And as far as I know, they have never disbanded this government agency. As far as I know, this guy still has a job. Or somebody has replaced him. And their initial mission was, and this was contained in a memo, 'to paint white hats on the Contras and black hats on the Sandinistas.' It was all done to maintain

Reagan's Nicaragua policy. That's why, if you ever said anything favorable about a Sandinista in a television show, you'd be in trouble. That's why anybody who went to Nicaragua to see for themselves what was going on was followed by the FBI in this country. The same way that under Nixon they had this thing called 'Cointelpro.' Which was like the United States government creating secret police to spy on US citizens—people who were suspected of being enemies of that particular administration, people who might be a threat to US foreign policy. Files were being built up on these people, they were persecuted, they were hounded, some of the were even—they disappeared. The guy you oughta talk to about that kind of stuff is A. West, the guy who did the cover for *Broadway The Hard Way.* Because he was involved with some of the people who had been to Nicaragua and they were being followed by the FBI. He's got stories about what happened to his friends. This is all just another case of the United States government going berserk, and in a way not even the US government, because government means the actions of people who have been elected. These were actions of people who decided that the machinery of the US government was so ineffective, 'we're gonna bypass it altogether.' And that's what Oliver North was doing. You heard him talk about, I believe the quote was, 'an off-the-shelf standalone self-financing governmental—.' I can't remember the rest of it, but the basic idea was he would be conducting private foreign policies, somebody would give him an instruction and it would be the world of dirty tricks. The self-financing part is the interesting part, because they financed these activities by arm sales and by drug sales. All of Oliver North's activities were involved with weapons and drugs. And so, after he was convicted of this small complaint that they finally stuck him with, what do you think his punishment was? He had to do a certain number of hours of public service in Washington D.C., working with some anti-drug force in the nation's capital. Now, if that isn't sending the fucking fox in to look after the chicken coop, I don't know what is! And the other thing you have to be baffled about is this guy William Bennett, who is the US drug czar. Under Ronald Reagan, William Bennett was the head of the Education Department in the United States. He was a miserable failure at that. Prior to that, Bennett ran something called the National Endowment for the Humanities. Now, how can a man who's been so massively unsuccessful in these other areas finally be handed the job of drug czar for the United States government? I think the answer is that he's just one of those holdover ideologues, that right-wing administrations like to have guys like that wandering around doing their bidding. He's just one of those kinda guys who's always gonna find a job as long as there is a right-wing administration. They find something for him to do.

CO Yeah, because it's almost a secret underworld of people covering up for each other.

FRANK That's right! And it's all being assisted by the broadcasters in the United States, because the real facts of what goes on will never go on TV, just won't!

CO How did control build up? I mean, would that go for newspapers as well?

FRANK Yes! Because remember, all these things are owned by people and the people who own them are not Democrats. They're Republicans. And when they get a phone call from their party leader—I mean, it's almost like Communism.

CO That's what I was thinking!

FRANK Under Communism, the people who were party members had privileges. They were protected. Everything that the Communist Party originally stood for was just thrown out the window in order to create this lavish lifestyle for the executives within the party, they all had limousines, they all had country homes. It wasn't brotherhood and 'we're all equal' and the rest of that stuff, it turned into something totally corrupt, and that's the way it is with the Republican Party, because if you're a member of the party you will have certain privileges, but you are expected to do certain things too. You're expected to always cover up for the other Republicans and it's exactly what happened with Communists.

CO You take it from the top and then it drizzles down.

FRANK Well, that's the trickle-down theory of economics and we've seen what that has led to.

By this time Frank was tired, and he asked to take a break. He left the studio, I used the bathroom, and there, hanging on the wall, I saw the original letter that Edgard Varèse had written to Frank. I'm not a thief, but I'd be lying if I said I wasn't tempted.

After half an hour, we walked back into the studio and sat down outside the drum booth. Bob Stone and Todd Yvega were still busy in the control room, working on 'Buffalo Voice.'

FRANK Somewhere you ought to get that actual Oliver North quote. Because he said it when he was testifying during the Iran–Contra hearings. He said a couple of other things: he described how he had put together this plan to suspend the US Constitution.

CO Do you want some more coffee, Frank?

FRANK I think we got some—I'm OK.

CO I'll change the subject. Could you tell us what the word 'wazoo' and the words 'waka jawaka' mean?

FRANK Well, 'wazoo' is a common word that's been used a lot in different contexts in conversation for years in the US.

CO It's a common word?

FRANK Yeah, people would say, like, 'up your wazoo,' which would be 'up your asshole,' so a 'grand wazoo' would be the grand asshole. I wrote a poem in '61 or '62, something like that, not exactly a poem, but this little thing about the 'Grand Wazoo of the hardware store.' It was a parody of the mentality of people who join lodges and organizations where men get together wearing funny hats and do things to each other in the dark, you know, and then—

CO Like the Flintstones?

FRANK Yeah! And have a secret handshake and, you know, that childish type stuff that certain adults like to participate in. So this character was the Grand Wazoo of the hardware store, and the final line of the poem was, '*I'm the Grand Wazoo of the hardware store / Fuck you if you don't like my hat!*' And 'waka jawaka' was something that Gail came up with on a Ouija board one night.

CO We're probably going to speak to Mark Volman and Howard Kaylan. From that period, the whole atmosphere around that band was definitely a live thing. Is there a lot of material that you still have from that period?
FRANK Not a lot. Actually, hardly any.
CO Because you didn't have the facilities to record anything you did back then?
FRANK Well, I was only starting to record . . . the very first time I started doing massive live recording was when we did the *Just Another Band From L.A.* album. I just bought a 4-track and that was the first of those recordings. And we used the 4-track on that tour, but the tapes were really kind of badly done, because there was no way to monitor them. And the guy who was running the machine wasn't really a recording engineer, he was like a roadie sound mixer, so the quality of those road tapes is not very good.
CO The big thing that attracted attention with them back then was the *200 Motels* project. They were in the audience when you played the premiere of that. The famous 'Hit It, Zubin!' thing. You don't own the product of that film—I mean, the record rights?
FRANK Right.
CO Do you ever play around with the idea of redoing some of that?
FRANK I don't own the tapes. I don't have the tapes.
CO No, I mean, you have the scores.
FRANK You mean having them performed again? Well, the piece 'Bogus Pomp' contains a lot of the themes from *200 Motels*, and of course 'Strictly Genteel' is one of the tunes from *200 Motels* and we've played that on stage, done that a few times.
CO But the concept as it was, for instance some of the material that was in the film but is not on the record and stuff like that, there must be—
FRANK Yeah, there are other things, but you know, they would require either a lot of typing to put it into the Synclavier, or once again hiring live musicians, which is something that I plan to spend a lot of time trying to avoid.
CO Is that—when we look at your liking Edgard Varèse's music, his whole views on the relationship, the music as it sounds, the composer and the

musician, I mean—is there any similarity between that and how you feel about it?

FRANK I don't know. I'm not that familiar with anything that he has said about that. My appreciation for his music has more to do with the fact that I like the way the music sounds, rather than any philosophical, psychological aspects of his work.

CO But what I mean is that we are now in an era that things like the Synclavier give a lot of work to do and give a lot of new ways that you can enter. Does that make you feel that some part of the activity of performing live could be taken over? I mean obviously it can, because you do it, but you are also somebody who has always made a strong point for the live aspect of music, especially in the days when all the Top 40 stuff came out that was so prefab.

FRANK I still think that live music is a good idea. Unfortunately, people who like live music are getting scarcer and scarcer. In the United States, most of the people who buy tickets to concerts are just as happy to buy hundreds of thousands or millions of tickets to see concerts performed by people who aren't even singing or playing, they're up there lip-synching. And they think it's OK. Nobody makes a fuss when Milli Vanilli appears there and they're not doing anything. They're just models hopping around on stage, or Madonna, or Janet Jackson, or a lot of these other groups that have been accused of having freeze-dried shows. And a lot of these shows, the bulk of them is being performed by Synclaviers. Or DAT tapes. And the people on stage are just dancing around, and the audience basically is seeing a dance revue with fancy lights, and the whole art of live musical performance is vanishing. The only place where there still seems to be any live performance tradition is in heavy metal. Most of those groups really get out there and bang it out and there is energy. And I guess if there are any punk groups left, they are still doing it the old-fashioned way. But the groups that get the most famous and make the most money are the ones most likely not to really perform live.

CO They're about as canned as the beverages they promote.

FRANK That's right! That's a very apt comparison.

CO But how far can that go? Do you sense already, for instance with a younger audience, a need for the live aspect?
FRANK Do you think for a moment that the people who are buying tickets to see New Kids On The Block care anything about live music? I mean, are they going to grow up to be sophisticated music listeners? I don't think so. I think that if they heard a live instrument they might be shocked at what it really sounded like. And also, the fact that most musicians who can really play don't dance that well. So they would be disappointed by real live music. And you know, it's not just a one-sided thing too, because these freeze-dried shows couldn't exist if it weren't for the fact that there are plenty of musicians who can actually play who would rather take one of those tours because they pay so well. You got musicians competing with each other to be part of the backup band for those fake tours.
CO Like digging your own grave.
FRANK Yeah! I mean, they think it's actually wonderful for their career, they can put it on their resumes that they were the bongo player for Madonna or something like that. And guys audition for those jobs and get really excited if they're accepted. Even the roadies who work on those tours think that it's a good—like a gold star on your report card, if you have participated in one of those frauds. So it's not just the evil beverage companies perverting the music industry—they have the willing assistance of the musicians involved.
CO And the whole appreciation thing for, for instance young kids, that might take part in kind of adjusting that. If it was possible, if it would be done in the first place.
FRANK Well, I see it as part of a whole package of brainwashing. The young person in America starts off being raised by a television set. And the bulk of what he appreciates on TV is what they call 'Saturday morning children's programming,' which is a lot of animated shows, each show basically being a half-hour commercial for a certain type of toy or a certain food product. The character in the show is the toy, which can be then sold. So they're raised on a steady diet of product-oriented entertainment. And then the other aspect of these children's programs is they are very heavy on violence, and the violence is committed in the name of justice by superhero-looking

guys, men with enormous muscles who can fly and all this kind of stuff. And they graduate from that to MTV, looking at heavy metal groups who are made up to resemble rather closely these same idiots that they saw on their Saturday morning cartoon, and maybe they go a little bit beyond that and they watch wrestling. Or this other horrible show that's on US television called the *American Gladiators*.

CO That's a nice title.

FRANK You have to see it to believe it. There is some really spectacular programs that you have to see while you are here. *American Gladiators* runs on Channel 9 Saturday and Sunday night, you should try and see that. And the other one is something called *The Love Phone*. It just came on. It's on WOR Secaucus New Jersey. The host of the show is Jessica Hahn, and the whole show is a commercial for you to call these phone numbers where you are charged anywhere from two dollars to twenty-five dollars to talk with a 'Love Counselor.'

CO Well, she had a good one once, didn't she?

FRANK Yes, she did! He is going back on trial again on another charge this week.

CO [Jim] Bakker?

FRANK Yep. Somebody has filed a huge suit against him, fraud suit. Some of his parishioners. I got to take a break here.

Frank left the studio to rest for a little while, and to find some more coffee. Menno and I chatted about the topics we should bring up, and the guys in the control room were still hard at work. It was about 9pm when Frank returned. He sat down in his lazy chair and we continued.

CO We've talked about the live situation, and the canned situation that is happening a lot now. You have a lot of music around you, for instance Dweezil, who is a guitar player. If a band is rehearsing right now—because music will go on, I believe—what would you say to those guys?

FRANK Well, I try not to discourage them so the less said the better. The musical situation in the United States is really quite drastic, because it's not based on quality, and the problem of getting your music broadcast in this country is really a disaster right now, because there is so much payola corruption. It is impossible to get a record of any description played on the radio unless you're paying off. Anybody who wants to have a hit rock'n'roll record has to be a part-time criminal. Meanwhile, the groups that are making the most money in doing the big tours all have support of beverage companies, or tennis shoe companies, or whatever, and the shows that they put on are not really—they're not about music. They are about show business. So if there is going to be any survival of live music any place in the world, I doubt whether that particular species will survive in this country. It will survive in Europe, it will survive in Japan, I think it's still pretty healthy in the Soviet Union and as far as I can tell in Eastern Europe, and probably in South America it's still OK, but in the United States it's a disaster.

CO Do you think that one of the results of that overemphasis on package and on money could be causing that? For instance, the rock'n'roll industry, which at a very specific point used to be the outlet for some contra ideas—

FRANK Not anymore.

CO For some revolt?

FRANK Not anymore. Not in this country. Because if you want a contract, you can't get a contract if the content of your music is too controversial. You won't get a record deal. If you manage to get a record deal, and you suddenly decide to do a controversial album, that will be the album that kills your career because the record company won't promote it.

CO But consider it from the other side. I mean, wasn't it like that for instance when you first—let's say in the first five to ten years, you were especially in Europe, maybe for a lot of wrong reasons, but you were taken up as some sort of cult figure representing a certain sentiment that young people had. I mean, they used that for their own purpose.

FRANK Sure!

CO Where do people find that sentiment now?

FRANK Well, that sentiment basically is not expressed in a positive way in the music today, it's expressed in a negative way and the rebellious sentiment is mostly contained in heavy metal, you know? Lyrics all about death and the devil and the rest of that stuff, and so a certain part of the frustration of growing up can be expressed in that kind of music. But the messages are really pretty negative, not really making a statement about real-world situations the way some of the music in the '60s used to. But it serves the function of relieving the emotional pressure. But the surprising thing about heavy metal is it doesn't get broadcast that much either, but it still sells well and draws large concert attendance. It is because there are so many frustrated young people out there, and it's the only type of music they can participate in that helps them get that steam off.

CO It's getting to the point that artists who are for instance threatened by censorship groups like the PMRC don't even seem to have the courage to open their mouth against the threat that's heading their way.

FRANK Well, they don't have any place to open their mouth. I am sure that a lot of people who are threatened would love to complain about it, but where can they complain? Nobody does interviews with them. Nobody goes out to interview the unknown group that's being threatened by censorship, because nobody wants to hear what they have to say.

CO But what about the big-time groups who are put on the spot by these organizations?

FRANK What big time group? Who? The big-time groups don't do anything controversial.

CO Some people are taking action against them. Take Prince, for instance.

FRANK All the noise that they made about Prince in 1985 had no impact on his career except to make him more popular.

CO So they just let it happen?

FRANK Yeah, he never spoke out against it, he never said a thing.

CO Which brings us back to that the people who might be in the position to keep certain activities alive just don't care, because it just promotes their career. You were a spokesman for these people. Did they ever call you up and say thank you?

FRANK No. I didn't expect them to, either. It wasn't the reason why I did it.

CO One of the things that amazed me is that you were never on one of those lists.
FRANK Well, they didn't want to put me on one of those lists, because if they ever would have really gone after me, then I would have really gone after them and they didn't want me to after them! I was a surprise for them, I wound up being the spokesman for the other side. I don't think they were too thrilled about that, because they couldn't figure out what to do about me.
CO When we look at your activities in the different fields of music—for instance, all your orchestral and ensemble pieces for smaller ensembles, the rock part—you have always been somebody who is best capable of comparing the different aspects. We have put a lot of emphasis right now on how the rock industry is becoming so packed with all the conservative-type sponsors, and so on and so forth. I have some earlier statements by you about the classical situation or the contemporary situation in the United States. What is your view on that now, in 1990?
FRANK Well, that's still about the same. The classical situation hasn't changed, it hasn't gotten any better and in a way it's just as conservative as rock'n'roll. The people who control the classical situation are the people who either have the most academic credibility, they may be composers in residence at universities or they are the social darling of a certain art clique in New York or something like that. You know, these are the most important figures in American contemporary music, the ones who go out and play that particular art-world game. So that's not too much different than rock'n'roll. The only difference is that rock'n'roll pays better.
CO Can you give us an example of one of the rules of that art game?
FRANK I don't know, that's not my world. I just know that there is a certain amount of corruption there, and you know, it's just—it's fake. The situation of music in the art world is about as sick as it is for painting in the art world. The only difference again is the painter actually is in a better economic position than the composer is.
CO So the people are driven into prearranged situations also? They get to listen to certain types of music and actually by that they get blocked off from things they might enjoy?

FRANK Well, the only type of music that's gonna get performed first of all is that which is economical to rehearse. And anything which is not economical to rehearse or mount isn't gonna get performed at all, no matter what the merits are. Which is one of the things that led to minimalism, because music for very few instruments which play the same notes over and over and over and over again is probably a lot easier to rehearse than music for a lot of instruments where everybody has to do something complicated and expressive.

CO And have you had any reactions from colleague composers from the United States scene, or critics or people on committees or any of those people who do that?

FRANK No, because I have no contact with them. I don't have any colleague composers, I never deal with those committees, because whenever I had any of my works performed, in the initial performance I was the guy who paid for it, because there was no way for me to go to anybody's committee and say, 'Put up the money to do this!' There was no way, I tried that for years and it just wouldn't work, as I stated many times before. So, the only way I was gonna get a performance is to pay for it myself, and that is so expensive you can only do that once or twice in your lifetime.

CO Are you still composing for orchestras, large ensembles?

FRANK No, no, I quit.

CO What is that like, to say 'I quit that'? Because obviously a composer wants to hear his music.

FRANK Well, I can hear music by writing for the machine in the other room. It's just that I can't really write for an orchestra because there is no way to get it played. And it costs so much to prepare the sheet music, it costs a fortune to just prepare the parts, so why spend the money? The same amount of money that I would spend to prepare a mountain of paper for an orchestral composition, I could buy another whole machine. So it doesn't make any sense.

CO You are one of the people in the industry who has a very fanatical following. There are people who collect certain artists, and you are absolutely one of the people who is really a collector's artist. If we look at that following, you can see people who try to get everything that you have done, for instance by exchanging tapes. I give you a tape, you give me a tape—Of course we have talked about this before, about people who try to make money off your work, it still goes on and on.

FRANK Yeah, but I think the real charm there is the thrill of collecting, having a complete collection. It has very little to do with me or what I do, but it has a lot to do with owning a quantity of objects and having a complete set. It's kind of like people used to collect toy soldiers or marbles when they were children, it's the same sort of motivation.

CO Hmmm—

FRANK There are a few exceptions who really just can't rest until they have listened to everything that is available, but the real collector mentality has more to do with owning every single artifact, to have a complete set, that's the motivation for collectors.

CO They see it more as stamps than an artistic product?

FRANK Yeah, it's like collecting stamps or coins. That's a lot of stuff to collect, and after you have collected it, what do you do with it? Listen to it day and night? No, you have collected it and then you may know somebody else who collects something and then you'll trade objects with him and uhm—it's commodities trading.

CO I think that goes for a lot of them, but like you said, there are exceptions, maybe more than you might expect. I can recall a conversation we had in about 1979, when you said, 'Who wants to hear my guitar solos? Nobody does!' And then you put out a three-record set and it sells like crazy. So even you can be wrong about that.

FRANK Well, I don't know whether it sold like crazy. The most surprising thing was the amount of copies that were sold in France, that was the biggest shock, because I think they sold eighty thousand units of a three-record set in France alone, which shocked everybody. And sure, I can be wrong, no question about that! That's part of what I do for a living.

CO Being wrong?

FRANK Yeah! I deal with all things which are wrong. You take a whole bunch of wrong stuff and put it together and you can make a unique artistic style out of it.
CO That'll be hard, to find a musical example of that statement. Maybe you have a suggestion?
FRANK Well, let's see. Hmm, yeah, that would be hard to illustrate that, but that's the philosophy that has worked behind a lot of it. Because there are certain things in music books where they tell you, 'Don't do this, this is wrong!' And I would go out and that would be the first thing I would do. So that is basically what I meant by the statement. I am not saying that I put together whole albums of wrong notes.
CO To go a little bit further on this, you seem to be a very practical composer. I mean, you aren't very much tied down by rules or whatever. You write what you wanna hear, and sometimes I wonder, if you have larger pieces, how does that develop? I mean, if we take for instance a song like 'Sad Jane,' or—well, not 'Bogus Pomp,' because that's like a suite of themes—for instance 'Sad Jane,' how would that develop?
FRANK Most of 'Sad Jane' was written in hotel rooms on the road and uh—

At this point the studio door opened. A little earlier, Frank had used the housephone to ask if someone would bring a large jug of water with ice cubes and more coffee.

His son Ahmet came in, together with drummer Josh Freeze, a skinny guy who played in Dweezil's band for a while. Josh was carrying a very heavy tray with the jug and the glasses.

AHMET I would now like to present—your coffee!
CO Great!
JOSH He makes me carry the fucking tray.
AHMET You got it like I got it, baby.
JOSH Where is this going?
FRANK On the floor right here.
AHMET Right there, Josh! Put it down, now!

FRANK Thank you.
JOSH Aaaargh, fuck!
FRANK Oh, it's good for you though. I mean, you feel good after that, right?
JOSH It's so heavy, man.
FRANK Fucking drummers! Always complaining.

We picked up our conversation about 'Sad Jane,' first recorded under the baton of Maestro Kent Nagano with the London Symphony Orchestra.

FRANK Well, the march at the end of 'Sad Jane' was a transcription of a guitar solo from the *Shrine Exposition Hall 1968* that Ian Underwood wrote down. And it happened to be in my briefcase I was carrying around on this one tour—I think it was the 1980 tour—I can't remember when the thing was written. But I remember I was working on that at the Hyde Park Hotel in London, because I managed to get them to bring in a little piano into the room, because I was there for about three or four days, and you know, the pieces are made out of other pieces. I know there is a theme over here that will fit with this, and there is a theme over there that will fit that, and you organize the material.
CO So you have all kind of things that you put down at home, while traveling, that maybe when you write them down nobody knows where it will end up?
FRANK Yeah, because there is no way to just sit down and devote yourself a hundred percent to music all the time. There is the real world that gets in the way, and you can't do all the work at one sitting. So you have to store things, and you have to remember what you were thinking of to put some continuity in there, and the actual work that you do to put a piece together, at least in my case, is always interrupted by things. Like for instance I would be in there working now but I am talking with you. There's always something that gets in the way. But eventually it gets done.
CO Would you like to do it? Would you like to have the opportunity to be a full-time composer? Or do you think that perhaps that relationship with the real world is what makes the music what it is?

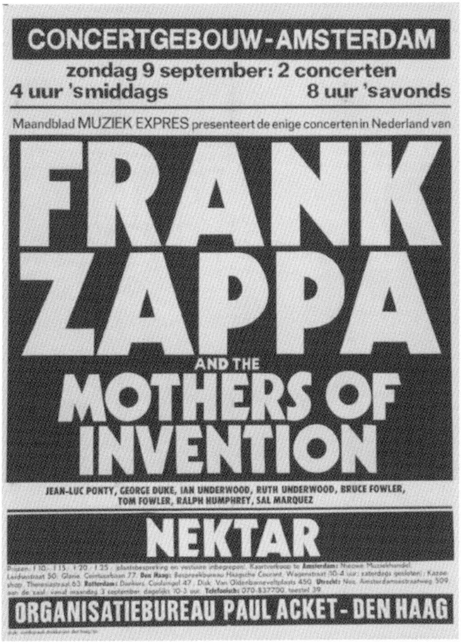

LEFT Original 1973 concert poster. *Courtesy George Duke.*
ABOVE Co's first Frank Zappa and the Mothers concert ticket, 1973.
BELOW Frank Zappa in the Pulitzer Hotel, 1977. *Co de Kloet.*

RIGHT A gift from Frank.
BELOW Frank and Co at the Amstel Hotel, 1975 (signed by FZ in 1980). *Jos Houniet.*

OPPOSITE Marriott Hotel session, 1984. *Ernest Potters.*

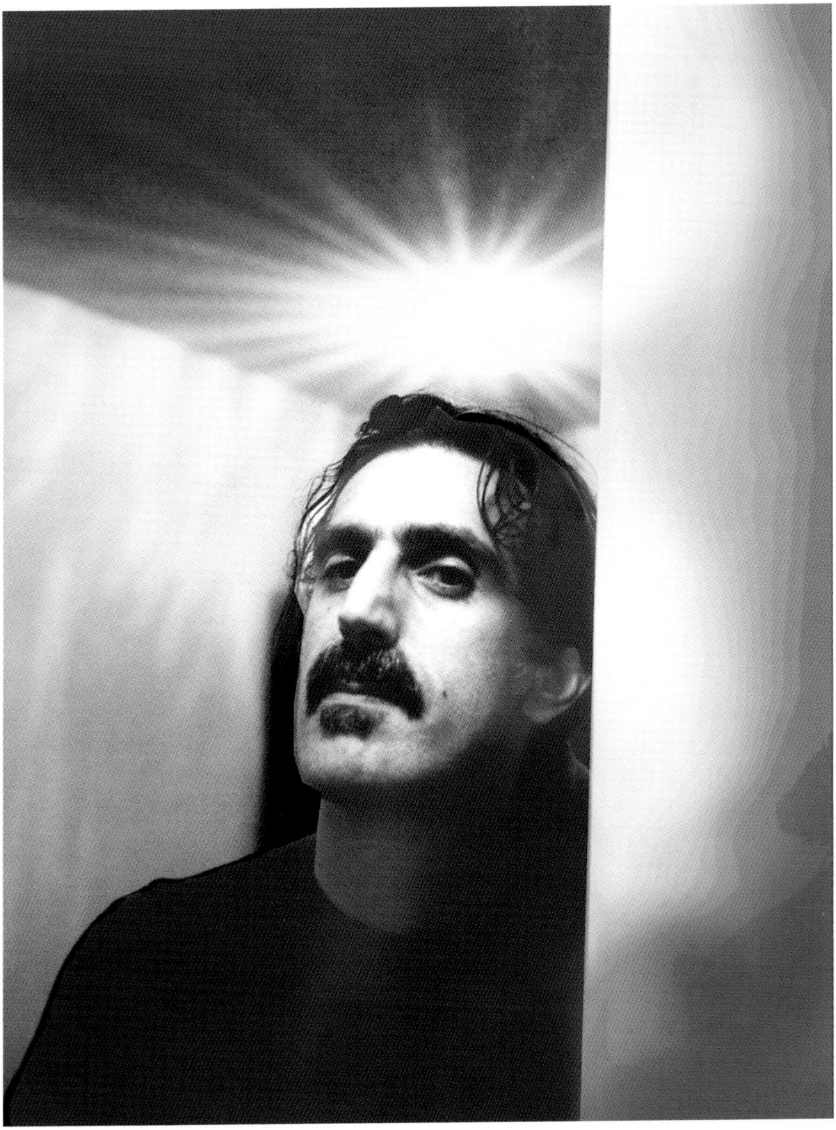

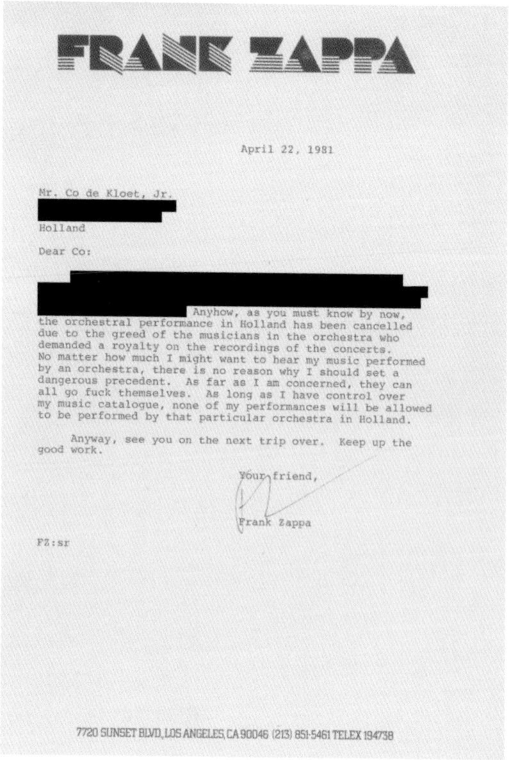

FRANK ZAPPA

April 22, 1981

Mr. Co de Kloet, Jr.
[redacted]
Holland

Dear Co:

[redacted] Anyhow, as you must know by now, the orchestral performance in Holland has been cancelled due to the greed of the musicians in the orchestra who demanded a royalty on the recordings of the concerts. No matter how much I might want to hear my music performed by an orchestra, there is no reason why I should set a dangerous precedent. As far as I am concerned, they can all go fuck themselves. As long as I have control over my music catalogue, none of my performances will be allowed to be performed by that particular orchestra in Holland.

Anyway, see you on the next trip over. Keep up the good work.

Your friend,

Frank Zappa

FZ:sr

7720 SUNSET BLVD, LOS ANGELES, CA 90046 (213) 851-5461 TELEX 194738

ABOVE LEFT Marriott Hotel session, 1984. *Ernest Potters.*
ABOVE RIGHT FZ-modified cover to the album *Ship Arriving Too Late To Save A Drowning Witch.*
RIGHT Holland Festival letter from FZ, 1981.

OPPOSITE Marriott Hotel session, 1984. *Ernest Potters.*

TOP The Dangerous Kitchen and basement, Los Angeles, 1986. **MIDDLE** *Supplement* recording, Los Angeles, 1990. **BOTTOM LEFT** Co at the Synclavier. **BOTTOM RIGHT** Flo & Eddie in New York City, 1990. *All photographs by Menno Kalmann.*

1992
THE NEW YORK FESTIVALS
FINALIST AWARD
PRESENTED TO
NOS
(Nederlandse Omroepprogramma Stichting)
for
"Zappa 50"

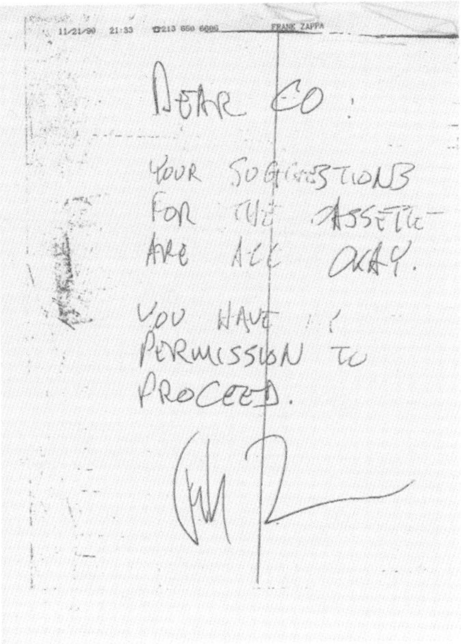

11/21/90 21:33 ☎213 650 6606 FRANK ZAPPA

DEAR CO:

YOUR SUGGESTIONS FOR THE CASSETTE ARE ALL OKAY.

YOU HAVE PERMISSION TO PROCEED.

TOP LEFT ThingFish in Liverpool, 2001. *Rob Heukels.*

TOP RIGHT Jimmy Carl Black, 2006. *Waitress!*

ABOVE LEFT New York Festival, 1992.

ABOVE RIGHT Fax from Frank, 1990.

LEFT *The Supplement Tape*, 1990. *Courtesy Siësta Productions.*

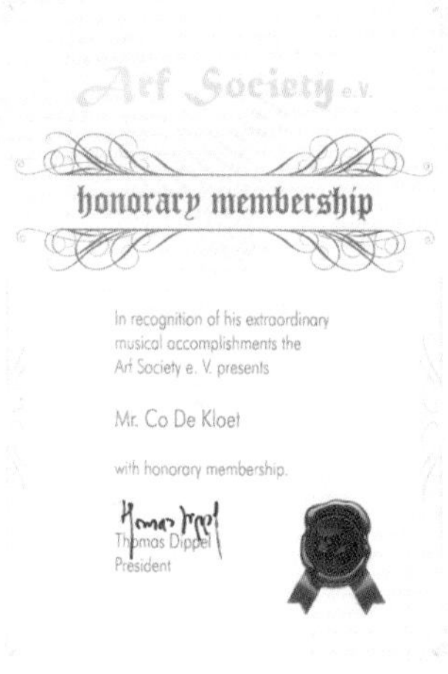

Arf Society e.V.

honorary membership

In recognition of his extraordinary musical accomplishments the Arf Society e. V. presents

Mr. Co De Kloet

with honorary membership.

Thomas Dippel
President

TOP LEFT Gary Lucas.
TOP RIGHT George Duke at Zappanale, 2011/2012. *Dieter Jakob.*
ABOVE The Gas Mask. *Mark van Schaick.*
LEFT Arf Society Award.

FRANK Well, I don't know. I think that to be a full-time composer and stop doing interviews about censorship and the rest of that kind of stuff wouldn't be a good idea. Because most of the interruptions for the last five years have been interruptions where I had to go out and say something on that particular topic, or do something about voter registration, and I think that was worthwhile, worth taking the time to do that. It would have been more fun to write music but you know, nobody else was doing it so I had to do it.
CO You practically fill your music with little hints—with little quotes from other periods, musical, text-wise. For instance, when I listened to the last *You Can't Do That On Stage Anymore* CD, suddenly I heard you say in a song, out of the blue, 'Pocket Fisherman.' 'Veg-O-Matic'—Not everybody will know that these are [Ron] Popeil inventions.
FRANK Ha, that's right! Well, the reason I said that was, if you can imagine this—we were playing in Chicago for Thanksgiving, and for people outside the United Sates, they don't even understand what Popeil means, or the whole idea of telemarketing and people who go on television late at night and sell you knives and gizmos, cheese slicers and little appliances like that, that's the Popeil syndrome. We arrived in Chicago to discover that there was a Popeil exhibition at some kind of industrial museum in Chicago, and everybody in the band was joking about this. The idea that there would be a serious display of Popeil stuff in a museum in Chicago! Either they were desperate for things to put in the museum, or it was somebody's perverted joke. And so just like a lot of other shows have a secret word which is whatever the band was joking about before we went on stage, that was a Popeil evening. There were a lot of references to Popeil appliances, and that's why those things came out.
CO And it was coincidental, wasn't it? Her being on some of your recordings.
FRANK Yeah.
CO The magic words that you pick and choose while on the road, like last time in Rotterdam with the fishbone down Martin's throat and stuff like that—these things tend to come back, and sometimes I wonder, does it ever happen that the people that you work with directly—like the guy

playing the keyboards on that tour—sometimes think, 'What is this? What is he talking about?' How far does the folklore reach with the people who work with you?

FRANK Well, anybody new to the band, it's a complete mystery. I would imagine there were some of the guys in the horn section who must have thought I was out of my mind doing that kind of stuff, but all that secret words stuff really works best with Ike, because he has a big storehouse of folklore and he's a good improvisor. He can take a word and deal with it. And Scott's good at that too: although he doesn't participate in the verbal part, he can follow the gag. It requires a certain amount of knowledge, you know, like at least a decade's worth of knowledge, to really play that game. That's not a game that you can pick up after three months of rehearsal. That's a game for veterans.

CO And you find some of those also in the audience?

FRANK Oh yeah, sure! You have audience participation with people that have been coming to the concerts for more than a decade, and they wind up being very specially entertained when there is something that is *so* inside that they are the only people who know it. And I like that, I like providing special entertainment.

CO I heard a version once that might be a good example. Sometimes you think these things don't just happen on stage. You switch around words and some songs seem to be suitable for that. On the last tour, when you did the song about the Madison Avenue girl, 'Any Kind Of Pain'—I remember when I heard that in the '88 tour you had done that with another band. I don't know if you ever did it live on stage—?

FRANK No. It was developed with the '76 band as a matter of fact. The very first chart was a sketch that was presented to the band that made the *Live In New York* album, but we never recorded it.

CO Some songs tend to get further back than most people suspect. I mean, a good example of that would be 'Easy Meat.'

FRANK Yeah, that was from the 1970 tour with Mark and Howard.

CO These songs, like 'Easy Meat,' and songs like 'The Torture,' seem to be real good vehicles for you to go pretty far in altering the original version.

FRANK Mm-hmm.

CO Are some songs more suitable for that purpose than others?

FRANK I think I could do it to just about any song. The reason that those songs have been the victims is that generally you can't stretch a song unless most of the guys in the band are so comfortable with playing the original that they can follow the stretch. The newer the song, the harder it is to stretch it, because the guys haven't played it that much. But the ones that stretch the best are the ones that everybody takes for granted. And also, when you're stretching, it also helps to have the audience be very familiar with the song so they can appreciate the stretch. Because if the song is brand new and unfamiliar then how can they tell you stretched it, you know? The more familiar it is, the more ridiculous it is to stretch it and the more entertainment value there is in the stretching process.

CO I remember being at one of your soundchecks and that you had 'Ms. Pinky,' which we all know was written for a Dutch girl—

FRANK Ha! Yeah, right!

CO And suddenly you added the end of the *I Love Lucy* show! I think we still have that on tape. That might be a good example for that.

FRANK Was that the very first time I stuck it in there?

CO Yeah, you were working on it with Tommy Mars.

FRANK Well, Tommy was great for stretching stuff because he knew so many showtunes. He just had a knack for doing that sort of thing. He was a good collaborator for that kind of stuff.

CO Correct me if I'm wrong, but some musicians that you have seem to have a certain ability to give a certain color to your band more than others. For instance, Tommy Mars would in my view be an example of somebody who represents—

FRANK A major coloristic element? There is no question about it. One of Tommy's drawbacks, though, you could never keep him from playing, because he always wanted to add something else into the arrangement, and if you build an arrangement to have a certain kind of a structure, and you have a guy who is so enthusiastic and he got his own musical imagination and he wants to suddenly stick in this 'event' in a place where there is supposed to be silence, obviously he is going to stand out, because there is nothing else in that place. There was never intended to be anything there, and all of a sudden you have a noise from Tommy Mars. Which is one of the reasons why it was so hard to keep him in the band, because he just kept—the arrangements would grow out of control, like they had leprosy or something.

CO You couldn't keep the lid on the Tommy Mars?

FRANK Yeah.

CO When you put out all the old stuff, you know, there are a lot of musicians floating around that were in your band, and some of them more than others were very colorful types for your band. Do you ever get reactions from them? For instance, do you ever get reactions from people who played on the first five albums and who see themselves in *The Old Masters* or in the CD shop?

FRANK No. Never talk to those guys. In fact, most of the guys who have been in the band don't even listen to the records that they have made. They don't like it. They don't like the records, they even didn't like playing in the band. If you really go around and check, I bet you'd find that most of the guys who have been in the band own few, if any, of the albums that they played on. And if they own them, they don't listen to them. And if they did listen to them, they don't like them. Being in the band is a job. If the guy owns the album, it's so he can show it to somebody else. 'Here is a record with my name on it.' But they don't like the music. They don't care about it.

CO But is that something that occurred in the process from, let's say the first album on, or was that from day one?

FRANK I think it's from day one.

CO Because people are still active with your music. In the 1980s we had the whole Grandmothers affair.

FRANK Yeah, but why do you think they were doing that? Because they like my music? I don't think so. I think they were doing it because they figured it was the only way that they could get a job, they could get hired for a gig. If they would go out and play their music under any other name they wouldn't have a job. The only reason they can get booked for a concert is because they were exploiting some aspect or tendency of the work that they did when they were working with me, and they are trying to capitalize on that and exploit it. And to go out and do it has nothing to do with any love or respect for the music that they participated in on the original albums. It's just another way for them to earn money.

CO Shall we wind this up?

FRANK Yeah . . .

Frank was visibly tired by this time. We drank one more coffee and decided to continue the next day. Menno and I headed back to the Hyatt on Sunset and had some wondrous experiences, which unfortunately will have to wait for another time to be told.

We returned to 7885 Woodrow Wilson Drive the following afternoon, where we were offered coffee and grapefruit juice. Frank was waiting for us in his studio.

The three of us made our way into the live room and sat down again by the drum booth. While Menno was busy setting up the recording equipment, I chatted to Frank about a CD I'd sent him a few months earlier. As a freelance producer, I was involved in a series of albums for Varajazz, a sublabel of the VARA broadcasting station. One of the projects was a remastered version of an album by the Pim Jacobs Trio, with guests. Pim played piano, his brother Ruud was on bass, with Han Bennink on drums. The guests were Wes Montgomery on guitar and Clark Terry on trumpet/flugelhorn. They'd recorded the album in VARA Studio 7 on April 2nd, 1965. Knowing Zappa to be a huge Wes Montgomery fan, I'd sent him a copy. To my surprise, he wasn't that into Wes's playing, but was very impressed by Clark, who'd switched back and forth effortlessly between trumpet and flugelhorn during the solos. We were still talking about it when Menno finished setting everything up.

CO He plays two!

FRANK Really?

CO He changes around, he has in one hand—I think it's on the cover.

FRANK No, it's not.

CO Is he not on the cover holding two trumpets? He changes around to trumpet and flugelhorn in one chorus.

FRANK He is fabulous!

CO I'm glad it arrived safely. Let's talk about *The Real Frank Zappa Book*, which is now available in a Dutch translation. I mean, you have not exactly been known for being the number one American reader of books.

FRANK That's for sure!

CO When and why did you decide to put out your own book?

FRANK It's been a couple of years, and the editor from Simon & Schuster kept calling me and bothering me to do it, and so I finally did it. The interviews were done at the same time as the rehearsals for the '88 tour, so that means December '87 and January of '88. I would rehearse from two o'clock in the afternoon till about midnight, and then I would do six hours of interviews with this guy each night, five nights a week. And then he transcribed all the tape and organized the material, and when I finished the tour he had this huge manuscript for me to look at. And I thought it was going to be real easy to do the book, just say it into a microphone and it would be done. But I didn't like the way it read when he gave the manuscript back to me, so I sat down at the word processor and spent three months and basically wrote it all over again from scratch. I took the basic organization that he did, same basic topics, and then fixed it so it sounded like the way I talk. Because what he had done with the tape transcriptions is that he converted it from the way that I talk into something that was what he thought a book should look like, and it was really boring, so I had to do it all over again.

CO And you also had a say, probably, in the big type and the illustrations?

FRANK Oh yeah! We worked on that for almost eight months, just a little bit at a time, doing all the cartoons, figuring out what kind of things I wanted to put in there. And there is a lot that didn't get put in the book, because the publisher was very concerned that the book not be too long. They could only have a certain number of pages, they could only have a certain number of pictures, a certain number of cartoons, they were really quite stingy with the preparation of the book. I would have preferred that the photographs be printed on gloss paper so it looked better, but they just didn't want to spend the money.

CO The choice of the buildup of the book—because there are some books already done about you by various people, and probably people who had to find their information from second hand, most of the time probably?

FRANK Mm-hmm.

CO Those buildups were what you would call historical. You start in 1940 and then you work your way up to whenever the book was published. What made you decide to make this topic-like buildup, and not a historical event?

FRANK I didn't feel like doing it the other way. I think that would be the normal way to do it. So I did it in a not-normal way. The reason for doing the book was just to have those essays in the back of the book where I could talk about those kinds of topics.

CO I heard you talking to Flo & Eddie, who are also helping out with this program, they said that your next book might be the road stories. There were some questions popping up right then, I heard—I don't know whether it was Volman or Kaylan, talking about a 'bulging sea of flesh.' A reference to a certain stewardess or something that came up? Or the Jack-In-The-Box stories and stuff like that? You had some pretty exciting stories in there, but there must be loads of others waiting around for the next book, aren't there?

FRANK Well, there's lots of other stories, but I have no intention of doing a book of road stories. I don't know where they ever got the idea of me doing that. I think writing books is a really boring thing to do. I have no plans to do a road story book.

CO So the folklore of the road should be found in the songs?

FRANK Yeah.

CO Well, there's plenty of that around, so—you told me one time that you had this idea about putting out road videos from the 1982 tour with Steve, and the first question is: what happened to that idea?

FRANK I don't have enough money to do it.

CO There might be, or do you think that there might be a circuit for some sort of output, audio or video, which could kind of go off the path of the normal CD release?

FRANK I am sure that there are people that would enjoy looking at it, but it's the production cost, I don't have the cash to invest in the video preparation. For albums it's easy, because all of the equipment that I need to do albums is right here in the house, but to do anything connected to video I have to rent studio time someplace else, and it's just too expensive.

CO You did the music for a program for the Cousteau Society. Could you tell us a little bit about that?

FRANK Well, they came to me kind of at the last minute before they were doing the show, and they asked me to do the score, and it was a very, very, very rush job. It was very difficult because I finished it just before I got on a plane to go to Moscow in January. And I am glad I did it but it was very hard.

CO What was it about?

FRANK Oh, it's about the Valdez oil spill in Alaska, and they traced all the different reasons why the oil spill occurred and how the Exxon company says they're cleaning up and they are not really cleaning up. It's kind of interesting.

CO We should make sure that we get to see that one.

FRANK It's available on home video. Turner put it out.

CO That reminds me of another thing that you talked about once, the thing that was in short called NEST, the National Emergency Security—?

FRANK Trust!

CO What happened to that idea?

FRANK I recommended it to a couple of people who actually were friends of George Bush and said, 'Why don't you suggest it to him?' But nothing ever happened.

CO But that was kind of a rotating system for emergencies to be paid for?

FRANK Yeah, you start with a trust fund where all the people who advertise in the United States would put in one percent of their yearly advertising budget, and if you started the fund off with that amount of money you could probably begin with a billion, a billion and a half dollars in the fund. And when there is an emergency someplace, the idea is that Congress always takes too long to appropriate the money, but the emergency fund would put the money out and Congress would in its time reimburse the fund, and of course the fund is gathering interest when it's not being used.

CO And for paying the money into the trust fund, the people who pay for that might get some sort of advertising?

FRANK Yes, what they do is, they get a logo that they can put on their product that says they're a contributor to the fund, you know? It's kind of like goodwill advertising. Makes people look a little more interested in the environment or a little bit more patriotic, that they would help out with something like this, and there are some advertisers that would respond to that. Especially if the request came from the president.

CO But until now he has failed to—?

FRANK He has failed to do—just about everything! [laughs] He just basically failed. He is really good at vacationing though. I haven't seen anybody so good at vacationing since Eisenhower.

CO In Holland, the word 'gulf' is spelled with an O, just like 'golf,' so we talk about a 'Golf Crisis.'

FRANK Ha, that's right! That's exactly what he's got.

CO This man can steer the world from a little cart that is driving around the lawn.

FRANK Well, he likes to give the illusion that he can, but I think that he can't.

CO You have a company, I read about this when you were in Spain discussing the project for the World Fair, I think it is?

FRANK Mm-hmm.

CO There was mention of a company called 'Why Not?'

FRANK Yeah, that's the company that I have established for doing all the international business.

CO Is that musical business?

FRANK Any kind of business. It's a Delaware corporation chartered to do licensing, consulting, and social engineering.

CO And what gave you the idea to establish it? What is your interest in that?

FRANK For all the different types of businesses that I do, in order to keep the books straight you should organize it into, uh—have some company that specializes in those type of activities. It's not a musical company so I had to have another corporation.

CO And where did the name 'Why Not?' come from?

FRANK Because that's the question one should always ask oneself when dealing with ideas of business possibilities. There is plenty of people who would like to see certain business ideas fail, and you always have to look them in the eye and argue with them. I think the best way to start when somebody says something can't be done, just look at them and say, 'Why not?'

We'd spent enough time talking about business, I thought, so I decided to try and lighten the mood of the show a little. Frank kept a steady supply of fresh coffee coming, and my attempt seemed to work.

CO This is maybe a somewhat weird question, but I would like to ask it anyway. There are two. I once heard from a friend of mine that 'Evelyn, A Modified Dog' had something to do with a pet you once adopted?

FRANK Yeah, 'Evelyn, A Modified Dog' is a reference to an echidna. The L.A. Zoo has a program where you help to pay for the support of the animals by adopting them. So we adopted the echidna, and that means that we gave money so that all the food for the echidna for its life would be paid for by us, and then you get a little plaque on the animal's cage. So that's Evelyn. The dog was modified so much it turned into an echidna.

CO Well, there are some other people or names that might be worth asking who they are or where they are now. For instance, whatever happened to Carolina laying on the tiled floor?

FRANK Oh, 'Carolina Hard-Core Ecstasy'? That was written actually for the girl who played the gong in a—uh, what's the name of that song? 'Eat That Question.' She used to work at the recording studio, and she was from

South Carolina. That was when I was in the wheelchair, and I was working there on the *Grand Wazoo* and *Waka/Jawaka* album. And I needed to have a gong overdubbed, and the way we were working, I wasn't in a regular studio, I was in a mix room, and in order to do an overdub, since we didn't have a studio facility, we had to run a microphone into the toilet which adjoined the mix room. So we had this girl in this little tiled toilet playing this gong, and I think she never had so much fun in her life as when she was just thrashing this gong in the fade out of 'Eat That Question.' The song was based on stories that she had told me.

CO So most of that is true?

FRANK Well, it's a fictionalized account. It's not anything that happened to me. It's based to a certain extent on Carolina folklore.

CO Billy The Mountain?

FRANK Where is Billy now? [laughs]

CO And what is he doing?

FRANK Well, I don't know. Considering that the rest of the world is in such bad shape, Billy has probably a bad case of acid rain right now and so does Ethel, and Billy is probably a lot smaller because he has been strip-mined down to a nub. He's probably not in very good shape right now.

CO And the Muffin Man? Is he still behind his little plate with his little head?

FRANK [laughs] I haven't thought about the Muffin Man for a while. You know, that was a very old text. That text dates from about the same time as that story I told you of the Grand Wazoo from the hardware store. They were all written at the same time.

CO You being one of the most interviewed musicians around, probably, I think that you would make—I saw that just now on the video from Poland—that you could make a pretty good interviewer yourself. I'd like to give you just a few names and see, if you had to do an interview with them, what your very, very first question would be after 'How are you today?' For instance, if you had to interview George Bush now, what would you ask him as a first question only?

FRANK Uh—George, who do you think you're kidding?

CO And Jimmy Swaggart?

FRANK Jimmy, who do you think you're kidding?

CO OK, let's go to Michael Jackson then.

FRANK Michael, who do you think you're kidding?

CO Same goes for Wild Bill the Mannequin Fucker? Is he still around?

FRANK I've never met Wild Bill, I only heard about Wild Bill from Crazy Jerry. I don't know where he is. You know, besides being a mannequin fucker he was also in the business of manufacturing speed. He had a laboratory in his house, and Crazy Jerry would work there for him and in exchange for helping him carry stuff up the hill and you know, working with him in his laboratory, I guess Wild Bill gave Crazy Jerry all of the drugs that he wanted, so that's what he was doing then.

CO So the use of speed might lead to the need to fuck mannequins then?

FRANK Not necessarily. I don't think you could draw that conclusion. I think that there is probably people who like to fuck mannequins that would probably be just as happy to do it using heroin!

CO What would you ask Detective Willis after all these years?

FRANK Hmmm.

CO What toilet is he hanging around right now?

FRANK [laughs] I wonder, you know, there was just this big story that just broke in San Bernardino about this family that kept the daughter, a girl, twelve years old, locked up in a closet for ten years. Maybe Detective Willis was in on that one.

CO Leonard Bernstein died a couple of months ago. You have been compared to him, because he was also a very outspoken American performing artist, composer. How do you feel about his music? Do you like it?

FRANK I very seldom listen to his pieces. The only one that I have heard all the way through was *West Side Story*, because I saw the movie years and years ago. But the rest of his orchestral stuff, I've never even heard it.

CO Did you ever meet him?

FRANK Yeah, he came to one of our concerts at the Fillmore East, in fact it was the night that Chicago was our opening act. And during the break between the first half of the show and the second half of the show some of the guys from Chicago and Leonard Bernstein and a couple of the guys from my band went next door to a delicatessen and had something to eat, and during that conversation he was giving us a lecture on the origins of gefilte fish.

CO That must have been—did you tape that also?

FRANK No, didn't tape it.

CO When we were talking last night about the situation with very popular bands right now, the way they do their performances, young bands that might have some kind of rebellious attitude, sincere or not or whatever—Menno and I were discussing last night that, could it be true that when you were building up your career, starting with the Mothers, that the climate then—maybe also in the minds of the people who were then sitting behind a desk—might have delivered more space for such things to occur? Can a young band find some space to do something like that? Or has the world changed too much?

FRANK Only if he gets a time machine and goes backwards.

CO So then that space was there?

FRANK Yeah, and it wasn't there because people were more aesthetically involved. It was there because they didn't know what they were signing, and most of them didn't care so long as it would sell. And nobody knew really what would sell because the artform was being developed right before your very eyes in those days. And so there was a little bit more risk taking in terms of the A&R men signing different bands. But those days are over.

CO So that makes a difference for the people?

FRANK Well, how are you gonna get a contract if you're doing something experimental? The criteria to get a contract in the United States is, first of all, what do you look like? Second of all, does your band sound like some other band that already has a contract? If it does, how does it compare to the other band that already has a contract? Next question is, how many records did the other band sell? And that will give the A&R man some clue as to how many you will sell, and that's all that matters. Unless you are just like somebody else they don't want you. Unfortunately, a lot of new groups know that, and what they do is they start off the beginning of their musical career, when they should be finding their own style, they go out and copy somebody else and the only thing that is unique about what they develop for their group is the way the look. They try to look sort of like the other band but a little bit more different and that's how they get their contract.

CO Well, the link is not new between how you look and how you are going to—

FRANK Yeah, but it's more critical now because of MTV. There was a time when if you're butt ugly you could still get a record contract, because people were listening to music. Now they *watch* music, and they don't wanna look to a bunch of butt-ugly guys.

CO You have been the starter, the initiator, of a lot of careers. Do you follow these careers?

FRANK No.

CO For instance, when you did the 1984 tour, George Duke was sitting in with you. How does that development of somebody who was a very vivid character in your band—

FRANK I have no idea what George is doing now. I never talk to him. He works in a realm of music that I have no contact with.

CO And one of the later discoveries that you made, Steve Vai, who is building quite a career of his own now?

FRANK Oh yeah, he calls me all the time. He stopped by about two or three weeks ago. He gave me my own copy of the gold record that he got for his album. He has been very nice.

CO Have you heard that album?

FRANK Only a couple of cuts. I don't have time to listen. I mean, I am busy *making* music, not listening to it. The only time that I have to listen to it is when I am not watching the news. So, given the choice between listening to music and watching the news, I usually watch the news these days. Because not watching the news can be hazardous to your health.

CO That's what you said in the documentary from Prague: you have been watching MTV, but you should be watching the news!

FRANK You *should* be.

CO Can it still have some entertainment value for you?

FRANK Watching the news? [laughs] Yeah, I mean it gets more entertaining. The more you know the tricks the more entertaining it is to watch the news, because you can laugh at how they try to manipulate you.

CO So you're getting to be an expert in that field?

FRANK I'm pretty good at it.

CO Maybe you should have a TV column yourself, like after the news.

FRANK They would never allow that. Never. That's the last thing they'd ever put on television.

CO You had that idea once, didn't you? 'Nite School.'

FRANK Yeah. They would never put that on TV, because the reason the news is the way it is is because they want you to think about the world in a certain way. All the news is designed to create a certain attitude in the population. It's all designed to control the way you think about the government and about products and about your job, and it's all about mind control.

CO While preparing a tour—because you have such an immense catalogue—when you decide to go on the road, how do you decide what you will put in the repertoire?

FRANK It depends on who is in the band, what instruments, which songs they already know, and how fast they can learn new material. Because if the band doesn't learn fast then you can't invest a lot of time teaching them new material, you have to be practical with your rehearsal time. If the band isn't quick then you find out that all of your rehearsals are being devoted to brushing up old material that they sort of know already. Because the goal of the rehearsal is to finish on the last day of rehearsal with a band that can play a show. With a band that can do a tour. And what it will play is related very directly to the skill of the people in the band. So that means that I can't always have the repertoire that I want.

CO For instance, the horn section on the last tour. However, that was added later—you'd started the rehearsals already, hadn't you?

FRANK Yeah, they were added about two months into the rehearsals. We rehearsed for four months, and I guess they were added at the beginning of the third month.

CO So then you decided to take the arrangements from the things from the *Weasels Ripped My Flesh* album?

FRANK Not necessarily. I took them from all over the place. And some tunes that had never had horns on them before had to be arranged specially, like 'Marque-son's Chicken' and some things like that, you had to develop horn arrangements to make all that work.

CO Did you do all those horn arrangements yourself?

FRANK Yeah. The only one that I didn't do was uh—

CO 'Strictly Genteel'?

FRANK 'Genteel' and 'Whippin' Post,' those were done by Kurt McGettrick. For 'Strictly Genteel' I gave him the orchestra score and he condensed all the melody parts that are in the orchestra down for the five horns, and for 'Whippin' Post' he listened to the Allman Brothers record and developed horn patterns based on their arrangement.

CO One of the surprising things was—

FRANK Oh, and another arrangement that I didn't do was *L'histoire du soldat* and the Bartok *Third Piano Concerto*, which were done by Scott Thunes.

CO Those were the things you put in 'Packard Goose'?

FRANK Yeah.

CO That also seems to be a little bit the story of your life. What did you say once about rock'n'roll journalists?

FRANK People who do interviews with—how did it go?

CO People—

FRANK Doing interviews with people who can't talk—in order to prepare articles for people who can't read, or something like that.

CO People who can't write.

FRANK Yeah! People who can't write, doing interviews with people who can't talk, in order to prepare articles for people who can't read!

CO You still remember our little press conference at the Sonesta?

FRANK No?

CO There was one time when there were all these journalists sitting around.

FRANK I remember the room, but I don't remember anything special about that press conference. What happened?

CO Nothing.

FRANK [laughs] So it was just another one of those, huh? Oh, the *classic* stupid press conference was the first time we went to Finland. When we were brought to this room and it had movie cameras and TV cameras and journalists all over the place. We walked in and sat down, and nobody said or did anything for ten minutes. And it was live. People were afraid to ask a question, so we just sat there.

CO It was live on TV?!

FRANK Yeah, that was a beauty. Once it got started it was kind of funny, but, you know, I guess we looked so horrible when we walked in that people were afraid to talk to us.

CO The whole part of your writing that you do—because you have written on covers, stories, and you talked about a little poetry that you did way back when—these writings, when you put them on paper, you are not an author, are these things that you need to put on paper outside of songs?

FRANK Those things were done such a long time ago, even before The Mothers Of Invention was formed. It was something to occupy my time.

CO One of the aspects we have not discussed so far is the guitar playing that you do, which is quite exceptional. Because the emphasis nowadays in our country, and I take it also in the United States, all these conservatories and training clinics are growing wildly. Very much emphasis on teaching and forming musicians. You are like a bit of an institute yourself. You are, in that respect, a bit of an odd guitar player because you don't seem to practice when you are not on the road.

FRANK I don't even play it. Hardly ever touch it.

CO How long have you not touched your guitar?

FRANK Well, I decided to play a little bit about three weeks ago, and for two days I plunked around on this acoustic guitar that I have upstairs, but other than that I haven't touched it since the end of the tour. June or July 1988.

CO You build up to it during rehearsals then?

FRANK Yeah. You have to. It was very difficult because my calluses are all gone, I don't have any facility, my hands are totally stiff. If I had to go out and play a job tomorrow I couldn't do it. I have to literally learn how to play the guitar all over again every time I put a band together.

CO Do you see a particular development in your soloing? You are to my taste one of the soloists that you could listen to over and over again, because you seem to be thinking on stage and inventing things on the spot literally. A lot of people might pretend that they are doing that—

FRANK I really do invent stuff on the spot. Some of it is pretty stupid and some of it works. It's a hit-and-miss proposition.

CO If you look at all the tapes you have here, do you see a development?

FRANK It's hard to say, because each tour there are some recordings, and you listen to that and say, 'Oh, that's a good solo and I have really improved there,' but then you listen to all the rest of the stuff that you are going to throw away and say, 'That's really horrible.' Every once in a while you play something that's satisfactory and then the rest of it is gibberish. Nonsense.

CO The guitar playing that you did on the last tour had some sort of an acoustic approach to it, the sounds that you had.

FRANK That clean sound? I always wanted to have some kind of a guitar that could make a clean sound that was still audible over the band, and I think I had a pretty good sound on some of the solos in the '88 tour.

CO Do you think that the solo on 'Any Kind Of Pain' on the *Broadway The Hard Way* album would be an example of that?

FRANK Yeah. I wouldn't say it's a great solo but it's one using that clean guitar sound. I think that on the *Broadway The Hard Way* album there is another solo on uh—

CO 'Outside Now'?

FRANK Yeah, I like that solo, I think that's good. And the solo on 'Green Hotel.' Those are two good solos. On *The Best Band You Never Heard In Your Life*, the one that is coming out, there is a really good solo on 'Zoot Allures' with clean guitar. I think there's another good solo in there, but I can't remember what tune it is.

CO Something that was very surprising in that period was—if we look at other performances in other years—the amount of covers that you did.

FRANK Yeah. They were easy to do, they were easy to organize, and the audience liked them.

CO You took some surprising stuff for that.

FRANK Well, I always like Ravel's *Bolero* and I thought it was a great opportunity with the instrumentation of that band to re-orchestrate it. Do a special version of it. There's a pretty good recording of it on that *Best Band You Never Heard In Your Life*. It's basically the version from Rotterdam which is on that album. There's a couple of other sections from other cities but most of it is from Rotterdam. In fact, there is a lot of stuff from Rotterdam in that album.

CO That's a novelty!

FRANK Why?

CO I don't know exactly how much Rotterdam there is on any other live albums.

FRANK Surprisingly enough, from the '88 tour there is a lot of tunes that were done in Rotterdam that were played pretty well between the two nights that we played there.

CO That's why I say it. Because you seemed surprised the minute you walked on the stage. I remember a quote, I think it was even in one of our conversations, where you say, 'Sometimes when I come to Rotterdam I have the feeling that the audience is painted on to the chairs.'

FRANK That's true. I experienced that a number of times there. And of course, this time, with the little emergency that we had with Bobby Martin getting the fishbone stuck in his throat—that's not a good way to start your concert off, with a medical emergency. But it goes to show you, you can never tell which concert the band is going to play the best at, you know? You can have really fantastic concerts in out-of-the-way cities, and you can play in major cities when the audience is really ready for the show and the band doesn't deliver. You just never know. So whenever the band does a good concert in a major city, then that is always nice.

CO And you get a lot of material mostly from that particular gig?

FRANK Yeah. I mean, what I do is after the tour is over, I try and remember which cities had the best shows and I start looking at those tapes first to see where the best performances are. But even in some of those shows I remember as being generally boring or lifeless, I will still listen to those tapes, because my memory isn't perfect and there will be one or two tunes out of that slow show that turned out to be played very well, or there is a good solo in it or some funny little thing and then I'll save that and edit it into the final version.

With this, I'd gathered the material I needed for the *Supplement* show. We recorded an opening for the show. Frank said:

> *Hello, this is Frank Zappa! There is a program called Supplement, on NOS, and it's supposed to be sort of a birthday celebration for my fiftieth birthday, and you might wanna listen to it, or you might wanna go get something to eat instead!*

It was already late by this time, so Frank offered to call us a cab. The dispatcher on the line didn't know who he was, and couldn't understand him. Frank was half-screaming into the telephone, spelling out 'Z-A-P-P-A,' and eventually rung off with a heartfelt 'Fuck!' When the taxi arrived finally, we thanked him again for doing the interview, and promised to send him everything once it was all edited.

That was the perfect time to present Frank with a little gift. My friend Spencer Streeter, from G&S Music in Hemel Hempstead in the UK, had given me a cassette tape with a recording of the Liverpool show on September 11th, 1973, two days after my first Zappa show in Amsterdam. I'd written the details on the cassette, and now I handed it to Frank. FZ unwrapped the gift, looked at it, looked up at me, and said, 'This wouldn't have a 1973 version of "Brown Shoes" on it, would it now?' We both grinned: he remembered what we'd talked about all those years ago.

On our way back to Holland after the sessions in the UMRK were done, we stopped off in New York. Mark Volman and Howard Kaylan had set up a flipboard in their offices, listing ideas for their show and displaying a motto that read, 'Eat Me/Eatus Meus.' The wall was decorated with a poster of two spectacular blondes in bikinis. We were offered water and coffee, and they welcomed us like old friends. We spoke of their reverence for their ex-boss, and the period that they described as 'the most educational years of our professional life.' Of course, the irrepressible Zappa humor made acquiring that knowledge a treat. Besides learning so much, they'd been exposed to another side of the music life also, having been known only as the largely well-behaved Turtles before their time with Frank. They were featured in *200 Motels*, which was way ahead of its time—and the first feature-length movie recorded on video—that narrated a life on the road, with great music, sexy girls, and Zappa's own surreal take on everything. Besides Flo & Eddie and the rest of the band, the movie featured a full orchestra, Keith Moon, Ringo Starr, Theodore Bikel, Jimmy Carl Black, Don Preston, and Pamela Miller (aka Pamela des Barres, the most famous groupie on the planet).

It turned out to be a hilarious interview. Volman and Kaylan clearly remembered every little detail like it had happened the day before. Every fan is aware that Frank regarded that period as an extremely important and inspiring time, and he'd gone on record as saying that Kaylan was the best singer he'd ever had in his band.

Just before Menno turned on the tape, Volman and Kaylan showed us some photos of gold-leafed plaster casts of the penises of several rock stars—the pet project of the now infamous Plaster Casters of Chicago. Flo & Eddie were trying to set up a rock'n'roll museum, and wanted the casts to be among the most prominent exhibits.

FLO They are owned by Frank Zappa's ex-manager, Herb Cohen—

CO I know him. Shall we start?

FLO & EDDIE Sure!

CO Right now we are in New York, and we have finally met the special guests of our show tonight. Maybe, gentlemen, you would be so kind as to introduce yourselves?

FLO I'm Mark Volman, and I'm known as Flo.

EDDIE I'm Howard Kaylan, and I'm the other half of our team. People sometimes call me Eddie.

CO So that would be Flo & Eddie! The famous Turtles, the famous Mothers, the famous singers! It's a real pleasure to have you in our program, as you know we are celebrating Frank's fiftieth birthday right now—

FLO Let's buy him a watch!

EDDIE [laughs]

CO So, before we start talking about that, what are you doing right now, here in New York?

EDDIE Right now in New York, we are on the radio every day in the afternoon between two o'clock and six o'clock. We do four hours a day, we're on a radio station called K-Rock, we play classic rock'n'roll records by The Beatles, and The Who, and the Stones, and Zeppelin, and the Dead, and that sort of thing, and then in between records when the mikes are turned on we're just ourselves. We don't have any scripts, we don't really know a lot about these records, like these other disc jockeys who have been doing this for thirty years. All we know is that we've been partners, we are partners, we were around during the '60s and the '70s while these records were being made, so we bring a unique thing to radio here in New York, because no other disc jockey in the afternoon can say, 'Yeah well, I sat down in a hotel room with Marc Bolan and we learned these songs and we got high together.' They don't have these memories, they can guess what it was all about but they can't *tell* you what is was all about. That, and our sense of humor, for what it's worth, I think is unique for New York radio. We're having a real good time.

FLO And we're still touring as The Turtles, the group that we formed in the mid-'60s as high school students, that had a real good run at the national charts in the United States, as well as all over the world, actually. The Turtles still continue to tour featuring Flo & Eddie. We do—until this year, we're doing over a hundred concert dates a year, and because of radio we've had to cut off our touring schedule down to at least half that this particular year, but we remain a pretty constant touring force in the marketplace, in terms of the fair circuit, the city festivals, a lot of theme parks in America. And the success of the music of the '60s has become a very high priority in radio around the United States and continues to flourish for The Turtles as a touring band. So, with our touring and our radio, this year hasn't really allowed us too much time to relax. Our radio show is four hours a day, five days a week. It's been a great challenge for us to hope to attain a success in radio like the success that we're known for, I suppose, in music.

CO Yeah, because people may think this is a revival thing, but personally I believe that maybe because of what is going on right now, there might be some sense of relief factor in hearing that material.

EDDIE Yeah there is, you know? I think you're absolutely right, especially because the music of the '90s so far is not so great. I mean, some of it is, I'm not saying it is all bad, there is a lot of good stuff out there but it's not like it used to be. In America in the '60s and the '70s, when you turned on the radio, you could hear Frank Zappa, you could hear The Supremes, you could hear Eric Burdon and The Animals, you could hear Otis Redding, you could hear everybody on the same radio station. And now in America you have to decide what kind of music you want to listen to. If you wanna listen to rap music, that's on one station; if you wanna listen to Black music, that is on another station; oldies are on another station, new stuff is on another station—

FLO Another point that Eddie—uh, Howard—was just making was that television in America has also become a very valuable tool to sell the music of the past as well. Shows like *The Wonder Years*, *Happy Days*; movies like *Good Morning, Vietnam*; *China Beach*, which is a very successful show—all of these shows recount what went on during the '60s, whether it was during Vietnam or just growing up in the innocence of that era, and from that they play the music of the '60s.

EDDIE A lot of people have attached a certain romanticism to the '60s that may or may not have been there. I mean, when we were going through that era and we were making music as The Turtles, it was by and large happy music, because what was going in the rest of the world was not happy at all. So we were trying to create some sort of a balance. Everybody thinks back and remembers how wonderful the '60s were, but what they don't remember was the only reason we were happy at all was because there was so much shit going on in the world that we tried to do something that was a little more 'up.' People look back and they think about all the great memories of the '60s, very few of them remember how many Americans were fighting during that time, it was not a very pleasant time in America. We tried to make it the Summer of Love. It *was* over here, the Summer of Love—overseas it was not.

CO And then again, the humor in the music was far more vivid then, wasn't it?

EDDIE Yes it was, it was a lot more vivid, it was a lot more old-fashioned. I mean, even though especially with Frank we pushed the envelope, so to speak. We really just tried to get away with as much as we could. By and large most of the music was not, most of the music was just reactionary.

FLO Well, Frank Zappa was really—I mean, there was a lot of humor going on from different types of artists. Stan Freeberg was probably most well known for being successful making records in the '50s as a humorist, but when Frank Zappa came along with *Freak Out* and *Absolutely Free*, which were the first two albums in America for Frank, Frank was actually taking potshots at the generation that was growing up with the love beads and smoking pot and the generation of love and peace, and Frank had a unique way of taking what was really happening and writing about it and making it fun, and still being able to sell to a certain audience. When those first two records came out, much of Frank's music never really got played until radio twisted around near the late part of the '60s, as college radio became much more influential and the formation of FM radio began to really take over, and album music became more important than Top 40 45 singles music. Frank became one of the forerunners of that alternative style of music, and one of the reasons that we probably have been fortunate enough to span—as we are now dipping into our fourth decade as a team, as a successful entertainment organization, as Flo & Eddie—probably has a lot to do with our leaving the '60s history of The Turtles behind and picking up with Frank Zappa and doing something that every '60s artist was really trying to do. Which was to get out of the pop mold, the Top 40 mold. And Frank picking up Flo & Eddie from The Turtles and bringing that pop-ism into his music did two things. It brought pop Frank, his ability to write more and vocalize the type of humor we were able to do, kind of based on rock'n'roll, but at the same time it gave Howard and I the beginnings of a new history which came as Flo & Eddie, which was to break out of the mold—

EDDIE And it also brought Frank into radio as much as it did the other way around—radio started taking notice of it because it was almost accessible. Frank is great, he's a brilliant, brilliant man, I don't have to tell you that, but part of his brilliance is that while hippies were out there marching with their protest signs and love beads, while the generations kept changing, while people kept smoking dope or trying stuff that was new to them, Frank never got caught up in the trends. Frank always stayed faithful to himself. So he would watch all these things going on and he couldn't believe it! And he would just write about it, he was just an observer, he was the best observer in rock'n'roll that our generation has ever had because he was never a joiner, he never joined any of these movements. He would always just comment about them, and half of the time the people he was saying rude things about were also the people who were buying his records and didn't even understand he was talking to them! He was always talking to the kids of America. Even in concerts he would always, and still to this day, say, 'Hiya, kids, how're you doing?' He treats it as they are his classroom, and they are. If they're very smart and they pay attention to what Frank is telling them and playing for them, they can learn an awful lot about music and an awful lot about culture, and if they take the time they can learn an awful lot about themselves.

FLO And not in a negative way. One of the things that came out of the Frank Zappa years with us was a statement that seems to have underlined Frank's whole conceptual way of writing, which was, 'It's OK to be hip and still to have a sense of humor.' And that was something that we really honed in on in The Mothers Of Invention, during the era that we were involved, because Frank was able to take the rock pop-ism of The Turtles' success and it allowed us to satirize the rock history that we had been a part of as The Turtles, and it was something that Frank had never, ever had. Whether he had aspired towards that or not, he never had that Top 10 rock business to fall back on at the time when we joined the group, and that became what we lashed out at comedically.

EDDIE On the very first album, where the quote on the back says, '*Clean you boys up a little bit and I can make you as big as The Turtles*—a noted Los Angeles disc jockey'—that disc jockey was our manager at the time, Red Foster, he was a disc jockey in Los Angeles. That was a real quote, and it was said to Frank. It seems semi-ironic that many years later we came to Frank and he turned us around and made us as hip as the Mothers. But we grew up sort of together in '65 and '66, when we were starting. We were all playing on the Sunset Strip, we knew Frank then, we knew his music then, so it was really a matter of proving more to our peer group, to other musicians, and to radio people across the country, that we were hip as The Turtles ended. And Frank gave us that ability to cross over and to show people that it was pretty close, I mean being The Turtles pop AM, and being the Mothers too rude to be played on FM, they weren't really that far apart, we were all just musicians trying to make a buck.

CO But I think you were the first famous musicians that he added to his band? Everybody became famous through the Mothers—

EDDIE That entire band of Mothers Of Invention that we joined, I think, was full of superstars.

FLO Frank used to say that it was the one band he had where everybody could go out and be the leader of their own band. Besides Flo & Eddie, he had Aynsley Dunbar, who had carved out a pretty successful career in England with The Retaliation, with John Mayall's Bluesbreakers. George Duke was in the band. At the time George was not known for what he would end up reaching out and becoming successful at, which was as a producer of Anita Baker, Philip Bailey, and many more successful stars. Donnie Preston, Ian Underwood, Jeff Simmons, who had made an album with Frank, *Lucille Has Messed My Mind Up*. It was a very unique experience, working with all those musicians—for us as well, because we had been pretty much in a band, a democratic organization where everybody shared and everything, and going into Frank's band—now we were in a band where we answered to a leader—

EDDIE Oh, a monarchy! No doubt about it!

FLO We learned, working with Frank—a whole other way of running organizations, which is the way we went and formed our bands after we left The Mothers Of Invention. We were the leaders and we learned through Frank's organization how that could work successfully. So there was a lot of giving to Frank of our experience, and our voices, and our success pattern in terms of our energy and our ambition and our drive, but we got back probably as much in the learning experience of the industry, and the fact that—One of the things that Flo & Eddie learned from Frank was that a career for us was not a year-to-year, album-to-album, project-to-project success, and artistically we were able to look at a career as a whole, which is something we still function under, realizing that people won't really judge what we've done as artists, forgetting just The Turtles and Flo & Eddie and working in radio and everything. When they look back at our career, when Flo & Eddie are no longer a part of the history of music but we are just a memory in the history of music, people will probably be able to see more of what we contributed at the end result, and that is what we learned by working with The Mothers Of Invention. And that's the type of man Frank is: he thinks of his career as his life's work, and that is something that we needed to experience by working with him and have been able to take in to our—every year after we left Frank Zappa, we have applied that same philosophy. That the important thing is not our year-to-year and what people get out of it, but what people look back at Mark Volman and Howard Kaylan, Flo & Eddie, and think of our career in that point of time.

CO When did you first decide to use the names Flo & Eddie? Flo being short for Phlorescent?

FLO Well, we had two members of our band who were actually crew members. A very wild flamboyant Spaniard, who was always leeching things in the band—wives, cigarettes, and money. We nicknamed him the 'Phlorescent Leech.' His real name was Carlos Bernal. We also had a fellow in our group who was a very straight, we always say fraternity president, class, short hair, simple fellow, very articulate, very smart, and we used to call him Eddie. His real name was Dennis Jones. When The Turtles broke up we were in a litigation situation, where the record company sued each member of The Turtles because we were signed individually and collectively, and Mark Volman and Howard Kaylan were not legally able to go out and make solo records when The Turtles broke up. So, joining Frank Zappa's band we made an album, we actually sing on about five songs on an album called *Chunga's Revenge*, and Frank said, 'The album is coming out, what are you gonna call yourselves?' and we said, 'How does The Phlorescent Leech & Eddie sound?' And he laughed and said, 'That sounds really good, let's use that!' And on the first album, the Phlorescent Leech & Eddie on *Chunga's Revenge*, Howard was the Phlorescent Leech and I was Eddie, because it didn't really matter to us. It was just kind of a—we looked around for a bunch of hip names and nothing really sounded good, so the Phlorescent Leech and Eddie were born, and by the time we did the white *Fillmore East Live 1971* album, we risked it all by just saying, 'We wanna be known as Mark Volman and Howard Kaylan.' And at that time we decided to use the names, our real names, and even then in the movie *200 Motels* the Phlorescent Leech and Eddie appear in the cartoon section as two of the cartoon characters when Jeff is stealing the room in the middle section of the movie. And when we left the Mothers, the record company, Warner Bros., felt that Flo & Eddie were known to a certain kind of audience that knew us from the Zappa days, and we kept the names the Phlorescent Leech and Eddie going into our first solo album with Warner Bros.

CO I've heard that the first time that you decided, or were playing with the idea, to be in the band was in the time that Frank was doing the previews with the orchestra in Los Angeles for *200 Motels*, is that right?

EDDIE Yeah. The Turtles had just broken up, I mean literally two weeks earlier, we had had a meeting and we looked at the other guys in the band and we just said, 'Look, Mark and I can't do this anymore.' Every time we were writing a song and bringing it to The Turtles, the rest of the members in the band would change the song around, that's how democratic we were. Everything was written as The Turtles, we produced as The Turtles, we had our own little company, we were trying very hard to be The Beatles.

So, while The Beatles had Apple, The Turtles had Blimp, and we would sign artists, we opened up a boutique on Sunset Boulevard for our wives to design clothes, I mean it was really sick. We were very, very sick. So when Frank came along with this opportunity—he had heard through the Hollywood grapevine that The Turtles had broken up—we didn't know what we were going to do. When the band broke up, we called our lawyer and we said, 'We just broke up The Turtles.' And our lawyer said, 'You guys are idiots. You're idiots because now you can't use the name Turtles to record, you can't use the names Mark and Howard to record, you can't do anything!' And so we were really depressed, we didn't know what to do. We were offered the West Coast lead parts in the Broadway production of *Hair*, we almost took it, I can't imagine how scary my life would be if we had gone into *Hair*. But instead we went to see Frank Zappa and Zubin Mehta and the L.A. Philharmonic do the previews to *200 Motels* at UCLA's Pauley Pavilion. It was a very nice program, and after the show we went backstage to shake hands with Frank and the members of the original Mothers that Frank had gotten together, and Frank said, 'Heeey, I hear The Turtles broke up!' We said, 'Wow, that was quick! Yes we did, we broke up about two weeks ago.' And he said, 'I'm putting a new band of Mothers together, we're going to go to Europe, we're gonna do this special in Holland'—that was the first thing we were scheduled to do, and he said, 'And also we are going to play a bunch of shows and then we are going to make a movie, are you interested?' And we said, 'Yes, absolutely interested!' And he said, 'Do you play instruments?' We said yes, because we both played saxophones at the time, and he said, 'Well, I'm having a barbecue on Sunday, why don't you come on over and bring your saxophones and we'll have a little audition.' So Sunday rolled around, we went over to Frank's house. We couldn't figure out why he wanted us to bring our saxophones, we knew he had Ian Underwood in the band, he was the best saxophone player we had ever heard in our lives, but instead he brought us during the course of the barbecue down to the basement. We took out our saxophones, we honked around a little bit, we did this audition. And after we played a little bit Frank just said, 'Yeah, that's real good you guys. OK, put away the saxophones, put them away, let's just try singing for a little while!' And that worked out really well.

FLO See, we had known Frank in Hollywood, as Howard said earlier—we would all work in the Sunset Strip. But we had also come to see Frank in New York many, many times. We had come to see his show at the Garrick Theatre, with the original Mothers Of Invention, when they were doing the show *Absolutely Free*, when he would play every night on Bleeker Street, and we had gone to his house—he had a small apartment underneath a building and it was very big and spread out—and we had actually been exposed to Frank's early creation of *Ruben & The Jets*. He played us a bunch of the early material.

EDDIE Those were the days in New York that Joni Mitchell was sleeping on his floor. It goes to show you how long ago that was!

CO Let's try some of that famous K-Rock coffee.

EDDIE Good luck!

FLO Actually, I think this came from outdoors . . . so our relationship with Frank was more as friends than anything else, and so it wasn't really that unnatural when we went and saw the band. We had relationships with Frank—kind of blood relationships . . . Howard was a cousin of Frank's original manager, and so going to see Frank, we had never intended to go thinking that we would join The Mothers Of Invention, and when we got the offer it was kind of—for us it was a safety. I mean, we didn't really have anything to do, we couldn't make records as The Turtles, we couldn't make records on our own, and basically this gave us something to do, a job to have. And we never really thought at the time that it would end up turning out like it did.

CO And for the Zappa audience, of course, it was a big surprise because he had disbanded the band that he had before you joined, a huge, very instrumental-oriented band. And then you came to Holland—
I know exactly what special you are talking about because I have it on tape—was it the *Piknik*?

FLO & EDDIE Yes!

CO They erased the video material of that.

EDDIE No kidding! Doesn't Frank have a copy of it?

CO I don't think so. But then Frank came back to Europe with you and everybody was very surprised—I even remember the set that you did. I think there was a real spiffy arrangement of 'Wino Man' in there, you remember that one?

EDDIE Sure do!

CO 'Call Any Vegetable' was in there, and that material was new for the Zappa audience, it was really new, and the color that we talked about earlier was the color put on top by you, some sort of icing on a cake.

FLO Well, I think that at time it was pretty rough considering up until that moment, as you say, Frank had pretty much been a very eclectic music band, with a lot of instrumentals and very strong in the music part of it, and probably fairly weak in the vocal part of it. So when we joined the band, as you say, that material to America was not new. 'Call Any Vegetable' and 'Wino Man,' he had been performing that with his other organizations, Jeff Simmons was singing 'Wino Man'—had actually recorded that on an album that Frank produced, the *Lucille Has Messed My Mind Up* album, so that was just an extension of what Jeff could add to the band. And then when we brought in 'Call Any Vegetable,' I think we were also doing 'We Are The Mother People' and 'Chunga's Revenge,' 'Primer Me Carucha (Chevy '39),' or whatever it was. We were doing mostly material that had already all been recorded, 'The Nancy & Mary Music,' the instrumental stuff that would eventually end up on *Chunga's Revenge*, 'Twenty Small Cigars,' there was a lot of that apart of the show, and we were doing 'Rudy Wants To Buy Yez A Drink' and 'Would You Go All The Way For The US of A,' which were things that ended up on *Chunga's Revenge*, and that was the extent of the original stuff that we had really added.

EDDIE Yeah, except that with 'Sharleena' and 'Tears Began To Fall' and stuff like that, it was Frank's closest attempt, now that we were in the band, to actually having a pop group. I mean, he looked at his new Mothers Of Invention as a pop band. And even though it was very, very close, Frank would never let himself just be in a pop band, so he would write these beautiful rock'n'roll songs and then right in the middle of it he would say things that were unbelievable. You would just go, 'Frank, you almost had a hit, we almost could have got it on the radio, but instead you sang about tits, you sang about holding somebody's dick—I mean, you're saying things that radio isn't gonna play!' That's just part of Frank that is still there, that still won't let him become too famous. Frank will never let himself become that big, he's got something inside of him that holds him back from super success. He really doesn't want it—I really believe that deep down inside he couldn't handle it if he got to be as big as he wants.

FLO Unless it was on his terms. Which was probably what happened after we left the band, when he had his two biggest pop hits in America—'Dancin' Fool,' which was basically a parody of the whole dance disco generation and he was able to slip that through, and then 'Valley Girl,' which became kind of a novelty record for the time, which were two hit records for Frank Zappa in America. Got to AM radio, actually were played as hit songs so to speak, they really did work for him. But then again, both of them were not unlike everything Frank had ever done, it's just the public bought them and became more aware of it, and 'Valley Girl' especially became a term that now fit a whole generation's style of child from the Valley that Frank was able to make jokes of, and 'Dancin' Fool' did exactly the same thing. But when we were in the band he was just kind of formulating that ability to do that. I think *200 Motels* closest resembled what he would eventually get into when we were doing songs like 'Daddy, Daddy, Daddy,' 'Easy Meat' ... things that were very pop, very rock-oriented but still were taking potshots at the rock'n'roll generation—

EDDIE And you still couldn't play any of them on the radio, not in America. I mean, it was still way too rude to play that stuff on the radio, even though it was real poppy, had a great melody, had real good vocals, Frank would always throw something in to make it impossible for radio to latch onto it, that's just the way he is. I think it's great, I think that's part of his creativity and his genius. The other part of Frank's great, great genius, or one of the many parts of his great, great genius, is his ability to take the best from his musicians and recycle it and put it out again—

FLO As Frank Zappa!

EDDIE As Frank Zappa music! This makes some of his musicians very, very angry because they wrote this part out or they said these things first, they tell it to Frank. Frank hears it, likes it, writes it down, makes it a song, and the author of the song is now Frank Zappa.

CO He even goes so far that this procedure that you're describing right now—the whole procedure became recycled and put into *200 Motels*.

EDDIE Right, it was a movie about a movie about a movie about a bass player quitting, and then the bass player quit! When he read the script he couldn't stand it and he quit.

FLO It was art imitating life—

EDDIE It was life then imitating art. So it became a vicious circle. We couldn't even tell, when that movie was being made, what was real and what wasn't real. I mean, we were all sitting around in that dressing room at the time when Jeff Simmons quit the band, we were already into rehearsals, we had to make this movie, we only had five days to shoot the movie in, and we were in our third day of rehearsal before the thing started when Jeff walked out, and we had no one to play his part. Frank brought in Wilfred Brambell from *A Hard Day's Night* to take the part over, and he freaked out after a couple of days and just couldn't say the lines, and when we all waited for the door to open, Frank said, 'The next person that walks through that door, I don't care who it is, is going to play the part of Jeff Simmons.' And we all just sat there waiting, 'Oh God, oh God, what's gonna happen, what's gonna happen . . .?' And when the door opened and it was Ringo's chauffeur, Martin Lickert, and he already had a rudimentary knowledge of bass playing and he had his cute little English accent and everything, Frank just went, 'That's it, this is perfect!' And it was! I mean, it worked out very, very well for everybody but it was one of the luckiest things I've ever seen.

CO So one day you are Ringo Starr's driver, the next day you are a movie actor.

EDDIE Yeah—Hollywood! That's the way it works, being a star. And then of course I am sure you know that Martin Lickert abused his privileges as far as Ringo was concerned, thought he was a real movie star. I mean after

200 Motels was made he went back to Ringo's house, and Ringo went on tour or on holiday, and Martin Lickert threw a bunch of parties at Ringo's house and drank all of Ringo's liquor, trashed his furniture. And Ringo just finally said, 'I don't know who you think you are, but you are fired!' So I don't know whatever became of Martin, but he wound up not even being a driver anymore, it just all went to his head.

CO The vocal part is what I want to dwell for a moment. You were doing the material that we have talked about until you joined Frank's band. From that day on you were not just singing words set to a melody, but you were also very instrumental singers . . . I have footage of you in which you sang like instruments. Was that new to you?

FLO Yeah, of course! We had sung in choir together for four years, and had learned the breakdown of music in terms of soprano, alto, tenor, first tenors, baritones, bass, and had been as musicians playing clarinet in high school and well aware of all the different textures. But going to work with Frank demanded something of us that we had never really experienced in rock'n'roll, which was fitting ourselves into a band not just as singers but as musicians, using our voices as musical instruments. This was a process that took hours and hours and hours of rehearsal time. And that was something that Frank never had any problem with. He was very, very caught up in the perfection of his music, even listening to an album like *Billy The Mountain*, which is filled up with a lot of off-the-wall improvisation. Those were things where the improvisation was given room to be created night after night, when we would get to a section that was meant to have the improvisation take place. Part of our job every night, Howard and I, when we would go into a town on tour, was to fill ourselves up with a town's history, a town's background, a town's major stars, whether it was a college or doing concerts. Part of our job was to learn the things and the people that we could draw humor from, and that continued.

EDDIE Just like *Just Another Band From L.A.* makes all these local references to things in and around Los Angeles. That show would only happen in Los Angeles. When we took that show to New York all the references were local to New York, so it was a customized show for every city. And that was our job: Howard and Mark had to go out and learn about the city and the town and the celebrities, and get to know what streets the kids cruised and got to know the hotspots they went to, so that in the improvisational part of our show we could say, 'Oh baby, where you're going? Well, I just came from the Paradiso—Oh, you do? Oh, that's a hot place! Well I gotta get up and fly out of here in the morning . . .' You know? All that stuff was modular—it was designed so that we could play with it a little bit. And when Frank laughed at something that we did it was much more important than whether the audience laughed or not. We existed in that band for humor but not necessarily for the audience's humor, for Frank's humor! When Frank laughed we knew we were funny. The rest of the stuff we practiced, as Mark said, for hours and hours, you know—eight, ten hours a day. The improvisational stuff was the most fun, because then we could really play around and keep an eye on Frank and when Frank started cracking up the shows really got good.

FLO Also, all of the musical things that are voices we ended up doing were challenges as singers. At the time we were twenty-two, twenty-three years old, working with Frank, and in The Turtles all we had ever really done was sing pop music. Even our attempt to do comedy during an album that we created in The Turtles, *The Turtles Present The Battle Of The Bands*, we never really challenged ourselves vocally the way that Frank taught us to sing. We probably weren't the greatest singers that Frank could have used to have done some of the vocalizations that ended up being done in things like *200 Motels*, where we had the entire choir—symphony choir singing along, where you could sing octave scales and do things that were kind of off-the-wall. But with just the two of us he was able to bend rock'n'roll a little bit by having the songs sung, and then get into a section where he would have us just do vocalization parts to work against the rock'n'roll band. Those were things that obviously we had never really done. They were very challenging to us as musicians. But as singers it gave us an insight to our potential that we've never probably even topped since working with Frank Zappa. Because you need a person who understood classical writing to know how to fit voices within the context of music and use them as instruments. And

Frank, obviously, with his history of who he enjoyed listening to—Edgard Varèse, John Cage, and the many classical writers that Frank was influenced by, who had used voices in classical music as instruments—he was basically bringing that to rock'n'roll by using singers who only sang rock'n'roll up until that point. So it was kind of a clash of many different influences and moods, and shaping it took many hours of rehearsal time.

EDDIE Not only that. I am sure that when we first joined The Mothers Of Invention there was a certain amount of resistance from the audience, because we were always perceived as being these lightweight sort of AM poppy singers. But you bring us in and you teach us 'Holiday In Berlin,' and all of a sudden you've changed the texture of what we brought to the group too. All of a sudden you could tell, 'Hey, these guys can sing and these guys are funny if you put them in the right context, if you know what to give them to do, they can do it.' And so we learned. We learned an awful lot, like you said, about how to use our voices as instruments, how to become more part of the band—

FLO How to hear! How to hear parts. You just said 'Holiday In Berlin,' one of the probably hardest songs to sing because of the octaves. It called on us, the notes we had to learn to sing to fit within his chord progressions. It wasn't just taking a song and singing a verse and a chorus, where you could pretty much, you know, improvise it night to night and have a little fun with it. With Frank it demanded learning notes and singing those exact notes or they wouldn't fit within single notes being hit by a piano, a saxophone, and guitar, and a bass, and our voices having to fit right into sections where we would do, [sings] 'We're on the road … tadadadadada …' Those things are embedded in our minds even to today. I mean, we sit and sing 'Holiday In Berlin' even today as we, like, mess around with just warming up or something, we will still sing those parts because it demands—it's almost like warmup exercises. But that's what a lot of classical music draws its influences from. The textures and tenure of warmup exercises, and Frank just took that and put words to it. And it was very demanding because we weren't allowed to just improvise the words to songs. We could improvise the bits and the comedic parts, but when it came to singing those songs, 'Shove It Right In,'

'Holiday In Berlin,' and on and on, with the music we were learning we weren't allowed to fluctuate. Those were notes that we had to sing the same every time out of our mouths, or it would sound wrong. Because of what everybody else was playing.

CO The B part of 'Holiday In Berlin' was never used in *200 Motels.*

FLO [sings] '*And when we began to play, a bunch of punks—*' Yeah, that was kind of sad.

CO I have it on tape though.

EDDIE In concert?

FLO That was one of the fun pieces to do, because again, as Howard said, being thought of as kind of namby-pamby pop singers and singing for a Frank Zappa crowd, those pieces, and seeing them and the respect that we gained by working with Frank and doing the job we did for Frank, it really showed us off as singers. Frank was always proud to display our talents, and he would sit there and smoke a cigarette and kind of like, 'Take it, boys!' And when we finished singing and he'd go into the guitar solo we would stand and watch Frank, and it became that kind of showing off for each other that really made that Mothers Of Invention such a unique band.

EDDIE You know what was also great about that too? When we would finish a section like 'Holiday In Berlin,' and it was real good and it went down very well in concert, you'd get a look of approval from Frank that was almost fatherly. Really, he would look over at you like, 'My boys, I'm so proud of you, you did it so well tonight.' It was like a pat on the head, it was a very nice appreciation. Frank really had an appreciation for the members of our particular band. Talking to some of the earlier members of The Mothers Of Invention, and even later members, some of them are so bitter about their lives. It's not what Frank did to them that makes them bitter, it's the fact that they were never able to do anything *without* him that makes them bitter. These poor people that—you know—are on the streets now, from the first Frank Zappa albums and they're going like, 'We got cheated, we got screwed, yada yada!' And the people afterward that say, 'Well, he treats his musicians like they're cattle, he doesn't pay them anything, he doesn't care about anything but himself!' Those people didn't carry the right message away from working with Frank Zappa and The Mothers Of Invention. It was a learning experience, we all threw our knowledge and our expertise into the pot, Frank stirred the pot and he came up with whatever stew was The Mothers Of Invention that year. That was the experience, we all profited from that experience, we still are. Whether or not those guys can get a job, whether or not they are bitter about the royalties they think they own, all that stuff is stupid.

FLO And being Frank Zappa's Mothers Of Invention, obviously, going in and knowing who's the leader, and who is not, was a very important stance you had to know going in. There was not a democracy, this was Frank's history he was creating, not mine. I was a part of Frank's history and as Howard said, fatherly, we were his children in that organization, because we were really allowing him to use us, take our experience and our voices and make this the best Mothers, we are the kind of people—and we said this many times—when we worked with Frank we wanted it to be as good an organization as we could be a part of, as successful as The Turtles. Any project we get involved in, we try and make it the best. There was no conflict over whose group this was and what we were there to do. If it meant eleven hours of rehearsal one day, you rehearsed eleven hours. And you put in your time. It was as Jeff Simmons used to say, it was your army and your rock band, and The Mothers Of Invention were what happened when you put the two things together. As long as you knew that you were the privates and he was the general, then there was no conflicts. And that's how Howard and I went in. When we left the band there was no animosity, we're still friends, we still have a genuine respect for his music and the man—I think more now than we did ever, because we are now grownup men ourselves. And our respect for him goes into his family, and how he has raised his family and the home he has built and created for himself and the lifestyle—

EDDIE That's the real measure for respect for a man. He can treat his band any way he wants to, but when you see how it spills over into his personal life, into how good a father Frank became, how well his children were raised, how well-disciplined they are, how well the household runs—

FLO How much they love him.
EDDIE Yeah, how much respect and love they have for the man, you know, nobody like that is a bad person. I mean, for all the people that may think Frank is evil, or Frank has done this or that, you can look at his family and know he is a genuinely nice man.

Menno switched the cassette. We were recording everything on cassette tape, and not on DAT—fortunately, because cassettes are still reliable and DATs aren't. We had some more of the K-Rock coffee and Howard/Eddie caught me staring again at the poster of the two very attractive blondes in bikinis, the California Twins. He laughed.

EDDIE These our are wives. They are home right now. They're probably getting dinner.
CO Is this one yours? And this one's yours?
FLO I think mine is the other one.
EDDIE We switch off. Havin' fun is the name of the game, and these girls are fun.
FLO They are real twins. They're from California. Which is pretty indicative of the Californian girls, I suppose.
EDDIE It's a good reason to move to California, I'd say.
CO It sure is!
FLO But Holland has always been endowed with some of the most beautiful women in the history of time as well so, I wouldn't look too far there, Co.
CO I don't. But sometimes you are in the States and sometimes you are not.
EDDIE That's right. Love the one you're with, as Stephen Stills once said.
CO I don't know if that's what he really meant by it. Would you know?
EDDIE Yeah, I think he did.
FLO Yeah, I do!
CO There are some things, for the real hardcore fans who are also obviously part of our audience tonight, there are some things that Frank did not put in the book.
EDDIE A lot of things!

CO And who should you talk to, to find out what he did not put in the book?

EDDIE [looks at the ceiling, whistling]

FLO Well, you know, that book—

CO I heard you talking about a 'bulging sea of flesh.'

EDDIE 'Bulging sea of flesh,' that could have happened any night. We had a couple of nights—gee, I hope this doesn't get back to Frank! We had a couple of nights that were pretty strange. There was one particular event in our lives, the night of the Winnipeg Rangers, which I don't believe made the book. I don't wanna even get into details about it. Let's just say that as a band—and we *were* a band, even though Frank was the boss and we were all the other guys—when we were out on the road, especially in the later days with Frank, we were a band and we had an awful lot of fun. And part of being in a band is being guys together, hanging out together, going to the clubs together, getting the girls together, and doing those guy things that only guys can do. Well, Frank didn't write a lot about that in his book and that's understandable. I don't think I would write about it in mine either, but rest assured they were there. We had our nights of unbelievable partying with Frank, oh my!

FLO Frank actually, in the book, covers three areas, and the one area that he sort of leaves out is his touring. That would be the fourth area. The three areas he covered, I thought very extensively, was the history of Frank Zappa as a man leading up to becoming the leader of The Mothers Of Invention, the middle section basically is the theory of music as Frank Zappa oversees the band and how he perceives himself as a writer and a musician, and part three was his political stance in terms of what's happening in the United States—probably a lot more than ever happened in Europe—which is the censorship and his involvement with the Mothers Of Prevention concept, which was his speaking out for the sanity of rock'n'roll, and lyric content, and so forth. And he only devotes about ten pages to touring and there's only one story that comes out in there, the girl with the champagne bottle, with Aynsley Dunbar and the promotor's girlfriend. But needless to say there was a lot of evenings that—when you're a touring band ... that was one of the things that I felt he left out of the book that would have made it to me, as a reader, more entertaining and more fun to have read, and maybe that book is yet to be written by Frank. The experiences of him on the road. He leaves out the experience in Montreux, he only talks about his accident from his point of view, which obviously when he was pushed off the stage and fell into the pit he kind of blacked out there—

CO Montreux is in there briefly!

FLO Very briefly, and he doesn't really talk about the band's experience of watching it burn down and the fire involvement of us going into England and reshaping the band with a lot of borrowed equipment.

EDDIE Oh yes! Because Frank wanted to go home—I mean after Montreux—and he doesn't really make that clear in the book. He makes it sound like he was a real trooper about it, but Frank, truth be told: you weren't. And as we were in the hotel across the lake watching the casino burn to the ground and wondering what to do next, Frank was the guy saying, 'I think we oughta go home, I think this tour is over.' We were the guys saying, 'Yeah but Frank, you're the guy with the Rolls-Royce, you're the guy with the big house, we don't have that stuff, we gotta keep the tour going!'

FLO It was Christmas time, there were two more weeks of touring, that was two more weeks of pay for the group, and they were all sellout shows on the English continent, so we pretty much forced the issue as a band that we wanted to finish the last two weeks. We would borrow equipment and go in and do it. Frank was really opposed to going into the Rainbow Theatre with borrowed equipment, to the four or five sellout days that we had there, and it was kind of a sad phenomenon that, on the very first show, that Frank would end up being pushed into the orchestra pit by the young fellow and experiencing the next eight months in a wheelchair and so forth and so on. But it also at the time—he doesn't recount the outside fact that, once Frank was in the hospital, that we were asked to continue the tour without Frank Zappa, that the Mothers were approached by the tour people involved with this tour, saying, 'You guys sing all the material, the music would still be intact without Frank, you could at least go and do the shows . . .' And that the band said, 'No!'

EDDIE It would have been horrible. I can't even imagine what would have happened if we would have showed up at some of these shows as The Mothers Of Invention without Frank, and that is what they were trying to get us to do. In the meantime, Frank was recovering for months and months and months. We had no contact with him whatsoever. We had no contact with his office whatsoever. What Frank doesn't get into in the book was . . . all these guys that were members of his band were sitting around their homes waiting for the phone to ring, wondering if they would ever work again, wondering if there would ever be another Mothers Of Invention. We couldn't get an answer. No one would tell us if Frank was ever gonna tour again or work, and eventually the guys in the band—Aynsley and Jim and Don—they came to us and said, 'What are we gonna do?' And we said, 'Well, we've always wanted to make a solo album.' We had the stuff that was left over from when The Turtles broke up and we said, 'Let's just go into the studio with you guys, we'll make the record.' We had a deal with Warner Bros., we put the record out. In Europe, and to Frank himself perhaps, for a while it appeared as if we had stolen The Mothers Of Invention for our own use, to make our record, but in fact everybody was just sitting around waiting for something to do, and it's a good thing they did decide to work with us because Frank never did call.

FLO Well see, there is a kind of an interesting twist here to all the stories. This really hurt us when Frank didn't call us, and began to make the *Waka Jawaka* album after the accident and began putting that band together. We thought that Frank was really—like, running away from the band and didn't like us anymore, and we kind of felt . . . kind of *against* Frank at that particular time. But in talking with Frank fifteen years later, Frank said his main reason for doing that is he had read—jokingly—Howard and I made a joke to the press that Frank wasn't pushed, Frank had jumped! And we made a joke of this in our own tongue-in-cheek—

EDDIE You can't take that seriously! That is ridiculous.

BOTH But Frank did!

FLO And Frank thought that we were making light of his injuries and his near—uh, you know, the negative eight months that he spent—He had a lot of time to really see the fact that we had made this joke at him. The English press, the European press took it and made light of it, and I think that that kept our distance from Frank for quite a few years, until we were able to say to Frank that obviously it had been made in a—just like we had made a comment once to the English press about Marc Bolan because we had sung on T. Rex. We made a comment that without us T. Rex would be nothing. Well, the press blew that completely out of proportion, and Marc Bolan and Flo & Eddie had a conflict and problems for a while until Marc understood that the way we had said it could never be put into the press properly. I mean, we had said that, but we had said it with a lightness—

EDDIE With a sense of humor. 'Where are their senses of humor?' we kept wondering. 'What's the matter with these people?' We make jokes, they print it up as headlines and they take it seriously. So we've tried to be very, very careful ever since.

CO We just talked to Frank yesterday, and he said that rock'n'roll journalism—You know his description of it? 'People who cannot write, doing interviews with people who cannot talk, and putting it out for people who cannot read.'

FLO [laughs] And especially who cannot see the sense of humor. So, basically the end of that Mothers happened too soon. Really, I mean, all of that negativism that broke up the band is what we have to remember as the way the band broke up. Montreux, the fire, and then Frank being pushed is the way the Mothers ended for us. So the opportunity to go back and work with Frank in 1988 in rehearsals, under the guise that we were gonna take out the tour with the material that we had done with Frank was very, very exciting. And we had gone to several rehearsals in 1988. Obviously the members that we working with were not brought in. They were all spread out. Frank had had some negative run-ins with Aynsley, George was now successful, the bass player Jeff was living in Seattle, Don Preston was suing Frank—there was no way that band was gonna get back together. Frank had remnants of his other bands—Ike, Chad, and many other really great musicians, and Howard and I rehearsed with Frank for two or three rehearsals, and the material that Frank was bringing to us was material we just didn't want to sing again. We had spent fifteen years cleaning up ourselves for the public in terms of—I mean, those three years with Frank Zappa were fantastic for us as singers and musicians but they were awful for us as trying to sell ourselves to the public. We didn't have a career musically, because the stigma of satire, humor, and rock'n'roll humor, and the pooh-pooh cocky humor we were doing really hung on. And we didn't fight it for the first album or the second album we did as Flo & Eddie. *Illegal, Immoral And Fattening* contained all of the sexuality and sensationalism that we had created with Frank and it was really—We had no real identity. We had our pop-ism from The Turtles and our Zappa-ism from working with The Mothers, but no real individual identity as Flo & Eddie, and it really hurt us.

EDDIE All we had was our past. And you can't exist on your credits. So it was very, very hard for us for a real long time to break this image that we had, of being nasty on stage. Even though we were saying Frank's words, *we* were the guys saying them, so we were perceived as being the rude boys. It took fifteen years to overcome it. It took doing a lot of children's projects. We did *Strawberry Shortcake,* we did the *Care Bears,* we did all these cute little projects for kids, we wrote for television and we were radio personalities in Los Angeles and we got very, very mainstream, and by the time Frank came back to us and asked us to rejoin the group, we had finally broken all those negative barriers. We were finally accepted on a morning show level, we could do TV shows again, people liked us, they called us—

FLO And we had also done the two *Happy Together* tours, in '84, '85, and even '87 we had gone back out to America as The Turtles to a very successful relationship of the Turtles' history and their music and Flo & Eddie's style and humor still in the show. But we were able to commercialize it enough to reach out to the American audience to the tune of a ten- to fifteen-thousand-dollar-a-night concert act. And when Frank brought us in to begin rehearsals, and we began singing those songs of sexuality and the sensationalism and the slap-in-the-face, balls-out humor, Howard and I were a little bit nervous.

EDDIE Very, very nervous. I mean, we didn't work fifteen years to clean our image up to do one tour and destroy it.

CO What songs would that be?

EDDIE Besides the stuff that is obvious, the 'Magdalena's—and I take responsibility for that because I was one of the writers of that song—

CO It's a good song!

EDDIE Thanks! But that was an awful long time ago, and I don't know now that I would feel comfortable, having a daughter who is a year and a half old, singing about, you know, seeing the girl by the lamp and reaching out—I mean that was then and this is now. We didn't feel comfortable with it, plus Frank added two other elements to this tour that kind of threw us off. One element was political overtones. Frank was considering running for president on the Libertarian ticket at the time, even though he really disagreed with a lot of the things they had to say. They were willing to give him a platform for his politics. We did not want to get involved in politics. Section 2a—the band was never going to be called The Mothers Of Invention. It was going to go out on the road as Zappa. Well, I won't be in a band called Zappa, or Santana, or Allman, or anything else. Anybody who thinks that they are the whole band has a problem. It's not really a band then, it's a guy and his support group, and because it's a guy and his support group, that's the way the money was structured too. On the third day of rehearsal, when Frank came to us and said, 'Well, you know what I usually pay my guys in my band, you know, you're gonna get fifteen hundred dollars a week,' or whatever it is, we looked at each other and said, 'Wait a minute! We got over a hundred thousand dollars of work coming up this year, and you wanna give us fifteen hundred a week? We can't do it, we're paying our guys that much money to go out and tour as The Turtles, so we can't accept that kind of money.' And Frank said, 'Well, that's all I got.'

FLO We were making good money by that time.

EDDIE We told Frank at the time that it was nothing personal, that we really enjoyed his friendship, that we were very, very glad that we were welcome in his house, and vice versa he was always welcome in ours, but that we had some differences material-wise and monetarily and we couldn't do it. Frank took it easier than Gail took it. Gail took it like it was a very personal statement we were making against Frank, and it wasn't. We had to talk to her for like an hour, or two hours, just to explain, 'Gail, this is our position, this is why we can't do it'—and she understood.

FLO Frank hadn't toured for a long time up until '88. He had done *You Can't Do This On Stage Anymore*, and when Frank and Howard and I started talking about touring, the family life around him was real up about that, everybody was real excited about Frank being interested in playing guitar and being a musician and going out on the road again.

EDDIE Because he had been downstairs in his basement doing nothing but editing for four years. Gail was just thrilled with the idea that, yes, get him out of the house! I mean, not to get him out of the house, but get him out there on the road where he enjoys being, so he can get a little input into his life so he can make contact with people.

FLO We weren't expecting to make a lot of money going out with Frank, but we were expecting that after doing all the years, the three years we had done, two and a half years, and the albums and the history that we had created with Frank, that he would've at least come to us and offered us maybe a lion's share of the bandmembers' money to have done it. I mean, we would have done it for maybe five thousand a week, twenty-five hundred each, to have taken the band out on the road again. You have to realize that his twenty-five hundred a week was really competing against our twenty-five hundred each a night, which we were able to do as The Turtles. We could go out for a week, five nights, and make ten thousand a week as The Turtles, each. So, for Frank to come to us and offer us seven hundred and fifty dollars for rehearsal and fifteen hundred for, you know, a week, the salary we were gonna make—I understand it, because it was gonna cost him a lot of money to put it out on the show, he does everything first class, first quality. But again, this was fifteen years later, we had busted our butts putting The Turtles out on the road, we had in a lot of people's eyes swallowed our pride as Flo & Eddie to create The Turtles history again, and it wasn't so much for swallowing our pride as again doing what we saw in what Frank had taught us, which was in the grand scheme of things, not the year-to-year but in the history of rock'n'roll, what you will be remembered doing. Those were very positive tours for us as The Turtles, those *Happy Together* tours. We were the headliners, it took us out to two hundred and eighty cities, we were away from home one year out of one eighteen-month period, we had created background parts for Alice Cooper, Ozzy Osbourne, Bruce Springsteen's 'Hungry Heart.' We had worked with Marc Bolan, we had created a whole history as Flo & Eddie after we had left Frank Zappa. And going back to Frank, there were a lot of problems in going back to it. It might have been fun, it might someday be fun in doing something like *200 Motels Part Two*, it might be fun doing an album with Frank, it might even be fun doing a tour again. But it would be something we would have to meet on more common ground. It wouldn't be something we would just be—as Howard says, we felt kind of funny being in a band called Zappa. Had it had been The Mothers Of Invention, had it had been Jeff and Aynsley and George Duke and Don Preston and Ian, and Frank and me and Howard, it might have been something we could have recreated and have done.

EDDIE Yeah, and maybe you can never go home again.

FLO Maybe not. And to recreate is not really to create anyway.

EDDIE That's what Brian Eno says, and he's probably very, very right. You know, the creation of something is not the repetition of it, you don't try to do it again and again and again, over and over.

FLO And as Turtles, that is our creation. That is something that we are repainting every time we go out and do it, and as Frank Zappa's Mothers we're just a cog in the wheel. As The Turtles we're the whole car. We are the leaders, we are our own Zappa, we are the leaders of the band.

CO And probably you are not trying to . . . when you go out—I have not had the opportunity to see that live, but you are probably thinking and saying, 'This is the '90s!'

FLO That's exactly true.

EDDIE Yeah, except for the music, and the music has to stay pure to the people's memory.

CO Yeah, but you are not pretending out there to be eighteen, are you?

EDDIE Come on! It's very, very sad. We do go out on some of these tours and a lot of the acts on the shows think that it's the '60s again, they wanna be just as big as they were thirty years ago, and they're crazy! You know? You see these lead singers and I won't even mention names—

FLO Mark Lindsay!

EDDIE Like Gary Puckett—

FLO But they think they have something to add to the music of the '90s, and maybe they do.

EDDIE It doesn't matter whether they do or not. There's somebody equally talented who is seventeen years old, who's cuter than they are, who's on MTV, who has the support of the teenage record-buying audience, who can do it better. I mean, there is no reason for these people to think that they're going to make a comeback and very, very few of them do. So we don't have any aspirations to make a comeback on that level, and that's part of what keeps us in such good spirits. We never lie to ourselves. I mean, we understand how old we are, we know that the audience we are reaching in concerts now are parents, and parents of younger children, and in some cases grandparents of children that we are seeing in the audience at the age of four or five years old, that are still singing 'Happy Together.' We have three generations singing 'Happy Together' in front of us, and that's a very, very good feeling. I don't think I could do that with 'Magdalena'!

FLO We do have a lot of Zappa fans who come to our show, because they know they're gonna get splatches of the same kind of humor that we brought to Frank. It's tossed into our live show, when we play the New York area, which we do every year at Christmas time—this will be our tenth year in a row in New York—we even do little medleys of our experience with The Mothers Of Invention. Every year we throw in bits and pieces of things that we created in and around The Mothers Of Invention, and that is still a part of our history and we can do that with a good feeling. And we would like to make records again but the records we wanna make are not Frankenstein-type records. We don't wanna make records that are a one-shot situation and putting our career on the line. We want record companies to reinforce our creativity by allowing us to develop a new history with the music that we would wanna make as writers and singers, and there is just not a marketplace. I mean, we're not gonna sell records competing against MC Hammer and Paula Abdul and The Nelsons and that audience. We have to aim our music towards the twenty-five to forty-five-year-old men and women who grew up with our history of music, and hopefully the music that we will make in the future that lies out there for us in this wasteland of making music. Much like many artists, we want the room to develop that sound and music on a more current type of music that we would create as people.

EDDIE And a less competitive level. I mean, I would never go out there again trying to compete against other groups for chart positions. I think it's ludicrous, I think we would really be fooling ourselves. But just the way we fell into radio here in New York City . . . if anything successful happens to us in records, it would be the same way. We will fall into the situation, it will occur naturally. Because everything good in our lives and in our careers has occurred naturally, without us having to actively go out and pursue it. So we exist now in a very, very good place. We have this radio show every single day, we tour all the time during the weekends, we have all this time off to do large tours, we have families, we have our households that are very financially secure, and we're living the good life. And I thank Frank Zappa for his contribution to my life, because I feel that it's major. Bigger than Frank knows.

CO I think that's a good note to end on. I have two mini questions and then I would like to do the promos. And then we're finished. Can you explain to the Dutch audience, and even maybe do it, where the (I don't know if I'm quoting it correctly) the 'Rentoontoon tennen' comes from?

EDDIE [laughs]

FLO Ren-toon-toon-toon-hen-toon-tennen!

EDDIE Hennen-tennen-tennen!

FLO That was just another thing that was created within the band as kind of—as Frank used to call it, folklore. It was a musical accentuation used to accentuate highlighted elements in the band, when we wanted to do a musical interlude that would connect vocal things and musical things, and it became something that we could use as spirited little accentuations musically.

EDDIE Yeah, see, we were really musicians, so when Frank wanted to teach us a part he would have to sing us the part the way he wanted it to be sung. When it was a part that, say, should have been done by the horn player but he wanted our voices to do it, he would demonstrate it—like, remember the old TV show *Dragnet* in America? 'Than tata than! Than tada da thaaan!' Well, that's the kind of way Frank would demonstrate to us the kind of things to do. So instead of just going, 'Tadada da dadaaa,' Frank would go, 'No, I want it more like more like 'HAN TAN TANTAN—TAN—TANTAAAAN!' And we'd get it, we would understand what he meant.

FLO More of a higher voice thing—where if he wanted a lower thing it would be like kind of a 'Toon-toon-toont.' Which he was highlighting kind of a cello-type thing or a baritone horn-type vocalization. So those became things that became part of the musical extension, when we would wanna incorporate a section-to-section bridge between vocal and vocal, if there was like a break, Frank would take advantage of that by latching onto a 'Ren-toon,' and those were things that we even satirized and that became part of the cartoon section of *200 Motels*. When we would wanna vocalize something, when he didn't wanna use an orchestral section and he wanted it to sound orchestral, but to use the vocalization.

EDDIE That even carried over further than that. We'd come to a place in the song, and this was used in *200 Motels* too, in a bizarre way, where we'd go, 'Taaaa padadam!' And to demonstrate that Frank would go, 'Raaaanze mohammitz' We would go, 'Ranze mohammitz, OK.' We would write that down and that's the way we would remember how that thing went. So, when it came time to name Theodore Bikel's part, the Devil's part, Frank said, 'Let's call him Ranze Muhammitz. Makes sense to me!' You know, and so—folklore!

CO Do you still remember the Dutch song you sang?

FLO No.

EDDIE I might—

CO It was only one line.

FLO I remember the German. When we did the German sections, which was the 'Sofa' and the fat floating sofa—

EDDIE We learned it originally in German. When we performed it in Holland we changed some of the pronunciations, but Frank was very wise and he said, 'You know, let's not really change too much of it because in Holland they will get the joke. If it's sung in German they are gonna understand it, and they get to authoriate, you know, that feeling of—'

FLO Us making fun of Germans!

EDDIE Yeah, under the gun, the German oppressiveness, they'll get it. They'll understand why we're singing it in German. And they did, you know. He was absolutely right, very perceptive in that respect.

FLO But we actually went to classes with a German teacher to learn the German, and we learned it phonetically and it stays with you, because you're learning it much like an actor is learning a role in a movie. We didn't know so much about the characters and what was going on as we knew we had to learn these words. So the words became something that we learned phonetically, and then we had to sing them in English as well, which was of course much easier. And then we could put the two together of what we were singing in German, because we were basically going to do it again in English three minutes down the line. That was an easy bit to do. But I do remember singing the bit in Dutch when we came there, but it was basically—I think you're right, we only learned one line.

CO The line was, 'Gimme some floor covering under this flat floating sofa.'

FLO Right, which was basically something we had learned when we doing the '*Ich bin der Himmel, ich bin das Wasser,*' and we did '*Ich bin der Dreck unter deinem Waltzen.*' And we had learned—I mean, I haven't sung that in eighteen years and I can still sit here and sing the 'flat floating sofa' song, because I had to learn those parts and sing them night after night after night. And there is another section that is left out of the book, I think Frank felt that his anti-Christianity stance that he kind of took in that, about God and the sofa with the little girl, and everything might have played a little role into the negative things that happened in Montreux and what happened at the Rainbow Theatre—and I don't think that Frank would ever admit to this—but I think he kind of felt his blasting out at religion during this 'flat floating sofa' era that we were going into with that might have had a very negative backlash, and was the cause of a lot of what happened in his history. And I know he stopped performing that piece after the accident and didn't even get back into it for many, many years after he was able to—kind of in his mind—accept the fact that that wasn't a part of it but—Frank's a Roman Catholic, and here is Frank taking potshots at God, and the ethics of it all and I think that he—

EDDIE But even by us, it perceives so heavily. It was never meant to be that heavy. It was always meant to be funny. Damn it, doesn't anybody laugh anymore? Don't they understand it was just a joke? Even Frank has to sometimes step back from his own creations and realize this is all a joke, and even he takes things way too seriously sometimes.

FLO Do you wanna write out the promos, or are they easy enough?

CO They're easy enough.

FLO Hi, this is Mark Volman, and I am Flo!

EDDIE And I'm Howard Kaylan, and that means that I—I—I—must be Eddie!

FLO And we want to wish Frank Zappa a very, very happy fiftieth birthday. Let's buy him a watch!

EDDIE Really, he's too old. December 21st, happy birthday, Frank! And we can all celebrate his birthday together.

FLO Eight o'clock. So tune in. And hear us talk about Frank, and Frank talk about Frank. December 21st, we'll see you then!

CO Again.

FLO Hi, this is Flo!

EDDIE And this must be Eddie!

FLO And together we're Flo & Eddie.

EDDIE Hey, pretty smart, huh?

FLO Hey, December 21st, on the show *Supplement* on NOS, you can join us.
EDDIE That's right, we're celebrating Frank Zappa's fiftieth birthday. Happy birthday, Frank! A special birthday party for you on NOS, eight o'clock, December 21st. Flo & Eddie will be there!
FLO Hey, fifty years old! Don't trust anybody over fifty, OK?
EDDIE No way!
FLO Let's buy him a watch.

[Tape ends]

Back home in Holland, I started work on editing the birthday special. I also made copies of all the interview tapes: Frank had asked me to send them to friends in Estonia and Lithuania, and of course I'd promised I would. Frank gave me a lot of stuff, including recordings of new music and an original version of 'Outrage At Valdez' that was almost twenty minutes long. He'd also shared a video production of his trip to Prague.

As I was busy assembling the material, I had the idea of producing a special cassette release containing fragments of music and the interviews that I'd recorded in October. It would be a small run, an exclusive deal, with a photo on the front from the sessions for *The Real Frank Zappa Book.*

I drew up a proposal and faxed it to Gail, and then kept my fingers crossed. On November 21st, precisely a month before our broadcast was scheduled, I received a fax at 9:33pm. There, in Frank's handwriting, it said:

> *Dear Co, your suggestions for the cassette are all okay. You have my permission to proceed. Frank Zappa.*

The *Supplement* tape was ready. And then December 21st was upon us. We had run several radio commercials and held a press conference to promote the broadcast, and now we were ready to go. Editor Piet Hein van de Poel and director/department head Carole Muizelaar turned it over to Vincent and me. The highlight of the show was when I called Frank to congratulate him live on air.

FRANK Hello?

CO Frank?

FRANK Hi, Co!

CO Hi, happy birthday!

FRANK Thanks a lot.

CO How are you doing today?

FRANK Well, I was sleeping.

CO So we woke you up on your birthday?

FRANK That's right!

CO Well, have you had your cake yet, or is that later?

FRANK Oh, that'll be later.

CO Well, on behalf of all your fans here in Holland we wanna wish you a very happy fiftieth. Flo & Eddie told us not to trust anybody over fifty, but does that go for you also?

FRANK Well, actually I was asked the same question yesterday on a French radio broadcast, they said it was once said in America you shouldn't trust anybody over thirty, and I said I think today it should be, 'Can you trust anybody *under* thirty?'

CO [laughs] Well, maybe the MTV influence goes that far that you can't.

FRANK It's possible!

CO What do we hear? Are they naming a school after you?

FRANK Well, somebody suggested it and I told them no, that unless I could control the curriculum that I didn't wanna have my name on it.

CO So maybe one day you will be a headmaster?

FRANK Oh, sure . . .!

CO Listen, we are almost at the end of our marathon here, we've been listening to our interview and to the music for almost four hours at a stretch, and I'm sure that everybody is waiting for you—because it's almost midnight here—for you to have some sort of closing message for our little radio show. Do you have one for us?

FRANK Yeah, I want everybody to think about what's going on in the Persian Gulf, especially this announcement by the US government that they are renting a ship from the Princess cruise line—they're gonna rent this boat for thirty-one million dollars and they're going to anchor this boat in Bahrein. And instead of sending the troops back to the United States on rotation, they're gonna send them to the Love Boat. And it's such an absurd idea because, when the troops go there, they have to buy their own booze, buy their own alcohol, except if you're in the navy you don't have to. So I can imagine fights breaking out on the boat between all people from the other services that have to pay for beer and the navy guys who don't. And meanwhile everybody is gonna be saying, 'Where are the whores?' And if the government doesn't do something to provide women on this boat, this is not exactly going to be the best vacation that a soldier can have. So, if they *do* get smart and decide to put prostitutes on the boat, the question then comes up: who is going to be Pimp Master General for the United States Forces there?

CO Do you have a suggestion, Frank?

FRANK Ah, well—Quayle is never doing anything constructive, maybe we should give the job to him?

CO And then on your next album, *Hot Rats Number 4*, will be 'Quayly The Pimp'?

FRANK [laughs] Could be!

CO Hey, listen, say hello to Rutger Hauer from us.

FRANK I will.

CO And have a very nice birthday. Your birthday will be over in a couple of minutes here, Frank, but we will try to put as much of your music on the radio as we can, and we hope to speak to you very soon.

FRANK All right, thanks a lot, Co.

CO OK, take good care now, you hear?

FRANK Yeah.

CO Bye-bye.

FRANK Bye-bye.

Four hours of Zappa, four hours of *Supplement* live: what a trip!

1991

Hello teenage Amerika

THE SUPPLEMENT TAPE WAS RECEIVED WELL. On January 22nd, I received a fax from Gerry Fialka, who ran the day-to-day operations at Barfko-Swill. He informed me that Gail wanted to make an official release of the cassette. Unfortunately, nothing ever came of it.

One evening that spring, my telephone rang, and I heard a lady's voice on the line.

'Hi Co, how are you doing?'

I recognized the voice but couldn't quite place it. The accent, the timbre, the pace of her speech—I recognized everything, even though I was certain that I didn't know here. Well, not really, at least—how often had I heard 'The Voice Of Cheese' in the hundreds of times that I'd listened to *Uncle Meat* (not to mention *We're Only In It For The Money*)? It was Suzy Creamcheese! Pamela Zarubica—the woman who'd lived with Zappa at the very start of it all. She'd accompanied him on his first European tour, and her name was listed first on the *Freak Out* cover.

So, this was Pamela Zarubica herself. I return to her later in this book. She'd received my telephone number from Spencer Streeter, my friend in Hemel Hempstead. Spencer ran G&S, a company that specialized in legal Zappa merchandise. She knew Frank was sick, and was trying to get in touch with him to express her sympathy and offer her support. Like so many others, she'd been unable to reach him. But she knew I had a direct line, so she asked if I'd let him know that he was in her thoughts. She'd been living in London for years by then, and had become a natural healer. I promised I'd pass on her message, and we exchanged addresses.

Besides the four-hour *Supplement* show, I was busy with another version of only an hour, which I called *Frank Zappa 50!* It eventually was selected as the Dutch submission to the prestigious Prix Italia festival, accompanied by a full-color booklet, and was aired by the Australian Broadcasting Company. After

Prix Italia, NOS submitted it to the New York Festivals 1992, where we were among the finalists—officially endorsed by Gerald M. Goldberg. To this day, I wonder whether that was one of those awards that was simply *for sale*. At any rate, we were now getting some recognition for our work.

I was still running Siësta Productions with Menno Kalmann. Thanks to Frank's personal involvement, we were presented with an opportunity to import a special project. As described earlier, Zappa always hated bootleggers, so he had come up with the plan to release the recordings himself, with better quality and better packaging. He introduced us to the people at Rhino Records (having apparently buried the hatchet with them), who were running the *Beat The Boots* series. On June 17th, we signed a deal with Rhino's Peter Pasternak. Although we didn't exactly sell millions, it was another step forward in the 'partnership' direction.

1992

The yellow shark

1992 ROLLED AROUND, AND ON FEBRUARY 14TH, THE RADIO SHOW SUPPLEMENT WAS READY WITH ANOTHER UNIQUE ZAPPA BROADCAST. We were allowed to share some more selections from the unreleased original *Outrage At Valdez* in a program called *Muziek en Milieu*. Music journalist Corné Evers put together an article for *OOR* entitled 'Zappa en de Wallevis,' in which he wrote, 'It's never been released before, and it doesn't look like it's going to happen anytime soon. Get your recorders ready!'

The Ensemble Modern had made Frank an offer to put together a program of arrangements of old and new work for their ensemble. The orchestrations were written by Turkish/German composer Ali N. Askin. That project is covered in detail elsewhere, and I mention it here only to include a small story. In the summer of 1992, I was on the phone with Frank, and he presented me with a choice—NOS had been selected to be the first to broadcast one of the *Yellow Shark* concerts on the radio, and Frank offered me either the first concert (in Frankfurt), or the final one (in Vienna).

When we were recording the birthday special, we'd already discussed that I'd be allowed to broadcast a full concert, albeit only a rough radio mix, for *Supplement*. So now I had a choice: the premiere or the finale? I went for the premiere, but only because it was scheduled for a Thursday, and my show was on the following day. Hot off the press!

Elise accompanied me to Frankfurt, and we spent a day watching the rehearsals. I was introduced to Mark Holdom, Frank's personal assistant, who was friendly and very helpful. I spoke with Frank briefly as well, but he was looking terrible: his face was bloated from the drugs he'd been prescribed, and he was moving like an old man. His music was clearly helping him hold it together. I spent a few moments chatting with his bodyguard Dave, who I'd met on the '88 tour. He told me that there was a big stink about smoking in Der Alte Oper—the same issue that plagued every Zappa appearance, wherever he performed. Someone had done some research, and discovered that smoking was permitted inside on one condition: if it was part of a scene *taking place onstage*. So, Frank wrote into the score that the composer had to sit on the edge of the stage on a sofa, keeping an eye on his performance, and smoke—his very own 'Sofa #3'! The artwork for the Yellow Shark features a photo. This was of course only for the rehearsals.

Egbert van Hees, the Dutch director, was in charge of the video recording. The audio was recorded in The Voyager, a top-of-the-line mobile recording truck from Paris. Frank's guy Spence Chrislu was at the board, and as soon as the concert was over he handed me a DAT tape of the radio mix. It wasn't as balanced as the album turned out, but it certainly sounded powerful—and complete! The following day, I jumped on the train, headed into the studio, and that evening we broadcasted the world radio premiere of the *Yellow Shark*—thanks to Frank. Frank wasn't at the second concert, but he was back for the third night in Frankfurt. Immediately after that, his sickness forced him to fly back to L.A., and he missed the performances in Berlin and Vienna. I'd been fortunate enough to broadcast the second-last stage appearance by Frank Zappa.

His condition was rapidly getting worse, and by now it was public knowledge that he was sick. Frank and Gail asked me to look into a possible option in the Netherlands. They'd heard of a clinic in Bilthoven that was booking progress with 'alternative' methods of cancer treatment, though I was to not allowed use the name 'Zappa' until I was sure it was worth doing. My contact at the clinic was a Dr. Hauer—what's in a name?

1993

Cup of cawfee

IN MAY I GOT A CALL FROM GAIL. She wanted some details on the VPRO TV footage from 1970, the documentaries made by Roelof Kiers. I told her that it would help if I had a letter saying I was acting on her behalf. One of the reasons that she needed the information was that one of the singers in the original cast was causing trouble: she claimed that by making her sing the word 'tinselcock,' Frank had negatively impacted her subsequent career. Thanking me for my 'faxulous assistance,' Gail wrote,

> *To Whom It May Concern,*
>
> *This is to authorize Co de Kloet to represent us in obtaining any information regarding the footage shot by VPRO of and authorized by Frank Zappa in connection with his project 200 Motels. This includes all footage used in whole or in part by VPRO to produce the two documentaries and all the outtakes supplied by VPRO to Frank Zappa for his use.*
>
> *We appreciate your co-operation.*
>
> *Respectfully,*
> *Gail Zappa*
> *12 May 1993*

Doing this research took me back to 1974, and watching film rolls at the VPRO villas.

In the summer of '93, out of the blue I received some money back from the tax authorities. I knew right away what I was going to spend it on: a ticket to L.A. I got in touch with Susan Rubio to ask if I could stay with her, to save money on my lodgings. It was discomforting to think that I'd be saying goodbye to my friend and my hero. Although I was aware, from firsthand knowledge, just how bad he was feeling, I knew also that he was still receiving guests, and so I arranged a visit. A friend of mine worked as groundcrew for Dutch airline KLM, and helped me to get a cheap ticket. As it turned out, I even got a business class seat! I sat down, took a sip of my champagne, and off we went.

I was sitting next to an older gentleman who reminded me a little of Jock Ewing from *Dallas*: a nice tan, with white hair and a whiff of aristocracy. As is often the case during long flights, after an hour or so we fell into conversation. He told me that he lived in California and that he'd been involved in real estate. He was retired now, and living a life of leisure. I asked him if he'd been in Amsterdam, but he was in fact on a connecting flight after two weeks in Bosnia. He was a member of some society, and had been visiting what was formerly Yugoslavia as its representative, to knight the president. This ambassadorship worked by a random system, and it happened to have been his turn. As if this story wasn't already interesting enough, he had more. He explained that he was corresponding with a writer to tell the story of his experiences during World War II. He'd been asked personally by President Roosevelt to lead an unusual operation. In northern France, the Americans were dealing with a high-ranking Russian intelligence officer who provided them with all manner of sensitive information. The Russian loved Coca-Cola, but of course he couldn't be seen drinking such an imperialist beverage in public. My new airplane buddy was contracted to build a small factory to produce crystal-clear Coca-Cola. This would then be shipped in plain bottles, with only a red star on the cap to identify it. The operation was codenamed 'White Coke for Red Russians.' He was working with the writer to prepare the story for a book and TV deal. To this day, I have no idea whether anything ever came of it.

I sat there listening to this fascinating story, and I realized that I hadn't had an opportunity to introduce myself. I told him who I was, and that I came from a small town outside Amsterdam. 'Pleased to meet you,' he replied, 'I'm Mladin Zarubica.'

I said that I hadn't come across that last name much, but that I actually knew a Pamela Zarubica. He was stunned. 'What? You know Pam?' As it turned out, he was her uncle, but they'd lost sight of each other years ago. I told him she was living in London and that she'd become a natural healer. He couldn't believe it, and asked me if I'd give him Pamela's address. I'm always careful about that kind of thing—you never know how the relationship was before the last contact—but I agreed to pass on a message, and I handed him my card. A few years later, I learned that they had indeed connected again, and Pamela was glad—especially because Mladin died not long after.

According to Mladin, he'd last seen her somewhere in the '70s, and the time before that had been in the '60s, when she was 'living with some musician.' He couldn't quite recall the name of the strange-looking man. 'Zeppo, Zappo, or something.' I told him I was on my way to Zappa, and that I'd been having these kinds of encounters with people all my life.

I arrived in L.A. and checked in at the Hyatt on Sunset—the same hotel where I'd stayed before with Menno, nicknamed the Riot on Sunset. I called Gail to let her know I was there, and she replied that she was glad and that I should come by the house the following day, around four in the afternoon. This suited me perfectly, since I only had three days before I flew home. The next afternoon I took a taxi to the house, where I was offered coffee and a grapefruit juice in the famous kitchen. 'Come on,' said Gail, and led me downstairs. We took the spiral staircase, outside, down to the basement, where Frank was sitting in a large, plush red chair—a birthday gift, it had been. The sight of him shocked me: when I'd last seen Frank a year before, he'd been a bloated man full of cancer medication. Now, he was skinny and sickly, with a full beard—but his eyes had lost nothing of their piercing gaze. He noticed my discomfort, and told me to sit down and relax. 'OK, Frank.'

I could hear drum tracks in the background, coming from the studio. He explained that they were busy remixing. It surprised me that now, with his life in its final phase, he'd have any interest at all in working, let alone the energy. 'The former more than the latter,' he said. I told him that Pamela Zarubica had been in touch with me, and that she still spoke fondly of their time together. I also told him that I'd sat next to her uncle in the airplane on the way out, and Frank exclaimed, 'You met Mladin? Wow! Thanks for telling me about Pam—but don't tell Gail!' My immediate thought was, 'Mladin couldn't recall the name, but Frank knew everything from thirty years ago. So typical!'

We chatted a while about Frankfurt, and Gail and Dweezil wandered in. Frank had received a gift from some German media friends—a big box of Cuban cigars. Frank just looked at the box as if to say, 'No way am I gonna be able to finish these!' As always, Frank asked about the situation in Holland, my own music, and my plans for the future. I told him that I had a memory of him during the *Supplement* time, showing me the original score to *200 Motels*—something of a holy relic for me. I asked about the possibility of getting the Ensemble Modern and the Metropole Orkest together, hand-picking soloists and getting a massive new and proper recording of the entire work. I knew it was audacious to even suggest, given how the Holland Festival business had gone down ten years before. Actually, I was surprised that Frank still inspired me so: driving me to the suggestion in the first place, when I knew very well that it wouldn't be possible *with him*—but that was something to selectively forget when sitting opposite the man.

What happened next I still can't fathom. I've told this tale to several people, and each time I barely manage to hold back my tears. Frank asked, 'What are you doing in L.A.?' I told him that I was there to see him and speak to him—to say goodbye. He'd noticed the absence of recording equipment this visit, and said, 'Yeah, I get it, but *why* are you here? What's your business here?'

He sounded a little agitated, as if I didn't understand the question. I replied, 'I've got a lunch with Susan, and then I'm going home.'

'So you've got nothing else to do in L.A. except sit here with me?' he pressed me.

'Yeah, Frank.'

He was silent, looked me straight in the eye, smiled suddenly, and said something that's left an indelible impression on me.

'Wait a minute! I get it—you've come for that cup of coffee, huh?'

I was speechless. The cup of coffee from the note with his address on it—from 1979!

I gave him a hug, felt how fragile he was, and whispered, 'Thank you.' As I left, I added, 'See you next time!'

That night, I stayed in Susan's house and watched some American TV by myself. My head was spinning, filled with thoughts of all the years with Frank, and realizing that I'd just looked him into his eyes for the last time.

I spent the following day hanging out with Susan and her friend Helen Sanders. We visited Dottie, who was one of Frank's employees—not just that, she explained how she was in fact taking care of him, rubbing his feet when his circulation was poor. I thought Dottie was lovely.

The next day, Susan took me to the Santa Monica offices of another legend she was working for: Johnny Carson. The great man himself wasn't in, but the offices (owned by Arnold Schwarzenegger) were decorated with all things Carson. One of the artifacts on display was a tall stovepipe hat, like the one President Lincoln used to wear. The reasoning behind the display was this: Johnny had never made a joke about Lincoln that went down well. I naturally asked Susan to take a picture of me with the hat—a once-in-a-lifetime opportunity.

The day before I left, Susan gave me a special gift, one that needs of a bit of backstory. During the time that Susan worked for Frank, she had her own little office in the house on Woodrow Wilson Drive, right near the nerve center of the house: the magical kitchen. Because of some political goings-on, Frank had been receiving threats, and his bodyguard, John Smothers, had moved in with the family until things quietened down. Frank and 'Dong,' as John was affectionately called, delighted in teasing Susan, especially with humor that was mildly, shall we say, 'sexual.' One morning Susan, dressed in a skirt, came into the office holding a handful of mail. As she was going through the mail, she sat down in her chair, and felt something strange. She jumped up and looked at the chair, where she saw a gas mask—something that for years has played a part in Zappa lore. Frank still had a few from his childhood, as described in *The Real Frank Zappa Book*. Hearing chuckling outside, Susan turned to see Frank with the huge bald figure of Smothers towering over him, howling with laughter like they'd pulled off the prank of the century. Grown men—a professional bodyguard and one of the greatest artists of the 20th century, a gas mask, and a girl. Well, what can you say?

Frank had given Susan the mask as a gift. Ever the sweetheart, she told me it was just collecting dust in her closet, and suggested I should add it to my collection.

The story has a coda to it. Before I could board the plane for my journey back home, I had to go through security at LAX. I'd checked my larger suitcase, and my carryon was a simple gym bag containing, among other things, the mask. Arriving at the X-ray machine, I was told by a customs officer to place my bag on the belt. I complied, and waited as he sat staring at the screen with an extremely bored look on his face. Then his eyes went wide as he saw my bag go past. Huh? A gas mask? He asked a colleague, a tall, friendly, Black gentleman who looked to be in his mid-thirties, to escort me to a private screening area, where I was told that I was 'naive.' I was nuts, it was explained to me, to think I'd get through security with the mask—even though it was old, it was still property of the United States Military! Realizing that I might soon have bigger problems, I hastened to tell him that I would leave it behind if necessary. He asked me how I'd acquired it, and I explained that a friend had gifted it to me because it had belonged to our mutual friend Frank Zappa.

'You know Frank Zappa?' he asked.

'Yes,' I replied, and told the customs officer about our relationship and that I was a Dutch radio producer. As it turned out, the customs officer was a big Zappa fan also. After a quick look around, he slapped me on the shoulder and said, 'Have a safe trip, my friend.'

Passing Dutch border controls didn't present any problems, and now a piece of Zappa Youth History hangs proudly on the wall of the Zivasound studio.

A few weeks after I returned home, a colleague at NOS asked if I had any ideas for rounding off a radio series about American and European composers. The series had run for five years, and I thought back to that moment when I'd held the original score for *200 Motels*. I sent a message to Frank, via Frank's assistant Mark Holdom and Gail, suggesting a production for the fall of 1996.

I'd bring together the Radio Philharmonisch Orkest (with Peter Eötvös at the helm), a rock band (with Mike Keneally at the helm), Mark Volman and Howard Kaylan (as soloists), and Spence Chrislu (as the engineer). We'd record *200 Motels* for Dutch radio and television, with the option of broadcasting it elsewhere in Europe. The production could also serve as a blueprint for further US shows. My proposal ended with, 'Production and publicity will meet the standard you are used to as far as NOS Radio is concerned. CdK/November 22, 1993.'

On November 26th, I received a fax from Mark Holdom, about *200 Motels*. Frank, in his last days, had apparently taken the time to reply to me.

> *November 26, 1993*
>
> *Dear Co,*
>
> *Thank you for your fax. FZ is thrilled with your idea, however, he already has plans to perform 200 Motels with the Ensemble Modern. Please hold your plans until these ideas are finalized.*

December 4th, 1993. My telephone rang. Frank had passed away. A *Supplement* broadcast was scheduled for December 6th, and we promptly upended it to play four hours of Frank's music. I spent the entire day in the editing room, visited by journalists and camera crews. I joined Golden Earring singer Barry Hay on current events program *NOS LAAT*, where I talked about my memories of Frank and his music. Barry spoke mostly of Connie from Little Rock—and quite right, too.

I needed to do something, but I wasn't sure what. I talked to Menno, knowing that the vultures would be circling shortly, and we decided to remove the *Supplement* tape from the market—we were partners, after all!

2000

Holland Festival

DURING MY YEARS AT NOS, I HAD A NUMBER OF PROPOSALS FLOATING AROUND. I wanted to do something with Brian Eno and an orchestra, and I was lobbying for a large-scale Zappa project. Dutch public broadcaster NPS has a direct line of communication with the Holland Festival, and my Zappa idea was taken up by Jacques van Veen and Ivo van Hove. This was wonderful news, of course: not only did the Holland Festival carry a lot of clout in the Dutch music scene, but there was also the curious historical aspect—the 1981 debacle. I was excited to finally have a *big* Zappa project in the Netherlands, and I was involved in two ways: helping to stage *200 Motels* with the original score (and a monster instrumentation), and an evening with the Metropole Orkest—conducted by Dick Bakker, and featuring Bruce Fowler as special guest.

Rob Heukels, Head of Radio at NPS, turned over the artistic portion of the projects to me, and we put together a team to handle the business side, with Rob in charge. Both concerts became legendary—fans lucky enough to be in the audience those nights still talk about them. The business side, however, seemed to carry a curse.

When the Holland Festival partnered up with the Zappa organization, Rob and I (dealing with the media side) stayed in close contact with Ivo van Hove and Jacques van Veen. Van Veen is a lovely person, and very good at what he does, and right away he saw how the scope of the project should be—large! Van Hove is a brilliant director, a visionary, and an inspiration to numerous artists. He did display one weakness, though: he let himself be won over by Gail's charms. Being very well aware of how Gail handled her affairs, I repeatedly warned him that doing business with her would be a real adventure, and that it was essential to keep an open mind—everyone should have their input.

One thing was paramount: a signed contract. At my suggestion, Mark Volman and Howard Kaylan, who were still in outstanding form, were asked to sing their original parts. Returning from a meeting with Flo & Eddie in

L.A., Ivo and Jacques told me to stop worrying about getting a signed contract.

'No problem,' I said. I know my place.

Mark and Howard were excited about the project. They realized that their involvement in the creation of *200 Motels* would lend some weight to the project. Not only that, they loved the idea of singing this material again. They had one condition: if a commercial release were produced of the concerts, they demanded a small royalty. This triggered a new 'phase' in the process. To avoid giving the impression that any of this was personal, I refer to Gail as the 'ZFT' (Zappa Family Trust) below.

The ZFT contacted Holland Festival and announced that Volman and Kaylan's participation was no longer necessary. When the Festival pointed out that the negotiations were already more or less complete, the reply was clear and concise: no Flo & Eddie. Pressing the issue, the ZFT added, would put the entire project in jeopardy. Without a signed contract in place, it wouldn't cost the ZFT a thing to cancel the project. Volman and Kaylan were canceled, and the ZFT had its own ideas about which local vocalists should be brought in to sing in their place. The locals were more than up to the task, of course—but Mark and Howie were missed.

My correspondence with the ZFT (which took place via fax) about the Metropole Orkest project was also taking a turn for the worse. All the faxes contained was business: some seemed to be boilerplate legal jargon, and some were covered in handwritten demands and changes.

By this point, Ivo and Jacques had changed their views somewhat regarding Gail's charms and her keenness to be involved. The project was still going ahead, but the conditions deteriorated—and for some strange reasons. *De Volkskrant*, a major Dutch newspaper, had agreed to sponsor the festival, but on the now famous Holland Festival/Zappa/Dutch soccer team poster the newspaper logo had to be blanked out. The financial cost of putting the event together without signed contracts was also substantially higher than it might have been, but I'll leave those numbers to the accountants.

However, none of this means that the project was a disaster. Artistically, it turned out to be amazing. The Metropole Orkest concert in Paradiso, with Dick Bakker and Bruce Fowler, still stands out in my memory as one of the best concerts I've ever heard. After Dick admitted that he wasn't well-versed in Zappa's music, and wasn't sure how to approach it, we spent two days in my house with the drummer, Arno van Nieuwenhuize, listening to music and talking about what makes Zappa so characteristically Zappa. Dick went away to study the scores, and when Fowler arrived for the first rehearsal he was surprised at how well-prepared the conductor was.

The setlist featured many gems from the whole of Zappa history, including 'The Hymn To Lumpy Gravy,' 'RDNZL,' 'Oh No,' 'Echidna's Arf,' 'Regyptian Strut,' and many more.

200 Motels in Carré was also a magical evening, prominently featuring Claron McFadden and Lieuwe Visser. One of my personal highlights (and to me, one of the most important musical pieces in twentieth-century literature) was the first public performance of the full version of 'I Have Seen The Pleated Gazelle.' I also struck up a friendship with Ali N. Askin, the composer/orchestrator who not only sorted out all the *200 Motels* scores but who'd been Frank's orchestrator and righthand man for the *Yellow Shark* in 1992.

Business differences notwithstanding, the ZFT eventually agreed to let me produce the recordings of both events. After the evenings in Paradiso and Carré, I set about mixing. I worked in the MCO studio in Hilversum for the Metropole Orkest project (with engineer Gert de Bruijn and supervisor Hugh den Ouden), and in Peter Vincent's personal studio for *200 Motels*, for which recording we selected the best takes from each of the nights.

Once the mixes were finished, I traveled to Berlin with Rob Heukels to play the *200 Motels* mix for Ali, and he approved the results.

Just when we were ready to broadcast, the ZFT came with one more demand: all mixes needed to be approved by the ZFT, and if there were any problems, they would need to be fixed in Los Angeles, on our dime. In spite of the fact that this would have been a technical nightmare to pull off, the legal department at NPS warned that we had to handle this with kid gloves, and my suggestion to broadcast everything as quickly as possible was rejected as being irresponsible and more than a little risky. Heukels wasn't sure—he knew me, and he knew that I understood how Zappa had done business.

And then one afternoon, all of a sudden, an army of lawyers and enforcement agents flooded into the NPS lobby, and they took all the recordings and scores into custody and handed them over to an independent third party to hold. Neither the ZFT nor NPS/Holland Festival had access.

No one has ever lifted the collection order, and at the time of writing the mixes are still in custody—so no one has access to them. The concerts have never been broadcast. And we suffered a further financial setback: the production depended on an investment by the *Stimuleringsfonds Culturele Omroepproducties* (a Dutch fund for cultural broadcastings) that was subject to the condition that it would in fact be broadcast, and so we never saw any of that money.

Later, our legal adviser (whose name I won't disclose here, out of respect for his family) said that we should probably have broadcasted the whole thing immediately. At least I wasn't crazy. One thing's for sure, though: the legal documents of the proceedings have all the makings of a best-selling thriller.

2006

Who could imagine?

I SPENT A FEW MUSICALLY SATISFYING YEARS WORKING AS A FREELANCER, BEFORE JOINING NOS ON A PART-TIME BASIS. That broadcaster was later split up, and its cultural division became NPS (subsequently renamed NTR, following a merger). Throughout my time with each of these organizations, I still felt a strong desire to promote Zappa's music, and the higher-ups were kind enough to give me quite a bit of freedom in that area. So, in 2006, I decided to spotlight the fortieth anniversary of *Freak Out*. My plan was to split the four-hour special into shorter blocks that each highlighted one side of the album. My approach was two-pronged: I wanted to use the original mono vinyl versions of the music, and I wanted to broadcast interviews with the people who'd been directly involved in recording it—I'd heard from Herb Cohen that much of the folklore surrounding how the record was made had become blurred over time.

The broadcasts were a big success. I included interviews with Carol Kaye (then a studio bass player extraordinaire, but who'd played 12-string guitars on *Freak Out*), Roy Estrada (the bass player in the original Mothers lineup), and Carl Franzoni (a dancer who is intrinsically linked to Zappa mythology). The interviews were conducted by Chris Opperman, who I'd met through Mike Keneally, and with whom I've built up a great friendship.

I'd found two more firsthand witnesses who'd watched (and heard) the whole process: the original Mothers drummer Jimmy Carl Black, and to my delight Pamela Zarubica, whose name (as mentioned before) was listed first on the *Freak Out* cover art. Both JCB and Pamela had been essential to the Frank's early development. I still had Pamela's number from when we'd talked back in 1991, and she agreed to do an interview—on the condition that I bought her lunch.

I met with Pam in London. The Cheese. Suzy Creamcheese. The weather was lovely, every now and then a train rumbled by in the background, and the cat occasionally came to make his presence known.

CO So just—

PAMELA You know that you're asking me something, like—you know, I might . . . uhm . . . I get a bit on the spot, so you can edit things.

CO Yeah, I'll hold it for a while.

PAMELA You don't need to hold it at all.

CO I want it . . . because I don't want you too remote.

PAMELA Too remote?

CO Not *too* remote.

PAMELA Too remote, you want me there?

CO Close, yeah.

PAMELA How about if I hold it, Your Honor?

CO Yeah—if you don't mind.

PAMELA I don't mind, are you kidding?

CO OK

PAMELA I love the media.

CO OK, then I'll just—

PAMELA Whoa! I don't know, this is getting pretty heavy now.

CO I'll just . . . what—
PAMELA Just kidding. [cat meows] Are you coming to sit on my lap, darling?
CO Hello—
PAMELA Are you coming to meow on my lap?
CO Just do as you like, cat. Meow!
PAMELA Come on darling, come on!
CO Okey dokey!
PAMELA C'mon!
CO I think this sounds pretty nice.
PAMELA OK

[Cat meows]

CO I like that.
PAMELA [laughs] I know, it's fabulous, come here.
CO We need the cats in.
PAMELA Come here, c'mon! Come here! Pss-pss!
CO Pets, they don't do—
PAMELA Did it register?
CO Yeah, yeah, yeah. I got it.
PAMELA OK
CO I think I'm already running.
PAMELA OK, cool!

[Cat meows]

CO I'm running. I'll change cassettes every once in a while, so—
PAMELA OK, whatever.
CO So—
PAMELA Whatever.
CO You know, it will be weird for me to focus it on the subject of my project, which is *Freak Out*.
PAMELA A daunting project!

CO Can you—before I ask you about the general scene that I also discussed with Jimmy Carl Black, can you tell me when—and I know that you're not into dates, but can you remember the vibe and the atmosphere when you first heard about the possibility of there being a *Freak Out*?

PAMELA We're talking about the album?

CO Yeah.

PAMELA The album was in work from when I first met Frank. He—uh, very shortly after I met him. Although I think I was one of their first genuine fans, because back then they were singing 'My Babe' by the Righteous Brothers. But very, very soon into our relationship he met Tom Wilson. And as soon as Tom Wilson came on board things moved very quickly. And I was going to school at the time, trying to finish school at the time and I was cleaning house for various people, Frank amongst them. [laughs] I was a really good cleaner. And he was living in Echo Park, and I don't think his place had seen cleaning actually. And it was really low. He lived in Echo Park, which was a Mexican neighborhood, and every time we'd go up the stairs to his place they'd call him 'Beardo Weirdo.' [cat meows] So it's really, really, really sweet. And so I came, and I cleaned the place. And I remember, uhm, I was there one day, and he was in the other room writing. And he showed me this piece of paper and it was 'Who Are The Brain Police?' And I said, 'That's really interesting,' and he said, 'It just came in the door' or something. And I remember him calling on the phone to a friend of his—that was Don Van Vliet—and we had our first conversation. So things moved very rapidly. I was going to school, I had finals. I was really trying to study amidst the work and everything else, and so he—the studio was booked, and he came to the house and said, you know, would I come to the session? And I was like, 'I don't know, I've gotta go to school, and whatever and whatever ...' But he was very persistent. So—it was over a weekend, I'm sure it was over a weekend, and it was really, really, really hot. And I went to the session, I was on the stairs, and I had pink sunglasses and he was like, 'Oh, those are really nice! Where'd you get those?' And it was just a studio full of people, absolutely full of people. And, you know, pulling back a bit, I remember him saying—there was a woman on bass, and he was saying,

'That's Carol Kaye,' and that she was a really famous hot-shit bass player. And I was so young and naive, it was all so very, very new to me, and so a woman being in the session was really amazing. And everything was just going crazy, just the freaks—the freaks were there. There were freaks all over the place, and it was the first time I ever met Tom Wilson. And it was quite an exciting—[train passes in the distance]—OK, let's cut that, OK?

CO It's OK with the trains.

PAMELA OK, cool. No, I'm not worried about the trains, I just need to cut myself mentally. So, Frank had written—he must have written—he went away to Hawaii, and he came back and he had written the bit about Suzy Creamcheese.

CO Mm-hmm?

PAMELA And then it was in the song. Oh! I'll never forget the first time I heard him play 'Trouble Coming Every Day.'

CO About the Watts Riot.

PAMELA Yeah, absolutely extraordinary! I can't remember if *Freak Out*, that was at—if that came before or after the album, when there was the Gig. And we came to the Gig and it was absolutely—there were just people everywhere, and you could not get into the Gig. And so my friends and I went up the fire escape, which is a big deal for me because I'm really afraid of heights. And we had to get up the fire escape, and we got up there and people are singing 'It Can't Happen Here,' so that must have been—that was post-album. But the power of that song! Absolutely—you know, to this day, the power of that song, extraordinary! So—

CO But you knew the band and Frank before the actual release of the album?

PAMELA Oh yeah!

CO How would you describe the scene that that band was operating in? Was he, like, already the boss?

PAMELA [laughs] Frank is a very dominant personality, and—you know, extraordinary charisma and persona. And I came into the Trip, I was young, I was homeless, and I was wet, and I hadn't had a lot to eat and I was just living on the streets basically. Only for a very, very short time, because Bob

Green, who was the doorman at the Trip, eventually took pity on myself and Julia and said—you know, I've been very fortunate that people have helped me in my life—and he said, 'As long as you stay in school you can come live with me.' And that was at 8404 Kirkwood Drive. So we went there to live with him, and we used to go to the Trip every night and I wore moccasins, which were not good when it was wet on the street, let me tell you! And so I'm sitting in the club and they come on, and they're singing 'Brown Shoes Don't Make It.' And I remember, like it was yesterday, sitting at the table and thinking, well, 'Are my shoes brown?' [laughs]

CO [laughs]

PAMELA And then I thought, 'Nah—fuck it, they're moccasins, it's notthe same thing.' And then they sang the song, as I said, by the Righteous Brothers, 'My Babe,' I think it's 'My Babe.' Don't quote me on that. And some other songs, and I thought, 'Fucking hell, these guys are good! What a raggle-taggle bunch of weirdos . . . if ever there were weirdos it's these guys. You know? They're hairy and they're older and they're—but very, very strong personas, each and every one of the guys—I think at the time Henry Vestine was on bass.

CO Guitar.

PAMELA Wasn't he the bass player?

CO Roy.

PAMELA OK, Henry was in the band at the time.

CO He played the guitar later, and then left—

PAMELA Yeah, yeah, yeah, OK. So, afterward, nobody was paying attention to them, they were just another bar band. Unknown. And afterwards I went up to them—we went up to them, and I said, 'I think you're really amazing!' And Frank said, 'Come downstairs.' And I think he was genuinely surprised that someone really thought their music was extraordinary. And we were friends ever since that time. And I do feel that our relationship was a driving force, it was something he required at the time. Because very shortly after they said 'fuck' onstage, and then they weren't allowed to play at The Whiskey or some shit like that. And so it was very hard for him, because Frank was—while there was a freak scene, Frank was all very ostracized, he was not flavor of the month and so I would say he's on the periphery. And the guys were very much behind him and with him, so I saw them very much as a unit, even though even then he had problems, he was always having problems. And I think Henry left, and Jim Guercio was in the band for a little while and, you know—It was always, always, always problems, because I remember meeting Elliot Ingber, who we lovingly called 'He Who No One Understands'—who was born on the same day as me by the way. And I remember we were driving in the car and we picked up Elliot. And Elliot had been—was fresh out of the army and he'd been working on Elvis's films. OK? So he was the new—he was the new one because it wasn't working with Henry and it wasn't working. But you know, the Indian, Jimmy Carl Black—the Indian of the Group and Roy Estrada, you know, who would literally fall asleep while he was playing the bass. Played extraordinary. I've always, always—bass is very, very, very, very important to me. So it was very much the uniqueness and power and the lyric. But I did see Ray, Roy, and Jimmy, and Frank as a unit.

CO Mm-hmm?

PAMELA Very much as a unit.

CO And you knew this unit before *Freak Out.*

PAMELA Oh yeah! Yeah, I knew them before.

CO Did something change with the chemistry when—uhm, a contract was actually on the table for an album?

PAMELA Oh absolutely!

CO How?

PAMELA Well, Frank then was able to fill the studio with musicians. And he was able to move closer to what were his personal goals as a composer. And I think that he always saw himself—I know that he turned me on to Varèse and Stockhausen and, you know, he saw himself as a composer, and I think that that was very difficult in the scheme of things.

CO Mm-hmm. Would he talk to you about that paradox?

PAMELA It just—things just evolved. And they evolved very quickly in those days. OK? Like, there was one night at the house when The Doors—before they were famous—came to the house to meet Frank. I was with Jim at the time, and there was some possibility about doing something with Frank. And we thought about—they were thinking about maybe having an impromptu session, or something, and I remember Jim going, 'But I don't play any instruments!' [laughs] So it really was worlds colliding, because I—you know, one of my most memorable nights, I was at the house and Tim Hardin was there, Frank was there in the bathroom with me. I was getting ready to go out, John Barrymore Jr. was there, and Lenny Bruce popped in. So it was very much everything was happening at the same time. The Buffalo Springfield came to town at the same time—practically at the same time—from Canada, and they were like, you know, local yokels and like, 'Gee, do you think we'll make it?' And uh—so Neil Young would be passing through, and it just really was an explosion. And it happened so quickly! And so Frank was propelled into his—on his artistic path very quickly. And I do know that it was always a problem because no one ever wanted to rehearse enough. But I've noticed this with musicians over the years, it seems to be a running theme, which I believe that Frank felt at the time was exclusive to him. And I remember—I don't know, it must be in books somewhere, but maybe it isn't because I think somebody told him he should take acid with somebody who believed in God. Is that—is that a known thing?

CO Tell me?

PAMELA That was—he was really, really upset about that. [laughs] Because he was so terribly anti-drug and had a huge, huge, huge paranoia because of, you know, he'd been busted before he came to Los Angeles. And uh—one of the more beautiful moments, which I've not really shared with anyone, that he was going away on tour somewhere and I was at the house. He had moved in with me by this time, and I was in college, and I just started—I just discovered marijuana. So, he went off and for some reason he had to come back. And me and my friend Julia were in the bedroom smoking dope, and he came back in, and we were like, 'Oh my God!' You know? 'What's gonna happen?' And he came in, you know, those very piercing eyes, and he goes, 'OK you guys, that's it. You're not getting any LSD for dessert.' [laughs] So, but that was a long—you know, it's all kind of—I suppose it's probably because I started smoking dope at the time and, like, he never knew when I was, and the only way he could see if I was stoned or not was if I was eating ice cream. I remember I had been out really, really late one night, and I was really, really stoned, and I came home. And it was in the morning and I was eating ice cream and he's going, 'You—you can't be stoned, it's ten o'clock in the morning!' And I'm going, 'Can't I eat ice cream without you thinking I'm stoned?' [laughs] But we went through very—we went through a long period—I mean, I suppose it seems like a very long period when you're hungry—and all that we had was peanut butter. We had rye bread, we had peanut butter. Sometimes if we were lucky we had cream cheese and a little bit of jam. And that's what we lived on, and we were very lucky to have that. So when the album came, I think a little bit of money came along and he started sending his jeans to the cleaners and stuff like that. But there were many times, you know, between Echo Park and my house, before he was living with me, that we put fifty cents in the car for petrol, and if we were really fortunate we'd have enough money and we would go to Greenblatt's and we would get one of those big white cookies with the chocolate drop in the middle. And we would split the cookie, and that was a really, really good day!

CO Mm-hmm?

PAMELA You know, and those are moments that will be with me forever. So atmospherically, in that time before *Freak Out*, just—you know, in that moment when I suppose, you know, I was naive, so I didn't realize—so a bit of money had come. And I had this cat called Dylan, and he was a really, really amazing cat. And he used to leap right into your arms when you'd walk in the door. He was like a Siamese—he had really long fur. And we'd had this situation where, when Dylan was born, his mom had four other kittens and Dylan left the mother to be with me. And he would come and climb up into my bed and stuff, and the mother was really, really, really angry. And something had happened to one of the kittens, it was on a Friday night, and it was brain damaged. And I made Frank drown the kitten. I tried to get chlorophyll or . . . you know? I tried to get something, but the kitten was really suffering, and I made Frank drown this kitten. It was very,

very intense. So Frank was having these animal experiences which he hadn't really had before. And I remember him saying, 'It fought!' I remember—I remember the look on his face. Because he had a great gentleness about him then, a great, great gentleness. And we all got crabs and they came from him, most definitely. And I gave to all—my friends had them, my friend's mother had them. Everybody had them—we were like, 'Why are we all itching, what is this?' Because he was very sexually active, and I wasn't at the time. And then we found these little crabs crawling around, and I remember him taking the crab to put it outside. He was very gentle.

CO [laughs] Like a Tibetan monk.

PAMELA Something like that. And uh, so we're sitting at the table and we have our, sorta, feet on the table, and it's a really lovely afternoon and this candle burning on the table, and Dylan walks across the table and Frank's talking on the phone, and his fur starts to singe. And Frank goes, 'Hold on a minute.' And he picks up the cat and goes—and he blows out the fur. And then he puts him back down and goes, 'Sorry about that, I had to put the cat out.' [laughs] But what I remember most of *Freak Out* and the actual sessions was the heat. It was so hot! It was so intense, and after the first big night when all the people were there, and then they decided that they wanted to have the voice of Suzy Creamcheese. So, Frank said to me, 'Go out there,' and, you know—microphone, 'and pretend like you're having an orgasm.' And I was like, 'I don't know how to do that!' [laughs] Because I was so young and innocent. So they got Jeanie of the Cherry Sisters, and she went out there and she did it very nicely, thank you. So, definitely not my voice on that one. OK.

CO And would you, uh—the sessions for such an historic album, of course people in hindsight look at it as a whole period. But actually, the recording sessions themselves were quite short, especially if we look at how albums are being made today.

PAMELA Well, when they saw how many people they had in the fucking studio, they were damn sure they were gonna not—you know, they were gonna let him have the people in the studio, but not for long. I think it was only over a matter of days.

CO Yeah, three days I believe.

PAMELA Yeah.

CO Did you—did Frank live with you while he was recording the album?

PAMELA Uh, he hadn't moved in with me yet. Because I remember him coming and knocking on the door saying, 'Are you coming to the session?' And me not being too sure, but then him twisting my arm and talking me into it, yeah. He was not living with me yet, but soon after.

CO Do you think he needed some feedback while he was doing the sessions? Just a glimpse or—?

PAMELA Well, we had plenty of feedback, there was plenty of feedback. He and I used to get into it quite a bit, because there were songs that he had written on there about myself. And 'How Could I Be Such A Fool,' which, even then, I was so young and I felt was a really, really beautiful song that someone like Frank Sinatra could have done, and then he put a lot of stuff on the end of it. So I really think often, and when I think back about it, I think I wanted to produce it. But little girls didn't do those things in those days. Because I definitely had—although definitely things I would have changed. OK? 'Cause I think that Frank could do with some editing from time to time. I think he fell into a world where he could be idolized far too much, and go on and on far too much. And that he would have done well with a little bit of genuine criticism at the time, and he got a hell of a lot from me. OK, whilst I was blown away by the songs and the material, I would have had a cleaner approach, definitely. But, you know, it was a thrilling time, and you know, it was very exciting and getting the album cover and seeing the album cover for the first time, which people often comment on the album cover and it actually was a complete mistake.

CO What was the mistake?

PAMELA I think their hair was supposed to be purple. And it was really devastating when we saw it and saw what a mistake it was. It was something like that, out of the hair and the eyes or something was supposed to be purple, but it was not supposed to be what it was. And it's interesting, because I don't think I've seen anyone ever mention it, but I remember being in the room with them. I think we were all there, like Roy, and

Jimmy, and Frank, and whatever and uh, the guy who did it. And it was like, ugh! But you know, there was no question that it was going to be done again. So we're like, 'Oh, whatever!' [laughs] What's a little album cover among friends?

CO You are very noticeable on the cover, there is the famous long list of people who have influenced the Mothers' music, and you're the very first to be mentioned.

PAMELA Yes, that was a great, great, great honor and a complete surprise, and I remember being in the house on Kirkwood and him bringing it, and opening it up and looking at it for the first time. I was deeply moved and, of course, I deserved to be. [laughs] So he got that part right, we didn't have to argue about that. And uh, you know, he used to say he could work when I was in the house and he was very surprised that I was able to—even though I was a woman, you know—that I was able to be a presence where he was able to create when he was around me. So that was, kind of, our understanding and something I carried on over the years with various artists I have known.

CO Was it weird—did you have any recollection of—that you considered it to be a weird situation? You describe yourself as young, innocent, a new world. You came into a really—because there was a lot of music going on—that you came into this niche of people that were, let's say, strongly connected to the likes of Lenny Bruce, than to any other teeny-bopper band.

PAMELA Yeah, yeah! Actually, it was myself that put Frank together with Lenny Bruce. I, uh, used to clean house for Lenny. And he was the loveliest—actually, the way that I met Lenny, I was sort of a teenage runaway and my father had a lot of influence. He was always harassing myself and Frank and everyone else. And someone introduced me to Lenny because he knew about the law! And I remember going to his house late at night, they said, 'This is Lenny.' I had no idea who he was, and him telling me 'if' was the biggest word in the English language. And so I needed to earn a living, and I didn't wanna, like, do whatever, so I cleaned house for him. And he was the loveliest, gentlest man. And I remember one day I was cleaning—actually the floor where he died eventually—and he came in, and he said, 'Oh, uh, don't worry, I'm not watching you. I just brought you this.' And he gave me an apple. We would eat brown rice in those days so an apple was a lot. And I remember his daughter was there and she was outside, and she said, 'Oh look, Daddy, look!' And up in the sky there was a bird, a big hawk or something, and her going, 'I love you, Daddy.' And so I was very attached to Lenny. He was like a father figure to me, and Frank came along through me. And I was never overwhelmed by any of it, because mostly I didn't know who they were. You know? I had a—quite a strong relationship with Philip Spector and I had no idea who he was when I met him, I just really, really liked him. And so it wasn't threatening in any way because it just was a natural evolution. Give me something more . . . where were we?

CO About you being young, innocent.

PAMELA Oh yeah, young and innocent. I was as young and innocent as they come. Let me think, let me think. Uh, when you said to me was it threatening, was it—?

CO How would you describe your relationship with Frank while he was making *Freak Out*? Because he was then obviously making the first huge step, a big leap in his career. He probably knew that was going to be the case. How would you describe it in a broadcastable manner?

PAMELA OK, I think that I would say that he didn't know it was going to be the case. I think that making *Freak Out* was an opportunity, and that when we were in the street that day and there were people lined up in the street, it was an enormous, enormous shock. It was merely the next step, and it did take a long, long time for Frank to really attain any kind of, you know—uh, the regard in which he was later held. So it was just the next opportunity. OK? And Frank and I were obviously very close and maintained a platonic relationship throughout our lives, because that's the way I chose it to be. But regarding the innocence . . . [laughs] I'm glad you asked me that, because I was in college at the time and I was in Pepperdine University, and it was a religious college. There was no mixed bathing, and oh God! They were very judgmental. It's now a surfer college in Malibu that is backed by the Church of Christ, in Christ, you can only imagine. OK? So I'm in college and my oldest friend Vicki, who's on—uh, 'Hi Vicki What's Happening?' [laughs] And her mother, who's a registered nurse and used to drink a lot, and she got phone calls for 'Suzy Cream Cake' for—oh, for years! For absolutely years, until they moved out of the house. They loved it really. And, uh, so Vicki was coming down from college and I said, 'Oh, I'm living in this house and I'm living with Frank and whatever and whatever, and I forgot to tell her anything what they looked like! [laughs] And Vicki came in the door, and Frank and Carl Franzoni were there. [laughs] And Vicki's like, 'I'm really glad you didn't describe them to me first!' Because even though Frank was only about twenty-seven then, which really isn't very old, but he was like—very much like a father figure to me. Even though I was only eighteen, we were much younger, we were much younger then and older than that now. And uh, but she just immediately fell into, you know, a very strong friendship with him, you know, it was just—it's the initial shock of how they looked. Because freaks being what they were, and all this running all over the place, not many people looked like Frank, looked like The Mothers or, you know, or looked like Carl Franzletoni, we used to call him. You know? So it was—it was going on looks. And . . . yeah . . . so I would say though the books, which are the history, might put it differently, I would say Frank and I maintained our relationship throughout our lives.

CO One of the songs, which is one of my favorite songs on the album, is actually very much linked to you by Frank in the liner notes, which is 'You Didn't Try To Call Me.'

PAMELA Right.

CO Does that song stand out in any way for you within the album?

PAMELA Well, I think that's, like, it's a really great song and it was a surprise to me, that was one he—I think I didn't know that before then, it just came on the album and I was, 'Oh, OK, that's what that's about.' Because it was about myself and Phil Spector at the time. But I think, uh, that that's a song that really stands up through time, because it's something that any woman can say to any man practically throughout history. And it's a really wonderful song and a great honor to have inspired it.

CO Because you obviously told him the story?

PAMELA Uh, well, he was around, you know? He was around and he was busy pursuing ladies, and I was busy pursuing Phil Spector. So we shared everything, you know, when you're that close and that poor, and trying that hard. I think I was one of the few people that really, really believed in him at the time.

CO Was your contact with Frank the same as your contact with, for instance, Jimmy in those days?

PAMELA Jimmy is my brother and great, great love, and Jimmy's just a very, very different individual. I just always loved Jimmy, right from moment one, you know? Frank's the great intellect and composer and bandleader, and Jimmy is the great human being, and a great drummer when he hasn't had too many. [laughs] And I give Jimmy enormous credit for—I, you know, it's—I seriously doubt that it's possible, anything's possible, but you know, would Frank have made it as far as he did without those guys behind him? I think the characters and the commitment were an enormous part of why it happened and the way it did.

CO Yeah.

PAMELA Because they could play! They were hot! They were like, you know, they're getting down with 'Trouble Every Day.' It was like a heavy rockin' blues boogie band.

CO But there's something that maybe you can clarify for me then. And I'll tell him that we discussed this, because I can totally understand what you mean, because that small group of the Mothers—as they were and how different they were later—were definitely part, of course, of that musical step that Frank as a composer could take. Jimmy says that also. He says, 'When I talk to later musicians,' he says, 'sometimes I say, Well, just realize that you are here because we were there in those days.' And half an hour later, in the same conversation, he says, 'I was merely the drummer, I didn't have anything to do with it.'

PAMELA No, I think that's, uhm—I think that Jimmy has one of the kindest hearts and absolutely no ego. And I think that that's just his gentleness talking, because they totally, totally, totally gave Frank a platform. You know? You're the lead singer and Frank's an amazing guitar player, make no mistake. But you can't do it on—in those days you couldn't stand up and do it on your own.

CO No.

PAMELA You know, they were a unit, they were a tight unit. And the songs were tight, and they worked, and—you know, and I got up and danced to them. And that was long before, you know, all the other stuff. The other songs, you know, weren't even—hadn't been conceived. He hadn't met me yet. So I think that Jimmy underplays his role, and that history has written a very different version of Frank as a composer and brilliant mind and, you know, the other side of history says he's a jumped-up Stockhausen or Varèse, you know, depending on what camp you're with. That it was a unit, they were there, they came forward together, they were a team—that's was how it was. It may have only been for a brief time, but that was how it was. And that was the platform upon which, you know—when Tom Wilson signed them, he thought he signed this great little blues band. You know? And Tom could—Tom was a guy who liked to boogie. I was very, very close to Tom, was the first woman he met in Southern California, and he's an extraordinary personality, and much, much missed . . . much missed. Very, very gracious, you know, in the uhm, in the Scorsese film about Bob Dylan. Have you seen it? Al Kooper tells the most amazing story about Tom Wilson. And mimics his voice so beautifully, and how Al Cooper eventually got to play the part on, uh—you know, the Bob Dylan track 'You Got A Lot Of Nerve.'

CO And wasn't it weird, because—Wilson being a famous producer, a charismatic person, probably a person with a strong opinion, how did that—? Because if you are my age or if you're even—if you're a young Zappa fan now, you pick up *Freak Out* you see 'Produced by Tom Wilson.'

PAMELA But Wilson was in the club, and Wilson liked to get down, and Wilson liked to boogaloo, and they were a hot-shit tight little blues band!

CO But would you say—?

PAMELA 'Blues' is the wrong word: rhythm and blues, rhythm and blues. Sorry fellas, rhythm and blues.

CO Would you say it's an—it's an appropriate description to say that *Freak Out* was actually produced by Tom Wilson?

PAMELA Tom Wilson was there. [laughs] Tom was definitely there, and I'm sure he had something to do with it. But, you know, it was Frank's baby all the way along. You know? Without question. Tom was—Tom was very laidback in his approach to producing records. You know, I've had many experiences, I've been to sessions with him. And he was always open to letting things happen, and I think that that *is* a good producer. I think the role of producer is not to go in there and, you know, and ride it like a cowboy. But to in there and go, 'Hey, that's working, make that—make sure the desk—make sure that it's switched on in case whatever comes up.' So I'd say that it was very much Frank's baby. Tom was there and definitely, I'm sure, definitely had a hand. But, you know, from my mind it was Ami and—Ami and Tom, the engineers, they were the ones. Definitely. And very, very gracious they were too. But they were the ones.

CO How would you describe their role?

PAMELA Well, you know, they were the engineers . . . they made damn sure it was switched on so it was there to be taken from. And I just—they were there, they were a very large presence without being large in themselves. You know? They were the consummate professionals and really, really holding the fort. And I know that Frank, in those days, gave great homage to Ami and Tom. They were the ones. And Tom Wilson was the one who signed them and made it happen and had a damn good time. And made sure it didn't run over too much.

CO History, kind of, makes you believe that if—the story that Jimmy told me is that Herbie Cohen took Tom Wilson to the Whisky and he heard them play 'Trouble Every Day.' And Jimmy said, had he heard 'Who Are The Brain Police?' as the first song we probably wouldn't have gotten—

PAMELA I absolutely—I totally—[laughs] Knowing Tom as I did, he would have run a mile, you know, at that point in time. Actually, Tom wouldn't have run a mile, but he would have had a damn hard time getting them signed. You know? Even back then it was, you know, this had to sound like that and so forth and so on. And Tom was like, you know, involved with Eric Burdon, and The Velvet Underground, and Simon & Garfunkel and, you know, things of that nature. So no, I don't think 'Who Are The Brain Police?' would have ever—in fact I would have to say that it is, you know, great whatever—the word escapes me. But to Tom, that those things actually managed to get recorded, I think that was the role that—I think he came in here, and saw that this was something completely wild, completely different, and that he managed to get that album made and all credit goes to him for that. I don't think it would have happened with anyone else at the time. And I did know a lot of producers and, you know, people who were working at the time.

CO Did Wilson and Zappa get along?

PAMELA Oh yeah! Yes, and they really cared—I think they, you know? They were very, very different people. But there was a lot of respect. They were both very intelligent, very good sense of humor. Tom and I certainly got along, and so there was a great respect throughout their lives. And I know that it was—the last time I talked to—I spoke to Frank right before Tom died, and I remember he said he had run into him and he looked—he didn't look well but he looked very old. And I think, you know, there was always a great respect there. I don't want to go into that too much, because it's very, uhm—it's very involved territory around family issues and stuff like that. I'll tell you about that later.

CO If you—when the album was done, let me see if this is still working . . . I think so, OK—I'll just put my other—

PAMELA OK, you're gonna use the stuff that's more related to the album.

CO Yeah.

PAMELA OK.

[Tape flip]

CO When Frank was around you while he was recording, of course he has this image of being very much in control and very certain of what he wants to do. Did you see—because even though it was just another opportunity, it was of course the first time he could make a real album—and even more, a double album. Was there any insecurity that you felt by him, or the Mothers as a group, like, 'OK, this is going to be our first album, are we right with this?'

PAMELA I think that part of him was delighted for the opportunity, and I'm absolutely certain that part of him was overwhelmed by the opportunity as well. You know? Frank was young and human. And it was an event, it was an event, OK? I don't think there was any assuredness of how it was gonna come out, what it was gonna be, or anything of that nature. So I don't think it was Frank controlling, you know? Like the later Frank who made *Lumpy Gravy*?

CO Mm-hmm.

PAMELA You know? It wasn't *that* Frank. It was a different Frank.

CO Do you have any recollection of what happened when it was actually released and it would be in a shop where other people could hear it or buy it?

PAMELA My recollection of that is, as I said when—it was the great underground artist's masked ball and something—Guambo. And *that* was a recollection. I don't remember it being in shops or us going to shops or—I remember, as I said, seeing the album cover. I remember holding the album in our hands. I certainly don't remember it being played on the radio or anything like that, my God! And then us going to the Guambo and there just being these crowds and crowds and crowds of people, and us all being like, 'Oh my God!' You know? *That* is my recollection. That's the moment when something has happened. Where you couldn't really call it an underground thing, it was the people on the streets, it was overground.

CO Yeah.

PAMELA But people were aware of it and people were into it, you know? Obviously on a very small level. But big to us. Very big to us.

CO Was it in those days, uh—there's another question that came in. Can you remember when you played it on an actual record player?

PAMELA No! [laughs] Did we have a record player? Let me think, I'm sure we did but I can't remember, and I have a very good memory as well. I remember looking at it, opening it. No, I couldn't honestly say I remember playing it on a record player. Though I'm sure we did, a gazillion times.

CO Do you have any favorites on the album?

PAMELA You know, I discovered the album recently. I got it on CD, and I think that it hangs together so well as an album. It's just unbelievable. I think 'Trouble Coming Every Day,' I think I probably have *many* favorites. 'How Could I Be Such A Fool,' 'You Didn't Try To Call Me'—really, really strong song. OK, I must remember playing it because he played me 'Bow Tie Daddy' for the first time. No, that's later.

CO That's on *We're Only In It For The Money*.

PAMELA No, 'Wowie Zowie'! He played it for me because he played 'Wowie Zowie.' I remember hearing 'Wowie Zowie' for the first time. OK?

CO The cover said he got that from you.

PAMELA Yeah!

CO [laughs]

PAMELA I've always been very, uhm—I'm a very enthusiastic person and like to express myself, so that was where I was then. Yes, it was. But I would say 'Trouble Coming Every Day'—I just think the whole album is fucking amazing. And I heard it, you know, quite a few times on CD, which I thought, 'Wait a minute, something's wrong here, it's not the same thing.' But I think it's an absolutely amazing album, it just hangs together extraordinarily. And 'Help, I'm A Rock' doesn't really rock my boat, OK? There's moments.

CO Also in our program is Carl Franzoni. How would you describe Carl in relationship to Frank during the *Freak Out* sessions?

PAMELA Well, you know, I know Carl and, but not that—you know? We were never close, and Carl was the dancer and the freak who sort of came along as, you know, the icing on the cake as it were. And filled the studio and did a lot of grunting and groaning. But for myself it's always been the Mothers. Exclusively the Mothers.

CO For somebody seeing the Mothers being born, how was it for you to later see totally different ensembles within the Mothers?

PAMELA Well, I remember it was heartbreaking that it had to be The Mothers Of Invention. That was really, really upsetting. Because the

Mothers was quite innocent, and for myself my cutoff point was probably, uhm, around the time of *Hot Rats*. That was probably my cutoff point, and I was never—I'm an early-Mothers fan and I find throughout life that it is very much divided between later and earlier and—except perhaps your own case where—that you have room and time for all of them. But I have found that it's very much divided. And that people that are into Frank are much, much, much into the later stuff, possibly beginning with *Hot Rats*, and that's kind of where I lost interest. Although there's a song called 'In Watermelon Hay'?

CO 'Watermelon In Easter Hay'?

PAMELA Yeah, unbelievable!

CO Yeah!

PAMELA That I play quite often. And I understand that later he—eventually he stopped playing guitar.

CO Well, he played on for a very long time.

PAMELA I must say that I think that Frank was one of the best, *absolutely* one of the best guitar players. An extraordinary guitar player, unique guitar player. You know, I'm not a lead guitar, Clapton kind of girl.

CO [laughs] One of my final questions is—maybe it's not even a question. What I'm doing in this program about *Freak Out*, which of course was one of many of the albums that came out that year, let alone in the whole '60's—one of the things I decided to do beforehand is talk, first of all, to very few people. And the people that I'm talking to—Roy I'm not sure about, but I will know it in a few days, the only people I've talked to are Jimmy Carl Black, you, Carl Franzoni, and the first person ever to write an article on Zappa in Dutch, which is about *Freak Out*. And he is now a child psychiatrist, a very famous professor, and he used to write for a Dutch underground newspaper, and he was there. So I've only talked to eyewitnesses. In the meantime, we have seen a lot of books and programs and films and documentaries—and for somebody who knows what happened, are you sometimes amused or puzzled by the way people will describe, for instance, the whole scene around the Mothers? People who were not there, like me?

PAMELA Well, I can only say for myself personally that I'm much written about, and that I haven't really read anything about myself that bears any bearing on the actuality. OK? So I think you kinda had to be there. And I think that, you know, it's tales told out of school probably. Because it was very innocent. It was a very innocent scene. And very, very much about the music. And I think, you know, that's the great thing that Hendrix has as well . . . you know, Frank met up with him as well? It was that sort of scene where people talk about Jimmy, and they talk about the women and they talk about this and they talk about that. He just was a very, very gentle, just unassuming guy who just really, really loved playing the music. And it really was about the music, and that's what it was about. It was about the music and it was about people and it was about looking at life a little differently. And I think it's very hard to look at that in retrospect for what it was really like. And I think that people write about Frank in a very—they have him up on a pedestal—that at the time it was just some guys from the sticks doing their thing. You know? Don Van Vliet as well, very intelligent and unique people, but guys from the sticks doing their thing, and I don't think I've read that yet.

CO Whatever happened to Suzy Creamcheese?

PAMELA [laughs] I think—I've always felt that there are many, many, many, many Suzy Creamcheeses out there in the world, that she lives in the heart of the world. And that there are many, many, many, of them out there, but there is only one Pamela Zarubica, and back then my nearest and dearest called me 'The Cheese.' [laughs] So she probably abides in a factory near your house, I'm not too sure. But I think—

CO Was it fun to be Suzy Creamcheese?

PAMELA Suzy Creamcheese was a device whereby I was able to communicate with other musicians on a musician's level. And it was a job. More than—more than fun. OK? They put me up there on the stage and it was very, very interesting to see what happens when you are in front of an audience of five thousand people, cheering, calling your name, and how insidious that can be. So it was a very good perspective to have had in my life. Fun . . .? I think fun is—fun wouldn't be quite the appropriate word. It wasn't designed for fun, it was a move, we had political aspirations, that just was the reason why. I was the safe face of the Mothers, they were just too old, too hairy, too weird, too diverse. They needed someone like me so that—literally, visually—by myself being that, they were OK. Not everyone was as open as I was, even in those days.

CO So you were kind of like there to legitimize . . .?

PAMELA I was kind of a little ambassador for the guys, you know? In that way. And it worked.

CO It was a unique move there, by the way. That was unprecedented.

PAMELA I think so, I think—I think Frank writing about Suzy Creamcheese initially, you know, was like when you'd think of spin doctors and stuff like that now? And then—you know, it was with my insistence that I was pushed into this—I wasn't pushed into it, it was with my insistence. I felt very strongly that they might not have the kind of acceptance they did in Europe. That they needed someone like me on the frontline to tell the world they weren't scary. To tell the world they were lovable. And then Frank and I had the pretty strong political agenda at the time in which I was involved. So it legitimized them, and it legitimized my own role as well, in terms of our political agenda. So it suited us both very nicely, and when all the other little girls in the world wanted to call themselves 'Suzy Creamcheese' that was just fine with me as well.

CO So there's also, let's say, still room for a Suzy Creamcheese in today's world, would you say that?

PAMELA I think there's room in this world for whatever it takes. That she's definitely still alive and kickin'.

CO This is going to be my last question for on tape. I have a very personal way of preparing for interviews, because I prefer to work by association. But knowing that, after I got your phone call—I sometimes have a dreamlike state in which I get ideas. And these are not just dreams that you forget, sometimes I even write them down. And I had this vague question that popped into my mind, and the question was just given to me, so I will ask it. Maybe I won't use it, but I *will* ask it. You had a very intense, important relationship with Frank Zappa, who later became the great composer, guitar player—somebody very much in control of his whole business, his image. As you know, I knew him, and he was always very gentle, I knew him especially as a gentle person. But I know that he could be mean to people, and of course he had the reputation of being extremely promiscuous and stuff like that, so free sex and everything around him . . . even though in his beginning he had you, as you said, as Suzy Creamcheese, as an ambassador, and also a person that he treated, obviously, as a person—with the respect of a person, the way you are on the *Freak Out* cover is maybe one of the best examples of that publicly. Very long introduction for a very short question. Did you ever discuss with him the fact that it is weird that both your last names begin with the last letter of the alphabet, and end with the first? With noise of the London trains rumbling past, I'm not afraid to ask this question.

PAMELA I definitely know that there was a very strong bond for us both beginning with Z.

CO And ending with A.

PAMELA Oh yeah, oh yeah!

CO So you begin with the end, and you end with the beginning?

PAMELA We were likeminded on many, many, many levels and that was definitely one of them.

CO So that was discussed?

PAMELA Oh yeah, oh definitely, yeah! You know, it's probably a little sign that said we were meant to be together, we were both weirdos. And when you grow up your whole life with your name beginning with a Z back then, you know, before things had changed. There definitely is a lot that goes with that, being last in line, being singled out, being different and, you know, the whole thing. We only later on went on to have our respective nicknames like 'Beardo Weirdo' and 'Creamcheese,' and whatever else the world had to offer. Long before the world started calling him Mr. Zappa. We definitely, definitely talked about that.

CO Well I'm glad that question came to me then.

PAMELA Cool!

CO And uh, so you went to see Zorro movies together?

PAMELA [laughs] I'm sure—I'm absolutely certain of that question. The subject of Zorro did appear from time to time. You're asking me to go back a long time, I've got quite a good memory, but I'm absolutely certain Zorro was the topic of discussion from time to time. [laughs] So that will give you a nice little—

CO OK.

PAMELA OK?

CO Thank you.

PAMELA Cool!

Pamela, The Voice Of Cheese—how lovely to speak with her! We made the trip into sunny London and got veggie burgers. Thanks again, Pam.

Later, Menno Kalmann joined me and together we traveled down to Höpfling, in southern Germany, where Jimmy Carl Black lived with his lovely wife Monika. We'd met before, and he welcomed us into his home. JCB seemed to enjoy talking about the record, and explained that he still felt that he'd made musical history playing on *Freak Out*.

We recorded our conversation, large chunks of which are presented here. I've left parts out, because some of the people involved (including JCB himself) are no longer around to defend themselves. However, the essence of what we discussed remains intact. We uncapped our beer bottles, put some extra water out as a standby, Menno started the recorder, and off we went.

JIMMY It's more like free jazz?

CO No, it's more like, it's more like—I think this is running. Well, what I do is I work for Dutch public radio, NPS, and run a whole team. But I also have my own shows on Sunday nights. And from '76 on I've been covering Frank Zappa's music, and I know Frank very well, as you know. And so a lot of the guys I got to know, like George, and Steve, and Mike—I carry their products, so I'm pretty involved in that scene. Well, we know each other from that but—

JIMMY From 1981, when we played at the Paradiso.

CO I recorded it.

JIMMY I know.

CO So, what happened is that my father was a producer, also for radio, and he introduced me to *Freak Out*, which was my first Zappa album. Very soon after that *200 Motels* was my second, and then I started collecting the whole catalogue and became friends with Frank. But in July—July marks the fortieth anniversary of *Freak Out*.

JIMMY It's been recorded forty years now.

CO Yeah, but it was released in July of '66.

JIMMY I know that, but it's forty years old.

CO Yeah.

JIMMY Because we were in—we were even back from Hayward California. We were playing at Frenchy's in Hayward at this time forty years ago. And getting ready to play at the Fillmore West for the first time, just a couple of weeks before the release of *Freak Out*.

CO So now what I decided to do is—because I always do something different in the summer—I'm going to devote probably four shows in a row on Sunday nights just—a lot is being said and written about Frank and the Mothers, and you guys—but I want to focus on *Freak Out*. And ask you some questions about *Freak Out*, and I have decided that I will only talk to people, not who are going to tell me how the history should be viewed, but who were really participants or were really close by to the process. So I won't talk to any later Zappa musicians or journalists or whatever. I have already—not me personally, but one of my guys has already done a two-hour telephone interview with Carl Franzoni, which was pretty wild.

JIMMY [laughs]

CO I'll talk to Roy. I'll talk—you'll be the main guest, and I will talk to Pamela.

JIMMY How about Elliot Ingber?

CO I don't know where he is.

JIMMY He's in L.A.

CO OK, well—

JIMMY I may have his phone number.

CO OK, if you have it, get Chris Opperman, because Elliot was of course also on—

JIMMY Well, he was on *Freak Out*.

CO But then I'll have the whole band—

JIMMY Except for Ray Collins. Good luck with that man!

CO I'm not gonna even try. And the thing I'm going to focus on, which is one of the nice things in my collection, is I'm going to focus it on the mono version of *Freak Out*, because I like that better than the stereo version. This is a mono and it's one of the first issues, because the later issues don't have this advert for the *Freak Map*.

JIMMY Right, that's definitely an original.

CO We're also talking to Carol Kaye.

JIMMY Oh, cool, man!

CO She was one of the auxiliary musicians.

JIMMY Yeah!

CO Well, Tom Wilson is dead, Herbie won't talk to me about it.

JIMMY He won't?

CO No.

JIMMY Why?

CO He says, 'I don't do interviews.'

JIMMY [laughs] He can be a hard guy when he wants to be.

CO But Pamela Zarubica is the first on the list of all these people who've influenced the Mothers, so—

JIMMY Yeah, I know. I've got her phone number as well.

CO Yeah, I have her phone number. Do you know she has a little record label called Ship Records?

JIMMY I don't know.

CO How old is Pam now? Early sixties or something?

JIMMY Gotta be.

CO Yeah.

JIMMY I'm sixty-eight.

CO So anyway, that's why I want to have this around because we're—I have some questions about it. And so let's just talk about it. I have some input from Franzoni, and he gave me some info about how some of the songs originated, like 'Trouble Every Day.' And so let's just see how it goes. I don't work with prep papers—

JIMMY What for? We got it right there on tape.

CO That's right.

JIMMY On the mini—

CO MiniDisc.

JIMMY MiniDisc.

CO Yeah, what I meant is, I don't prep interviews on paper. I'm not gonna run by questions because I'll just zoom in on what you're gonna tell me.

JIMMY Ask what you want, man, and if I can answer it I will.

CO Well let's go back. You have told me in the past about how it went with The Soul Giants, a band that you participated in. Frank came in, sorta took over, said he was gonna make you rich and famous. And then you had to do all—

JIMMY If we played his music.

CO If you played his music.

JIMMY And to play his music before he'd make us rich and famous.

CO But you guys said yes.

JIMMY Well, that's what I moved to California to do, is be rich and famous. I had no idea what he was gonna—what he had up his sleeve at that time that we said this. I thought we were gonna try to be a commercial hit.

CO Mm-hmm?

JIMMY When I first heard *Freak Out* I said, 'Man, there's not a damn thing commercial about this thing.'

CO But because The Soul Giants played pretty straightforward commercial gigs, Frank wanted you to start playing his music. Can you remember what one of the first few songs was?

JIMMY I know the song, the very first song we ever learned was 'How Could I Be Such A Fool?' The second one was 'I'm Not Satisfied.'

CO Mm-hmm, and he also demoed those, right? Because he just released some, the—

JIMMY Well, we did a demo for Columbia Records one time. Billy James produced that. You know? This is before we got the record deal. And at that time Henry Vestine was in the band, it wasn't Elliot Ingber.

CO The guitar player who later joined Canned Heat?

JIMMY That *started* Canned Heat. I'll never forget the day, it was the day we got the contract for *Freak Out* from MGM. And the reason we got it, Tom Wilson only heard us play one song at the Whisky A Go-Go. He walked in, he heard us play 'Trouble Coming Every Day,' and Henry was playing. And it sounded like a John Lee Hooker song at that time. It did! And he left after that. They called New York and said, 'Yeah man, this is the band, it's a blues band. We could sign these guys, this could be the new Rolling Stones for MGM records!' So, the day we got the contract, we were rehearsing at the Trip in Hollywood, because we were playing there at night, and Frank pulled out the music to 'Who Are The Brain Police?' And Henry said, 'No, that's it. That's it for me, no more of this weird shit. I'm gonna get starting a blues band. I can't play this stuff, Frank. See ya later, alligator!' And he split. Man, Herb really had to work really hard to keep that contract.

CO Herb Cohen?

JIMMY Herb Cohen had to *really*, really do some heavy-duty stuff to keep that contract, because those people wanted Henry Vestine. They liked the way he sounded. Tom Wilson liked the way he sounded. And anyway, we hired Elliot. Elliot had just gotten out of the army, as you can see. His hair is really short, as opposed to the way he looked as the Winged Eel Fingerling, for instance.

CO That was his name when he was with Beefheart?

JIMMY Yeah.

CO But let's go back a bit. You were in the Soul Giants, you make a decision to play Frank's music. Then the name change came.

JIMMY Well, we changed the name to The Muthers. M-U-T-H-E-R-S.

CO Yeah?

JIMMY The Muthers. And we had that name right up until we recorded.

CO So then you started playing . . .?

JIMMY We didn't change the name. MGM changed the name.

CO Mm-hmm?

JIMMY They said, 'We called up all these radio stations, see? Would you play a song by a band called The Muthers? And they said, hell no, we won't man because that's a reference to motherfucker, we won't play that.' So MGM said, 'Well, we're changing the name of the band to The Mothers Of Invention.'

CO So they did that, it was linked to the contract. But there must have been a period between you getting a contract and being The Mothers? Playing Frank's music, obviously.

JIMMY And other music—I mean, we still had to work, you know? We couldn't play—nobody wanted to hear original music, man. Especially the titty bars that we were playing in. You know? They wanted to hear 'Louie Louie' a thousand times a night. So we still played that, we still played 'Wooly Bully.' We still played all the bullshit that we had to play, but we were—when we rehearsed, we rehearsed Frank's music, and every once in a while we could throw in one of Frank's songs.

CO Were those rehearsals fun?

JIMMY Yeah, they were OK.

CO How were they?

JIMMY Yeah, they were OK. They weren't—I mean, it wasn't like it was later on, where he didn't even—later on, Frank didn't even show up for rehearsal half the time. Ian was the musical director.

CO Ian Underwood?

JIMMY Yeah. Later on—you know, when Frank was too busy.

CO So you rehearsed Frank's music, you did gigs with a mix and match because you have to work, you have to do commercial stuff also. Can you remember the first time anybody—be it Herb, be it Frank—told you, 'We got ourselves a record contract'?

JIMMY Well yeah, when Herb—Herb told us, when Tom Wilson came in, he told us a couple of days later, 'You guys got a record deal with MGM.'

CO So you thought, 'Money and fame!'

JIMMY Well, that's what we were all working for, was the 'big record deal.' And it was a good record deal with MGM! I mean, Tom Wilson was a producer. It was really funny, the first night of the recording at TTG Studios.

CO Tell us about that.

JIMMY We got set up—it was forty years ago last month, by the way, is when all that happened—we got to the studio, and the first song we played, the very first song that we recorded for the *Freak Out* album, was 'Who Are The Brain Police?' And Tom Wilson *immediately* was on the phone to New York City, the head office of MGM, saying, 'We didn't sign a blues band. I don't know what the hell we signed, but it damn sure ain't a blues band!'

CO And then?

JIMMY Tom just kinda—Tom was a great guy man, one of the nicest guys I ever met in my life. He pretty much let Frank do what he wanted, man. He never said no, he didn't produce us that way. He let Frank produce us, 'cause he knew it was the only way. He didn't understand this music, first of all. It was just completely beyond him, man.

CO Were all the songs rehearsed before you went into the studio?

JIMMY Oh, yeah, man! Oh yeah, we rehearsed in this movie—it was an editing room, or a small studio, on Seward Street. It was owned by the guy who Frank had done the soundtrack for *Run Home Slowly*. The end of the stuff from *Uncle Meat*, the soundtrack to the movie he did when he was sixteen.

CO The cowboy movie *Run Home Slow*?

JIMMY Yeah, the cowboy—what is it?

CO *Run Home Slow*.

JIMMY *Run Home Slow*, yeah. So this guy is the guy that had done that movie, and he hadn't paid Frank all the money—he didn't have the money. I mean, the movie was a flop, man. So he let us rehearse there for two months, seven days a week, man. Baloney sandwiches. We'd buy a big pack of baloney and a loaf of bread and that's what we ate while we were rehearsing for the record. This is after we had the deal. We had the record deal, so it was January and February in the studio rehearsing.

CO '66?

JIMMY '66. And that's when we almost had a keyboard player play with us. He tried out and he would have been the keyboard player had he not been a junkie. And his name is Mac Rebennack, alias Dr. John. The Night Tripper. He played on *Freak Out*. He played on 'Help, I'm A Rock.' He didn't get credit for it, but he played the part on the piano. That's Dr. John playing that, man.

CO That weird solo?

JIMMY Huh?

CO That weird solo on there?

JIMMY That's really strange that they never gave him fucking credit for that, man. I don't know why they didn't. It was wrong.

CO So, well-rehearsed as you were, you went right into the studio, you scared Tom Wilson by starting with 'Who Are The Brain Police?' But in those days, when you were rehearsing those songs, what was your personal perception of what you heard? Did you already have in mind what kind of an album it would turn out to be?

JIMMY I didn't have any idea what was happening. I mean, I just played it because that's what Frank wanted. I thought some of the songs were—I thought some of the songs were really—*most* of the songs were actually good songs, man. I like all of 'em, but they were pretty strange. I know that the lyrics were really strange, first of all.

CO Especially for those days.

JIMMY I mean, and we're talking about the regular songs on this, Side One and Side Two. We're not talking about Side Three and Side Four. Because after this record came out I said, 'What in the shit is this, man?' Roy was saying to me also, 'What in the shit is this?' We didn't understand it. I had to take an acid trip and listen to *Freak Out* and then say, 'Oh, OK. Now I get it. Now I understand what's going on.'

CO We'll go through the sides later, but can you give me a description of, when you went in, how the complete mood was? Like for instance, if this was going to be Frank's big chance to prove what he had conceptually in mind, to lay it on the tape—was he nervous about it? Or how did you guys communicate?

JIMMY Well, I mean, the thing is that we never thought of it as 'Frank's tape.' I mean, because we were all partners on this record contract, we all got the same amount of money for signing the deal. We got five hundred dollars for doing the—for the signing. But that was in '66, it wasn't that bad, it was OK No, it wasn't any of that—I thought we were partners, you know? We had all agreed that we're doing Zappa's music. There was no question about that, nobody cared. You know? We didn't care.

CO So how was the vibe in the studio?

JIMMY Maybe Ray Collins might have cared, but Ray Collins is a fucking weirdo anyway.

CO Describe to me just the room. How did you feel behind your kit when you were doing that?

JIMMY Good, man! It didn't bother me a bit. Maybe because after two months of rehearsing this shit every day, six, seven hours a day, that was—we knew it, I knew it in my sleep. I still know this stuff in my sleep. You know? It's because of all that rehearsing that we did. And three or four of the songs was The Mothers Auxiliary were playing with us, man. You know? We did this whole album in three days. The whole thing was recorded in three days. Two sides of a record—the first record, with a two-record set like this, to come out with this kind of music, ever.

CO Yeah!

JIMMY We did it in three days.

MENNO Did you record more tracks for each song? Or did you—how did it work? Did you stop, for instance, halfway and have to start over? Or—

JIMMY Not us! What for, man? We knew this stuff backwards and forwards, man.

MENNO Because I understood it was a 4-track recording.

JIMMY It was a 4-track recording.

MENNO How did that work? You recorded with bass, drums and—

JIMMY And then they ping-ponged it around. Then they'd remix it down and put that on one track and then—they had ways of doing it man. All the Beatles stuff was done on three tracks. *Sgt. Pepper*. Because they bounced it—but that's all there was back in those days. That was state-of-the-art studio, man, 4-track. And then of course we did the orchestra pieces, the thing that we did with the orchestra was all done live. We did it one take. Because the record company was paying these musicians, and we're a new band, we're not an established band, and they only had so much of a budget. I think we had a twenty thousand dollar budget to make this record. I think it was twenty thousand—no, more than that.

CO That was just for the recording, or also for the whole—?

JIMMY Well, that's including us getting our five hundred dollars each. But twenty thousand for the whole thing. That's paying those other musician's, renting the equipment that we had to rent—all that shit, and paying guys to play.

CO But if you tell me it's three days for such an amount of work, did you feel a lot of time pressure while playing? Or could you just focus on your playing?

JIMMY I just focused on what I was supposed to do. He'd just call a song out, I already knew it, not a problem. We'd go in and we did the basic tracks, we did one take on the basic tracks and that was perfect. I mean, shit man! You know, we might have gone through maybe half the song before we recorded it, to make sure that the levels and everything were set right. But then when the recording started, man. I mean, 'Let's do this shit, let's get it over with!' Move right on along.

MENNO But how many instruments did you play on the first track? Bass and drums and guitar—

JIMMY Bass, drums, and rhythm guitar.

MENNO And all the rest later?

JIMMY And the overdubs came later.

MENNO By ping-ponging and—

JIMMY Yeah. [phone rings] Me! [crosses the room] Yeah, hello? Hello? Oh, man—

CO Yeah? Change the tape.

MENNO Change the tape, yeah.

[Tape change]

CO OK, so.

MENNO Ping-pong was the last words—

CO We go back to the—I want to, before we go back to the actual album, I want you to tell me a little bit more about if there was any change within the band, mood-wise, when you guys knew that you were going to change from playing bars and actually going—aiming for a proper release on a major label? That must have been quite a turnaround.

JIMMY Well, you know, nobody really thought about it at that time, because we were still playing in bars even after we'd recorded the record. We played a month in Hawaii.

CO How was the scene then for the Mothers? How was the scene in general? Because we talked to Carl Franzoni—

JIMMY Well, the scene in L.A. was it was just the beginning of the freak scene. Frank told us we had to let our hair grow long, go to the Salvation Army and buy your clothes. We didn't do any of—I didn't do any of that shit, but I did start letting my hair grow long. I wasn't gonna buy my clothes at the Salvation Army, they didn't have anything I like there.

CO So where did you get your clothes?

JIMMY I didn't buy very many clothes, man. I used to get some in San Francisco, in the psychedelic shops up there, you know? When we were getting psychedelic, after I took my first acid trip.

CO But how was your day-to-day life then? Because playing drums in a band, was it like going to work? What did you do? What was your day like?

JIMMY Well, we were rehearsing. That was like a job, man. Except we weren't getting paid for it.

CO So how did you get by?

JIMMY It was hard man. I was living with my father-in-law, I had five kids. We were all living in that house—and she had six brothers that are all living in the house, so there were about fifteen of us living in this house in Santa Ana. And that went on for quite a while, man. Even after the record came out it didn't really change that much, man. I mean, there were only a few places that you could play. Looking the way we did, San Francisco was one, L.A. only in Hollywood—[loud bang] what the fuck was that?

MENNO Maybe an Indian thing.

JIMMY Could be! [laughs] Who knows?

CO So it was, like, financially you went through rough times then?

JIMMY We financially went through rough times after we had four albums out. We were still going through rough times.

CO So did that have an effect on the vibe within the group?

JIMMY Well, I never could figure out how we could have all these fucking records out and not have any money.

CO Mm-hmm?

JIMMY Have you heard *Uncle Meat*? [loud bang] God, I've got to shut something.

CO Yeah, shut something.

JIMMY Something's driving me crazy here. Took care of that little problem.

CO Great! So, we were talking about the financial situation of the band that came to be within—also in Europe—came to be famous.

JIMMY Not monetarily.

CO No?

[Banging in the background]

MENNO I'll take a look, OK?

JIMMY I don't know what the hell is slammin' around here.

CO Has it always been there, or is it just since we arrived here?

JIMMY No, no! The wind's blowing outside, I got the windows open.

CO This is a beautiful place you've got here. Nice and quiet, man.

JIMMY Oh yeah!

CO Is it a big change from—? Have you adjusted to the pace here and—

JIMMY Oh yeah, I've been here nine years.

CO Yeah, it's pretty cool.

JIMMY I just don't know what the hell, what door's open or not open. [loud slam] I'll shut all the fucking windows, then there *can't* be anything banging around.

CO [laughs]

JIMMY I'm sorry I can't offer us any more beer, but I don't have any.
CO That's OK, we'll get a pub later.
CO So, the whole recording process was finished within three days.
JIMMY Our part of it. Zappa spent probably two of three weeks mixing and editing that record. But we had nothing to do with that. Nothing whatsoever to do with that part of it. We didn't even hear the record until we—until it came out.
CO Why was that? Didn't you want to?
JIMMY Well, he never—it was none of our business. But that's the way—but that's Frank.
CO Yeah, OK. But you could also say that that's how Frank became. But was it already that—being his music, was it so distinctive that there was already a separation between him and the rest of the guys?
JIMMY Yup, there definitely was.
CO Did you talk to each other about that?
JIMMY You mean with Frank?
CO Like you, Roy, and Elliot.
JIMMY Oh yeah, we did.
CO And what did you say then?
JIMMY We couldn't figure out why it was the way it was. But hey man, if that's the way he wants to be, I don't care. Let him. We're getting more pussy than he is anyway. [laughs]
CO [laughs]
JIMMY It's true, we were.
CO I won't argue with it because I wasn't there, but—
JIMMY But how in the hell could he get pussy if he was always writing songs, man? That's all he was interested in.
CO That's not something you can combine?
JIMMY Well, I could, but he didn't.
CO But you talked to each other about that? Because it was definitely presented—the whole package, from the outside—as a group effort.
JIMMY Well it *is* a group effort, the reason it was a group effort is because Frank couldn't play all the instruments at the same time, how could he?

You know? So whether he liked it or not it was a group effort. All the Mothers Of Invention stuff was. With the exception of two songs on *Cruising With Ruben & The Jets.*

CO Because they were co-written?

JIMMY No, there are two songs on *Cruising With Ruben & The Jets* that Frank did everything himself. Played the drums, played the bass, played the guitar, played the keyboards, sang all the parts.

CO What songs are those?

JIMMY 'No. No. No.' and 'Cheap Thrills.' And that's because we all refused to go to the studio that night.

CO Why was that?

JIMMY Well, 'cause he wasn't paying us, man. We were doing all this fucking coming to town—and I was living in Woodstock at that time, man. I had to drive ninety miles one way just to come to the studio, and he wasn't paying any gas. We weren't getting any fucking money for this. We were recording at that time. *Uncle Meat* and *Ruben & The Jets* were recorded at the same time. In the same studio.

CO This was in the New York period.

JIMMY In New York City, Apostolic Studio.

CO So then *Freak Out* was released pretty soon after the recording.

JIMMY Fairly soon after the recording

CO July '66?

JIMMY Yeah, June or July. Something like that.

CO And then what happened? Did that change anything for you?

JIMMY Not really. Well, we did go to New York City. We finally made the break from the West Coast, and we went to New York City and started playing the East Coast a little bit. And things started looking up then, a little more, for us. But hell, it wasn't—*Freak Out* had only been out for about three months—about three months, and then we started recording the second one, *Absolutely Free*. And it was right after July, right after the release of *Freak Out*, maybe a month after, we were playing at the Avalon Ballroom and that's when Elliot Ingber got fired from the band.

CO Why?

JIMMY Well, he took an LSD trip on the stage, and we started playing the song, and Elliot had to play a lead, had to play a solo in the beginning of the song. I can't remember what song it was, one of the songs. And Elliot was wailing away on this solo, just fuckin' kicking ass, and Frank just kept staring at him and said, 'Your amplifier is not on.'

CO Wow!

JIMMY 'Might be nice if you'd turn the fucking amplifier on so you can hear, so the rest of us can hear what you're playin'!' [laughs] That was it.

CO That was it then?

JIMMY That was it for Elliot. Frank fired him when we got back to L.A. And that's when he hired—Billy Mundi came, Don Preston came, and Bunk Gardner came. That was when those guys came, because they came on the second, *Absolutely Free*, the second LP.

CO Yeah. Does *Freak Out* stand out for you, being the first album of the—

JIMMY To me it does because that's the album I was the original drummer on. I was the only drummer in this band.

CO Yeah. Because already on *Absolutely Free* you had Billy with you.

JIMMY Billy, and then after that Artie Tripp was in.

CO So . . .?

JIMMY *Freak Out* I was the only drummer in the band.

CO Did you like the drum sound when you heard the final album?

JIMMY On *Freak Out*? Yeah, I did, man. I think they captured the drums good.

CO Because you have a very distinctive way of playing, which is a very clear signature of all the early Mothers stuff. How would you describe your own playing in those days?

JIMMY Well, a sweet, sweet steady beat, that's what Elliot Ingber used to call me. The best 'time' drummer. All those other guys play circles around me with that fancy shit, but they can't keep time better than I can. And after all, that *is* the purpose of the drummer, is to be the timekeeper, no matter what time it is. If it's in 7/8, in 5/8 time, or 9/8 time, it doesn't matter. It's still gotta be—the 'one' has gotta be where the 'one' is supposed to be in order for everybody to be together. So, to me, the bass player and the drummer are the most important guys in the band. We're the backbone of the band.

CO And how was your interaction with Roy Estrada?

JIMMY Mine with Roy was great, man. Absolutely great with Roy.

CO Because *his* steadiness is also pretty—

JIMMY Oh yeah, man! It's really good, man, with Roy. Not a problem at all with Roy Estrada. Billy Mundi I had a hard time playing with. I couldn't play—It was really, really hard for me to play with Billy. Because, first of all, it's two rock drummers playing, and his time was like a fucking rollercoaster. He was taking all the speed all the time, man. And I mean he would just... fast. He'd start out at a tempo and by the end of the song that thing would be twice as fast. And Frank used to tell me, 'Jimmy, hold him back.' I said, 'Jesus, Frank, I can't hold him back, he's a freight train! Look at him. He's twice as big as I am, man. How am I holding a freight train back?' And then when Billy quit, and Artie Tripp came, then was the best for me, man. I enjoyed playing with Art Tripp more than anything in the world. Because Artie was a percussionist. He had never played rock'n'roll before, he'd never even played trap drums before. He was a—Before he joined the Mothers he had graduated with a Master's degree from Juilliard School of Music, and he was principal percussionist with the Cincinnati Philharmonic before he joined the Mothers. So it was easy to play with him, but then again Artie wasn't on *Freak Out*.

CO No. And going back to *Freak Out*, your role as the timekeeper, your role as the drummer, and already laying down a signature for the beat that would carry on for all the years of the early Mothers, did you ever reflect on the fact that your steadiness and your very direct approach of the time had to interrelate with all the weird shit laid on top of it?

JIMMY Yeah, I did.

CO How did you cope?

JIMMY I just played my part, man. I didn't listen to what those other guys were playing, necessarily.

MENNO Did you play, let's say, for yourself and—?

JIMMY No, I never played for myself, I always played for Frank, 'cause that's what Frank wanted man. I just gave Frank what he wanted.

MENNO Yeah, but I mean keeping the time?

JIMMY Well that's what Frank wanted me to do.

MENNO Yeah, if somebody is losing it, like the bass player, then you just go on—you just follow him, or . . .?

JIMMY Well, see, that didn't happen. That *never* happened. The bass player never lost it, that's why I enjoy playing with Roy Estrada so much. That's why I *still* think he's one of the best bass players ever in the history of music.

CO He goes right to the essence of stuff.

JIMMY Well, see, because we came from a rhythm and blues background. That's where Roy and I *both* came from. You know, when he was fifteen or sixteen years old, man, he was playing with Johnny 'Guitar' Watson, man! Roy was. Being on the West Coast, so, you know . . . and I was playing in Kansas. I was playing with bands, Black bands called The Smart Brothers and stuff—and playing R&B shit, man.

CO Mm-hmm?

JIMMY Where you had to—the time is important, man, in that kind of music. And you know Frank was a really big fan of rhythm and blues, first of all. He learned a lot from it, him and Beefheart. When they were in high school out in the desert. Always, man, listening to blues and stuff. And you can hear it in all of Frank's music, man. The blues is there, man. Even when it's in weird music it's *still* there man. I still hear little things when I listen to Zappa's music. He was definitely influenced by that.

CO When *Freak Out* was released, you were still in the freak scene, you were still doing the commercial gigs. Did you witness any response from the audience or the peer group that you were approaching when it came out? Did something happen, or was it just another album?

JIMMY Well, no . . . to us it was just another album. I have to say this, man: things were changing for us. First of all, we started playing in Hollywood more. We got out of playing in the titty bars. Herb got us gigs at the Whisky A Go-Go, and we became the house band at the Whisky in 1965, the last part of '65. Because that's where Tom Wilson heard us play. And we were playing the Trip and we were playing at the Action Club. Herb was the best thing that happened to The Mothers at that time, because he had so many connections. We played up in San Francisco our first time way before *Freak Out* came out, not *way* before—about three months, four months before *Freak Out*. Before we recorded it. We went up and played the last Longshoreman's Hall gig that they had up there, and it was a coproduction with Bill Graham and Chet Helms. You know? Graham, after that, went to the Filmore West and Chet Helms opened up the Avalon Ballroom.

CO Yeah?

JIMMY And they became—they were in heavy competition with each other by that time. But we played that gig, and the reason I say it was the last one was because we were playing when the riot happened. And it just so happened we were playing the song 'Rumble.' This fuckin' riot happened and Herb Cohen's the one who started the whole fucking thing! Some hippie came up and did something, and Herbie just fucking coldcocked that bastard, man... you know? Probably called him 'peanut.' That's fightin' words for Herb. You want to get in a fight with, him call him peanut. Don't mention that I told you that! [laughs] It was really funny, man, and Herb started this fight and they broke out all the fucking windows in the Longshoreman's Hall. I mean it was supposed to be the City of Love and this blah blah, and this blah blah. And as it turned out it wasn't the city of all that lovey-dovey stuff, as it... you know? That wasn't exactly the case that night.

CO Right. Was that in a period you shared the stage with Lenny Bruce?

JIMMY Lenny was still alive. We shared the stage with Lenny Bruce about one month after *Freak Out* came out.

CO Mm-hmm?

JIMMY We would have been playing at the Filmore—we started playing the Filmore West right after Hayward. Right after Frenchy's. And it was about three weeks before *Freak Out* came out and Herb got—I don't know... him and Bill Graham, I think they were friends but sometimes I didn't know for sure if they were friends.

CO Did you have a lot of contact, in those *Freak Out* days, with Herb?

JIMMY Uh yeah, quite a bit. Not as much as Frank did but . . . in fact the guys in the band—nobody liked Herbie at that time. We thought he was ripping us off but actually, in reality, it wasn't Herb that was doing it. It was Frank.

CO That's a bit contradictory. Because you said you had a very clear and open situation in the pre-*Freak Out* days, and even during the *Freak Out* days, that you just knew you were getting your money, you were playing his music and that was it. But I also sense some sort of contradiction when you say that there were things going on and—

JIMMY There were things going on and it was all laid—it was pretty much all laid on. In other words, Herb took the rap for everything. But as it turned out, it wasn't really Herbie after all, really. You know? We didn't have near as much contact with Herbie as Frank did. Even though Herb was our manager the same as he was Frank's. I mean, we had that management contract between us.

CO So then the album came out, and were there within the guys—besides Frank—were there . . .? When it was released and available in the shops, did you have certain expectations for it after having heard it?

JIMMY I didn't think we were gonna sell shit, man! But that was my own personal opinion, you know. I didn't know. I just thought, 'This is pretty strange music, man. I don't know if this is gonna happen or not. Maybe it will.' Especially Side Three and Side Four, man. 'The Son Of The Monster Magnet'?

CO Would you call Side Four—

JIMMY 'Help, I'm a Rock.'

CO Would you call Side Three and Side Four legitimately ahead of their time?

JIMMY I would consider everything that's on that record legitimately ahead of its time, because as it is right now that record is not dated. You play it right now for young kids, they're liable to freak out. Saying, 'Man, who is that new band?'

CO [laughs]

JIMMY Hell, those guys only did that forty years ago.

CO Yeah, if you look at the charts of those days it's a total different universe.

JIMMY But this record stayed on in the Top 100, on the *Billboard* for two years, over two years. It was around 98, 97, 95. You know? And the other records that we made, like *Absolutely Free*, went up to number 40. *We're Only In It For The Money* made it in the Top 20—it was a pretty good seller, and it still is.

CO Mm-hmm.

JIMMY *Ruben & The Jets* did OK. *Uncle Meat*, pfff! Too fuckin' far out, man. It would just—I mean that's way too . . . that's out there man. What is that? I don't even *know* what kind of music it is. People would say jazz, classical, rock . . . there's a little bit of everything on it.

CO How would you describe—

MENNO We have to change for the tape.

CO Change tape?

JIMMY You don't have a tape though, do you?

CO Loads of 'em!

JIMMY I've got some if you—

[Tape change]

JIMMY When are you guys going back? Tomorrow?

CO Tomorrow morning.

JIMMY So we'll have to go out and eat dinner tonight.

CO Let's see, what's this? OK, it's running. OK, ahead of its time we've covered. I have a few more questions. Do you have any favorite songs on the album?

JIMMY *Freak Out*?

CO Yeah.

JIMMY I have several, man. I like 'Hungry Freaks, Daddy.' I think 'Wowie Zowie,' man, is a cute little song, 'How Could I Be Such A Fool?' 'Go Cry On Somebody Else's Shoulder' and 'You're Probably Wondering Why I'm Here.' And of course 'Trouble Every Day,' man.

CO Yeah!

JIMMY I like 'Help, I'm a Rock'! [laughs]

CO Carl Franzoni told us about the 'Trouble Every Day' content, and that he actually was near the riots in Watts, and that actually the fact that a woman was killed while sitting behind the steering wheel of her car was actually all reality and true.

JIMMY Well it was on TV, man, that's where I saw all that shit.

CO How did you look at that situation? What was your—

JIMMY First of all, Roy and I had to go right—sorta right through Watts to get there on the autobahn—on the freeway, to get to Hollywood to go rehearse every day. We had to go—we'd be drivin' on the fuckin' autobahn, and we'd see this smoke off to the right and it was in Watts.

CO What happened?

JIMMY Well they just—The police is what happened, man. The LAPD. They've caused *both* riots. You know? They did it—they had another riot again in the 1990s, when this guy—

CO Rodney King?

JIMMY Rodney King got beat up and that—the same thing happened again. More trouble coming every day. But exactly the same thing, man. Frank used to watch it on TV. 'About to get sick from watchin' my TV, been checkin' out the news until my eyeballs fail to see.' He was watching it and he wrote this song about the Watts riot, man. The Black people got tired of being treated like shit, man, by the cops. You know? Prisons are full of Black people in America.

CO How—Because Roy Estrada is originally Mexican?

JIMMY Yeah, he is . . . *still*. He hasn't had the operation! [laughs]

CO Oh Jesus, no! It costs a lot of money.

JIMMY [laughs]

CO How was it, as an Indian and a Mexican, to watch so much racial unrest?

JIMMY Better them than us! [laughs]

CO Is that what you thought?

JIMMY Well, in a way, yeah. I'm glad *they're* doing it and not me. But I can understand, I was full of sympathy for 'em, man. I understand why they were doing it. You know? Nobody likes to get—minorities don't like to get treated like shit, man.

CO Did you feel like part of a minority in those days?

JIMMY Yeah. I was pretty dark-complected. I grew up in El Paso, Texas. Eighty-five percent Mexican people living there.

CO Mm-hmm. And how different was L.A.?

JIMMY Not that much different, man. You know, like Santa Ana was a very big Mexican population in L.A. Huge Mexican population in L.A. So there was—and Blacks also. But the Mexicans kinda stayed out of the Watts thing, man. You know? Because they didn't live in Watts, the Mexicans lived in El Monte. East L.A. And Watts is more in Central L.A. Just a little bit south of downtown.

CO When the producer, Tom Wilson, heard you record, at the *Freak Out* session, the song 'Trouble Every Day,' could you see a—witness a response on his behalf?

JIMMY Well, he didn't get to see that until the last day. Us recording *that* song.

CO Really? While that was the song that got you your contract.

JIMMY That's the one that got us the contract, but that's not the one we—that was the last day, right after we did that we did 'Help, I'm A Rock.' And then after that was the . . . well, you know, it wasn't even *called* the 'Son Of The Monster Magnet.' There was no name, we just jammed. That's a jam session.

CO Mm-hmm. That's Side Four. But I want to focus now about what I just asked you, about Wilson and the song 'Trouble Every Day.' Did he have any urge, being a Black guy, to pick that song and maybe get it on the radio?

JIMMY Not really. Tom Wilson was a different kind of a Black guy. He was from—I think he's from Connecticut. He's from upper class, you know? His family had money. He was married to a White woman at the time. He wasn't really what you'd call a Black man that came from—that's from the ghetto . . . from Mississippi. Or that's been—that their parents—watched their parents get hung by the Ku Klux Klan or something like that, you know? He didn't have *that* kind of an upbringing, man. So he was a different kind of—and also Tom Wilson was, I think he was half-White to begin with, because if you see the pictures of him he's very light-complected, man. He's a mulatto, they call 'em mulatto. Hell, most of 'em have blue eyes, and ... yeah, he wasn't a full-blood Black boy. Not that—I shouldn't say 'boy,' but ... could cause another riot here.

CO Well. In Bavaria ...? I don't know.

JIMMY I doubt it either! [laughs]

CO But that song, that 'Trouble Every Day' song—which was heavily edited on the European version, by the way—that kind of was the introduction to two other pieces on Side Three and Four, which are totally from a different world than Side One and Two: 'Help, I'm A Rock,' with the whole 'It Can't Happen Here' stuff and 'The Son Of Monster Magnet.' Well, I'd like to talk about both of those pieces. Like you said, Side Four was like a jam. What happened? Because all that we see on the cover is that probably there was a big assembly of people, and Herbie Cohen complaining about rental for percussion instruments.

JIMMY Well, that's exactly what it was. It was a jam session with all those instruments.

CO So what happened? What time was it?

JIMMY About two o'clock in the morning. It was the last thing we did. After that it was finished.

CO So how was it organized? You just got people from the street?

JIMMY Well, no, that was the freak scene. It was those people from—Carl Franzoni brought most of those people down. Vito and that whole crowd of people.

CO Mm-hmm?

JIMMY The freaks. That's how that happened, it started out as 'Help, I'm A Rock.' And we played the 'Help, I'm A Rock' thing because we played that a lot at the Trip before we recorded it. 'Help, I'm A Rock' was kinda like a jam session, but an organized jam session. It's like 'King Kong' is a jam, but it's an organized jam, it's got a head on it and it's got an ending on it. We used to do that there, just because we didn't record it until *Uncle Meat*, we used to play 'King Kong' for years, man.

CO So that was just a big jam session, and probably edited? Down to . . .?

JIMMY Oh yeah, and then he added voices and he added the overdubs and all kinds of crazy shit like—you know? Getting really psychedelic. For a guy that never took any acid—

CO That is pretty far out.

JIMMY But a guy that *did* do baby woodrose seeds.

CO What are those?

JIMMY Well, they're like morning glory seeds. [laughs] You get high on 'em, really psychedelically high.

CO So how many people were at that jam?

JIMMY Probably about twenty or twenty-five.

CO And what were the beverages, or the other kind of things that you could consume like at that night?

JIMMY Well, nothing in the studio, but there were always trips outside. Mainly we just smoked pot, we drank beer. But we didn't really do it in the studio because Frank didn't really go for any of that shit, man. You know? We are supposed to be there concentrating on doing a job.

CO Mm-hmm. And 'Help, I'm A Rock' is actually like a little suite that has various parts. Were you involved in the—what he calls the 'barbershop' singing?

JIMMY Of course I was!

CO Was that conducted, or improvised, or what was it?

JIMMY Everything was conducted by him. You know? Frank is a control freak. He really is a control freak. He doesn't really like to let things just 'happen.' It's not like the Grateful Dead, they just let things happen. I mean, you can't really knock the Dead. I mean, look how long they were together, a lot longer than The Mothers Of Invention were together.

CO Mm-hmm, but like the 'It Can't Happen Here' stuff and the vocal stuff, did you get a chart for that? Or how was that—

JIMMY Well yeah, he had a map laid out. Yeah, he knew how he wanted it done, and that's the way it was done, that way. You know? He was the one who invented this word 'freak out.' That word was never used before in any context whatsoever until this record came out.

CO But was it a term that Vito used that he copied, or did he really think of it?

JIMMY I think Frank thought of it.

CO Because it is a truly addition to the English language.

JIMMY It *is*, man. And it wasn't in the English language until this record came out forty years ago. And now all these kids use it. I mean, man, it's freakin' out. Freak out!

CO Is it true that is the first double album in rock?

JIMMY Yeah. Another double album came out about this same time, although it wasn't in rock. It was Bob Dylan—it was his folk stuff. This was the first rock double record. And it sold for three dollars and ninety-nine cents. That was the retail price of that record when it came out. There are copies of that record now that you could probably get two hundred dollars for, or more.

CO Like this one.

JIMMY Yeah!

CO Because this is—the funny thing is, what I'm using in these shows is the mono version.

JIMMY Well, I don't know the difference between the—to tell you the truth, I don't really know the difference between the mono version and the stereo version. I never was really . . . I'm a drummer, man. I don't know about—what do I know about stereo shit, man?

CO Three more phases I want to go through in this talk. The first of all is 'people involved.' We already talked about Herb Cohen. There are two other names that pop up a lot if you read books or if you talk to other people about that period. And I'd like you to tell me about those two people in your perspective. Namely Carl Franzoni and Pamela Zarubica. Let's start with Carl Franzoni.

JIMMY The Laughing Lion. He had a tongue longer than the guy from KISS. Not only that, but he was a card-carrying Communist.

CO What was his role in the whole scene?

JIMMY Just a—he was in the freak scene—

CO He was a dancer, right?

JIMMY He was like—yeah. He was, like, a first lieutenant. Vito was the main guy in the freak scene, Vito the Sculptor. He taught dance to young kids and stuff like that, was just really a weird guy. Nobody ever knew how old Vito was, but we know that he was pretty old, and I know that he had a very young wife, Sue. So Franzoni was the lieutenant there, he'd recruit all these young girls off the street. You know? And they were all dropping acid—because acid, LSD, was legal then, 1965. The police had no idea what the fuck was going on, man! All of sudden, all these people were growing their hair long and wearing all these wild-colored clothes… the police had no idea. 'What the hell is going on here, man?' They were dropping LSD, man.

CO So Franzoni was in on that?

JIMMY He was there right in the middle of that whole scene.

CO And then when—because 'Hungry Freaks, Daddy,' the first song on the album, is dedicated to Franzoni. So how did he connect with Frank, who was not really an LSD-type of person?

JIMMY Well, Frank used to… when we first started and Frank—we were playing out in Pomona, but Frank was living in—he moved to Echo Park near Hollywood. And he started hanging out at Canter's. Trying to get into the scene, that's what he was trying to do. And he met these guys, and you know? Frank was a pretty strange guy anyway.

CO Canter's was, like, a delicatessen?

JIMMY Yeah, a delicatessen, where all the freaks used to hang out. Vito and all of 'em would go down there at twelve or one o'clock at night, two o'clock in the morning, and stay till six or seven in the morning, just generally freaking out. Not doing anything, just making a scene, making a statement, is what was happening. Against the establishment. Which in a way was against the war. Not—you know? Because the Mothers never did any anti-war songs during all this Vietnam time. We didn't do anti-war songs, but we did anti-establishment songs, which were the guys that were causing the war in the first place. Frank was even going farther than the… just—you know, Country Joe was singing about the war.

CO So through Canter's he got connected with Franzoni?

JIMMY And through Herb Cohen he got connected with Lenny Bruce. He was a big fan of Lenny Bruce's. He liked what Lenny was saying, and that influenced Zappa's writing of lyrics.

CO And was Franzoni present at the concerts that you did, with his dancers?

JIMMY Yeah! Always at the Whisky A Go-Go, he was always there. And at the Trip and all those places that we played, even to the Action Club . . . you know? All those places at that time were run by the mafia. The L.A. mafia. You know who Mickey Cohen is? He was the head of the L.A. Jewish mafia. Herb's uncle. I rest my case.

CO Did you know Herb's brother, Mutt?

JIMMY Oh yeah, very well! I like Mutt a lot, man, he's a good guy.

CO I think he passed away.

JIMMY Really?

CO Yeah. What was the audience like in those clubs then?

JIMMY Well, in Hollywood the freaks were there, man. And there was more and more freaks every day, man. Just a lot of freaks. San Francisco was really freaky, the whole city was freaked out in San Francisco. You know? It was a pretty wild scene. The Filmore East and the Avalon Ballroom were all—a lot of LSD going on, you know? And then of course they had just invented the birth control pill, so that meant of course that free sex was everywhere.

CO Yeah.

JIMMY And there was no AIDS. The worst you could get was the clap or syphilis, cured with a shot.

CO Those were the days.

JIMMY I have my memories! [laughs]

CO Who's the girl that Frank refers to, and who is audible on *Freak Out*, as Suzy Creamcheese?

JIMMY I think her name was Sherry. Pamela Zarubica isn't the original. That girl Sherry—

CO Yeah?

JIMMY Although Pam was living with Frank in Kirkwood, with Sherry, with Cherry, with Gail, there was about—he had a harem up there, about six chicks.

CO Because Pamela Zarubica is pretty—is the first one who is credited as an influence on his music, on the *Freak Out* cover. Later she came to Europe with you guys as Suzy Creamcheese, in her role as Suzy Creamcheese. In the *Freak Out* recording period, was she a notable factor?

JIMMY Yeah, she used to come down to the studio. She wasn't that noticeable, I mean, she was living with Frank at the time. She had to ball Tom Wilson.

CO Why?

JIMMY Well, because Frank wanted to get the producer on his side. [laughs] You know? He took LSD on the night that we did 'Help, I'm A Rock,' he was fucking blown out of his skull, man, when we were recording 'Help, I'm A Rock' and the 'Son Of The Monster Magnet.' [laughs] And all *that* shit.

CO Wilson, you mean.

JIMMY Yeah. He had never taken that before.

CO So, rounding up. You already said a little bit about something, about the actuality of the album, but how do you—After having such a long career and experience in music, how do you look back now on the album?

JIMMY I still like it. It's not my first recording but it's the second. I did a single in 1962 with a band called The Keys, in Wichita, Kansas. That was my first recording, did a single. That was the first recording I did, and the *Freak Out* was the next one. I know I've never made any money out of the music business, man, never have made any fuckin' money out of the music business. I'm a legend, as the boys in England call me.

CO But, being the original drummer of the original Mothers and on the original first album, it has steered you probably in your musical career?

JIMMY It has. Not so much the music, but the idea of doing it and all that. You know? I still have a lot of drummers that say I'm still their favorite drummer. When there are guys like Vinnie Colaiuta and Terry Bozzio, they play circles around me, man. But the reason they play circles around me is because I never wanted to play like they do. I'm not interested in that, that's not my trip. Never have wanted to do it and I never will.

[Tape change]

JIMMY [looking at the cover of *Freak Out*] You see this guy right here?

CO The guy with long hair?

JIMMY Yeah.

CO What about him?

JIMMY As it turns out, he turned out to be one of Manson's boys.

CO Really?

JIMMY Yup. He killed that musician up in Topanga Canyon. Bobby was his name, and I couldn't fucking believe it when I heard it, man. Because he was such a gentle guy, man. Just a *sweet* guy, man, and turned out to . . . I guess Manson got him up there in San Francisco and indoctrinated him. But he became one of the Manson boys.

CO What I was asking was, Frank being the documentalist that he is, is there any footage? Was any footage shot? You know, photo or film outside this, that had to do with *Freak Out*? Why wasn't that jam filmed?

JIMMY With what? There really much—It's not like it is nowadays, man. Nobody had movie cameras, nobody had—I mean, there weren't any such thing as a video camera. There wasn't certainly anything like *this*, this little thing right here, you know? There weren't even cassette players, man! If you were gonna record a concert, you had to have one of those Uher portable tape recorders and hopefully two good stereo microphones, or a good mono microphone, or something like that, to do it, man. Because there just *wasn't* anything. I mean, hell man, we played the first—I bet we played three years before I had even saw, and didn't even know what a monitor was, because there *weren't* any monitors on the stage. You got up and sang through two boxes at the theatre, big boxes out there. And you never heard anything that you sang. Had not a clue what was going on, man.

CO So actually this cover that I'm holding up now, is actually the only real documentation that there is? You're on there quite a bit.

JIMMY That I know of.

CO Yeah. If you look at the cover, and if you look at the . . . this is the original band on the outside of the cover, and on the inside we see a lot of people. We see Les McCann, we see Vito, we see Emperor Vito, Crown Prince Carl, Mother Elliot, Mother Jim, Mother Ray . . . explains the Great

Society and stuff like that. P.F. Sloan. If you look at this, what does it say to you today if you look at this as a concept?

JIMMY Ha! I don't know man. I'd think, 'God, these guys are crazy!' You know? Paul Butterfield right there.

CO Paul Butterfield Blues Band.

JIMMY Well, he was at the *Freak Out* thing, he played on it. They were hanging out in L.A. at the time that *Freak Out* was being recorded. That's why they were down there, they were playing at The Trip. The Paul Butterfield Blues Band was. Paul was a good friend of ours, we played a lot of gigs with him, a nice guy too, man.

CO When did, for you, the band The Mothers Of Invention stop being The Mothers Of Invention?

JIMMY When we broke up.

CO '69?

JIMMY The last record was '70 or '71. *Weasels Ripped My Flesh.* But that was the end of the original Mothers Of Invention.

CO Was it weird for you to see totally different ensembles?

JIMMY Well, sure it was, man! And then calling themselves The Mothers. And I used to watch these guys, they all tried to be really clever and really funny. And they really didn't know *how* to freak out. And you know, in the original Mothers Of Invention we didn't even have to try to. We *were* freaked out! [laughs] That's the difference, man. I mean, Frank always tried to get—he never could get the humor back that the original Mothers Of Invention had. That's why all these people got all pissed off at him when he took Roy and I off of *We're Only In It For The Money* and off of *Cruising With Ruben & The Jets*. When he said, 'Oh, the tapes are all fucked up.' Well, then how could Rykodisc put it out in the original form? They didn't put out *Ruben & The Jets* in the original form, but they did *We're Only In It For The Money*. And all you have to do is copy—a really good copy of the record, and they've got studio enhancement stuff that you can make that thing sound good.

CO You made a very clear statement about the, let's say, the separation of the old Mothers and the ensembles later to be called Mothers. Yet you are one of the few from the old days that would appear later in Frank's work. Of course you had a *major* role in *200 Motels*.

JIMMY Well, I don't know. It wasn't *supposed* to be a major role. I sure didn't get paid for a major role.

CO But you got the chance to say *that* in the movie.

JIMMY That's true, and I only did actually one other thing with him after that. And that was in 1980.

CO 'Harder Than Your Husband.'

JIMMY Yeah. On that whole LP. But he paid me good for that, man. Frank took real good care of me with that.

CO So the fact that you went out and because ... of course the role of Zappa, who's the main character on *Freak Out* as a composer, his role later became something which is now the subject for books and shows. And I did shows with him, and about him as well, together with Menno. Do you think that the picture that people try to draw of the old Mothers and Frank, but also the other Mothers—books are being published ... every time I read those books, my first question is, 'Is this something that you could write down, and is this really what happened?'

JIMMY You can write ... I'm trying at the moment. I'm on chapter 12 of my book. I'm already finished with the Mothers section of it, I'm up to 1985 at the moment. End the book from '85 to '90. I want to try to finish the fucking thing soon. It's a lot of work, and for somebody that doesn't really know what the fuck he's doin'. [laughs]

CO But probably one of the first 'eyewitness reports' on that period?

JIMMY But this book is not about Frank.

CO That's what I'm saying.

JIMMY This book is about The Mothers Of Invention.

CO That's right, what I'm trying to zoom into.

JIMMY Yeah, that's what—I didn't want it to be about Frank.

CO But there is no eyewitness report on that Mothers period.

JIMMY Well, hopefully if I get this book out there will be one. They're just stories that happened to us during the time. I actually had—I never said anything bad about Frank because, first of all, if I do there'll be a lawsuit. Immediately, if not sooner.

CO Yeah. But... I was going to ask you something but you kind of distracted me now. That's OK, that's OK. Do you think disbanding, and not for financial reasons—I'm purely talking artistically now—do you think disbanding the Mothers was a mistake?

JIMMY Well, I always did. And so did the rest of us in the band. We couldn't figure it out, man. You know? How he ended the whole thing.

CO Tell me.

JIMMY Well, we just came back from a very successful tour of Canada, and got back... you know? We had still quite a bit of work lined up, man, after that. And he just called up one day and said, 'Oh by the way—.' He was talking to me about something and said, 'Oh by the way, I decided to break up the band. Your salaries have stopped as of last week.' That's pretty fucking cold, wouldn't you say?

CO And what did you say?

JIMMY What *could* I say? 'Why?' He said, 'I just told you, I decided to break the band up.' And that was the end of the conversation.

CO Has there ever been a moment that you and the guys—because it was a big band then, it was like a ten-piece or eleven-piece band then—

JIMMY Yeah.

CO Was there ever a moment when you said, 'We'll carry on as The Mothers Of Invention?'

JIMMY Well, we were gonna. In fact, we even went into the studio with Tom Wilson as producer to do an album called *The Grandmothers*. We did one session and then found out what they were gonna call the record, *Frank Zappa Presents The Grandmothers*, and we said, 'Fuck you, man!' Not after what he just did. Frank Zappa's not presenting *anything* to us. He tried to get the band back together about six or seven months later.

CO How?

JIMMY He tried to get us back, he tried to start the band again. But I mean, everybody was just so—I mean, because of the way he broke the band up, man. You know? It could have been done with a lot more class than that. It could have been, 'Well yeah, we'll finish out the rest of the tours, we've got six more months of work to do, six more months of this, and we'll finish up and we'll make a big farewell thing.' *No!* That's not the way Frank did it.

CO Mm-hmm. A year and a half later you were in London, doing *200 Motels*. So there was a moment that you met him again.

JIMMY Oh yeah, I kept in contact with Frank. Just because he broke up—the band broke up . . . I did keep in contact with him, unlike some others. Well, Bunk would never *ever*, never would speak to Frank ever again. And there were others. Roy didn't, Roy stayed—he didn't really stay in contact with Frank, but he did in a way.

CO And later he toured with him again.

JIMMY '75 or '76, and got fired by him again. I heard Frank fired the whole band in Tokyo.

CO OK, what will be your last statement on *Freak Out*?

JIMMY I think it's a—

CO You've got nine minutes.

JIMMY Well, I think it's a—it's still, in my opinion, one of the best records I ever made. It's the first LP I ever made, and I have fond memories of that, I have fond memories of the time when we made this record. It was a good time. And it was an important piece of work, actually, as it's turned out. At the time, we didn't know what kind of a piece of work it was going to be. Had not a clue. But as it turned out, it was a good piece of work.

CO Do you ever play it?

JIMMY My wife does. [laughs] Nah, I don't. I don't play any of that shit, man. No, I don't want to listen to it anymore. I've already . . . I know the—I know it. [long pause, followed by a sigh]

After we'd rounded off the interview, we all headed into town to eat at a local restaurant—more like a cafeteria than a real restaurant. JCB's order still makes Menno and me laugh: 'I'll have a very large beer and a *Kinderschnitzel*!'

The *Freak Out* documentary was one of many Zappa radio projects that I have very fond memories of. It was also the last time I met Mr. Black, the Indian of the Group.

2011/2012

Link your mind

IN NOVEMBER 2011, I MET GEORGE DUKE FOR DINNER AT THE PARK HOTEL IN AMSTERDAM. Afterward, as we drank our coffees, we reminisced about our projects with the Metropole Orkest; the Amsterdam Halloween show in 2009, with Jules Buckley conducting and featuring guests Izaline Calister and Napoleon Murphy Brock, is still a highlight. Every day during that project week, George came back to my place after the rehearsals to relax, talk, and listen to music. Out of the blue, he said, 'Co, tell me in all honesty—do you think I should play at Zappanale?'

The following excerpt is taken from *We Are The Other People: 25 Years Of Zappanale*, the gorgeous book written to celebrate Zappanale:

> *George spent some nice beer- and wine-oriented times in my house in Kortenhoef, along with the great Herbie Cohen: video material of Herbie and I dragging George into a cheese farm near my house exists on the internet. God, I miss those guys. I was and am an Orbeccian, member of Mr. Cohens religious movement honoring the Great Duck Orbec, I may tell you about that during a future Zappanale. And then there was the George Zappanale Question. I honestly do not know what I would have answered in 2010. Many Zappa Festivals have this semi-religious vibe to it that I really don't like. Also: I do not like bootleggers. Or shitty cover bands. I did not really have a negative feeling re Zappanale, but in 2010 I would not have felt comfortable to give advice to a man like George. It also struck me that he asked me for my opinion, I mean come on, he was George Duke! But it was not 2010, he asked me in 2011 and in that year I had visited my first Zappanale to do a performance with my dear friend, the amazing Gary Lucas. We performed the piece based on the last interview Captain Beefheart did with me, called I Have A Cat. It*

was a great success, and it enabled me to find out what Zappanale was all about. A celebration of the music and the attitude of one of the greatest musical phenomenons in the 20th century and beyond. With enormous respect and a lot of fun. So I said to George: YES!

And he did play Zappanale, with Jean-Luc Ponty. I did not have plans to attend in 2012 but George asked me to be there, so I suggested to Thomas to do a staged version of my Supplement Tape Project. And George promised to be part of it.

The first time I saw George was in 1973 with FZ in Amsterdam, with Jean-Luc in the band: I was just a kid. So can you imagine how good it felt almost forty years later to introduce George and Ponty on stage (thanks for letting me do that, Jim Cohen . . .) and to become an Honorary Member Of The Arf Society together with them, also on stage? You think you can, but you can't!

You can read the rest in the book. It's a wonderful, must-have volume.

2016/2017

DZOF

I'VE ALWAYS HAD A SOFT SPOT FOR ORCHESTRAL ZAPPA. I think it's because *200 Motels* was the only record (besides *Freak Out*) I listened to every single day of my teenage years. My orchestral projects with Steve Vai carry on the tradition that Zappa started: we work with elements from various 'sound worlds' without ever mentioning the difference, and certainly without ever putting any of them on a pedestal.

Artistically, I have been, and continue to be, challenged by my good friend Marcel Mandos, the Artistic Director of NNO, the North Netherlands Symphony Orchestra, based in Groningen. Some years ago, I was considering the possibilities for a project that Marcel had proposed to me. Having always wanted to organize a performance of Zappa's orchestral works, my idea was this: an evening to celebrate Zappa, combined with work by someone he himself had discovered. Steve Vai has never been shy about saying what a huge influence Frank was on him, and had become a musical phenomenon in his own right. We could then combine his work with new music written and performed in part by—Dweezil Zappa!

I pitched my idea informally to Zappa and Mandos, and as always I had support from NTR Editor-in-Chief Wijnand Honig. On September 13th, I wrote them an email:

> *Dear Mr. Mandos, Marcel, dear Mr. Zappa, Dweezil,*
>
> *Let me start this introductory email on a personal note: I am pleased to introduce you to each other (since I know both of you), because I am convinced we have the opportunity to create an event that will write history!*
>
> *For Marcel:*
> *For a long time I have been harassing you with the idea of producing a concert with Dweezil as the main focus. Your unique attitude towards orchestral programming is what makes this a possibility.*
>
> *To Dweezil:*
> *My history with this fantastic orchestra and our huge projects, especially those with Laurie Anderson, Steve Vai, and Todd Rundgren, makes me feel very confident that we can create a wonderful event.*
>
> *To both of you:*
> *I am audacious enough to call myself a friend of Frank Zappa's. Why? Because HE told me so. It is a known fact that since the late '70s I alone have been responsible for more than 75% of FZ (and DZ for that matter) airplay on public radio here. Also, I have an impressive track record of projects WITH and ABOUT FZ.*

Therefore I feel comfortable proposing this:

Let's create this Triangle:
1: DZ as the main soloist/focus.
2: Marcel as the Man in Charge re the orchestra and the overall production (he is also you contract partner, Dweezil).
3: Me, via my company Zivasound, as the artistic producer, program sparring partner for DZ, and media consultant.

I've also discussed with Dweezil the role of his orchestrator, Kurt Morgan, as well as Fringe Programming.

In other words:
I suggest we set a date, perhaps by email, to finalize a deal for
AN ORCHESTRAL EVENING WITH DWEEZIL ZAPPA
MUSIC BY DWEEZIL AND FRANK ZAPPA AND OTHERS
REHEARSALS NOV 28–30, 2017
SHOW(S) DECEMBER 1 AND 2, 2017

I have a lot more thoughts and ideas for this, but I think it is better to take it from here. I am thrilled.

Kind regards,
Co

After countless emails, phone calls, meetings, and demos, and endless planning, the project was finally realized in November 2017. It was Marcel's wonderful idea to bring in conductor Hans Leenders. With a background as percussionist, Leenders had a strong grasp of the rhythmic characteristics of Zappa's and Vai's music. Kurt Morgan and my good friend the amazing Tom Trapp orchestrated Dweezil's material (including the world premiere of 'The Adventures of Dindoo'). The other Zappa material included 'Sad Jane,' 'Bob In Dacron,' 'Watermelon In Easter Hay,' and 'Strictly Genteel.' Vai's music was represented by 'There's Still Something Dead In Here,' and Dweezil's other music included 'Preludumus Maximus,' 'Shampoohorn,' 'Truth,' and 'Marmux Buhdardux.'

It was an amazing week in Groningen, with Dweezil, his wife Megan, Kurt Morgan (who played bass for Dweezil also), and Martine van Zelst, who produces my show *Co Live!* The two concerts met with a favorable response from a very diverse audience: both regular visitors of the NNO (who mostly enjoy the classical music that makes up most of that orchestra's usual program), and diehard Zappa fans from around the world. Overjoyed to see that Zappa's orchestral DNA was alive and well, I named the project *Dweezil Zappa's Orchestral Favorites*.

2019

Essence

MY DAUGHTER JASMIJN ZIVA HAS SOME FAVORITE ZAPPA SONGS: 'Cheap Thrills,' 'Electric Aunt Jemima,' 'Baby Snakes,' 'Goblin Girl,' and 'The Handsome Cabin Boy.' One day when she was eight, we were in the car playing these songs with the volume up, and she suddenly proclaimed, 'You know what, Dad? What I like about Frank's music [she refers to him as Frank—and why not?], not only is it funny, it's so very well made as well!' Later, when I told this story to Mike Keneally, he commented, 'It takes the average music journalist about fifty pages to come to that conclusion.' Amen.

Semi-fraudulent bonus track

One of the legendary people I met through Zappa was the totally unique and unbelievable Don Van Vliet, a friend from Frank's younger days, also known as Captain Beefheart. I worked on many projects with Don, and for the *Supplement* show I phoned him for a long interview. I later learned that it was the last interview of any length he ever did. Don passed away in 2010.

Together with Mr. Gary Lucas, Beefheart's former manager, virtuoso guitarist of the last Magic Band, and now a dear friend of mine, I used that interview to create a 'soundscape' piece. It was entered for the prestigious Prix Italia competition, and released via Okay Music. As a bonus track, the full transcript accompanying that release is included here. Enjoy!

– I HAVE A CAT –

Music based on a telephone call, Don Van Vliet & CdK, July 23rd, 1993
By Gary Lucas & Co de Kloet

I Have A Cat (part one)	38'22'
I Have A Cat (part two)	29'00'
Total Time:	67'22'

Dedicated to Garland & Bob

Transcription interview: Tom Trapp
Original 1993 interview recording produced by Piet Hein van de Poel & Josephine Veldhuijzen
Recorded in the Poelroom, Heideheuvel, Hilversum

Music recorded January 17–19, 2008
Mixed February 10–11, 2008
Studio MCO 3, Hilversum, Holland
Engineer: Frank Mathijssen
Music performed by Gary Lucas
Creative Catalyst: Co de Kloet

INTRODUCTION

From the original submission to Prix Italia, 2008.

DON VAN VLIET, AKA CAPTAIN BEEFHEART, IS A PHENOMENON.

After having a major impact on the history of popular music—creating music in the sixties, seventies, and eighties that is still ahead of its time—he decided to leave the music scene in 1982 and focus on his other talent, painting.

Legend has it that with one painting he earns more money than in his entire musical career.

Not only is it quite unique that an artist voluntarily leaves the musical arena, Van Vliet also withdrew more and more from public life altogether.

Co de Kloet, radio producer, musician and composer, met Van Vliet in 1975. In 1980 they met again during the recording of the last show Captain Beefheart and the Magic Band would play in Amsterdam. His manager and part-time guitar player at that time was Mr. Gary Lucas.

In 1993 CdK decided to devote a 4-hour special to The Captain for the famous Dutch radio show 'Supplement.' At that time Van Vliet had already decided not to do any more interviews. However, based on their good relationship, he did agree to an hour-long telephone interview, most likely the last lengthy interview he ever did (in this period he also delivered quotes for the short, yet impressive Anton Corbijn film 'Some YoYo Stuff').

On one hot summer night, CdK conducted one of the most intense interviews of his career. The material was used for radio and quoted in numerous articles and books.

So, there it was, the last long conversation on record with a phenomenon.

But over the years, the Thing itself collected dust on one of the many shelves in CdK's NPS office. All that time there was a question mark hanging over it... there was more to it than just the words. But what?

It took yet another decade for CdK to hear the light, as it were. Besides merely a conversation—the weird noise of the phone, the way Don spoke, the pauses, the ambience, the bizarre associations, the contrasts—everything pointed toward the idea that these tapes should be regarded as a music track for a larger recording, whereby the words themselves would be overruled by the pure sounds and dynamics, sort of like Instrumental Vocal Music (not to be confused with Instrumental A Cappella).

With this paradox in mind, CdK approached Gary Lucas, his '1980 link,' and asked if he was interested in participating in 'scoring' the interview, wherein the new music and the old tape would be equal in importance.

Gary said yes, CdK sent him the transcription of the basic material and a few months later, in January 2008, the recordings took place. First recorded was a basic layer to the complete track, then inserts which consisted of Gary Lucas improvisations and lines as well as ideas that were the result of thought-exchange between CdK and Gary.

CdK requested sounds, notes, and sometimes conducted Gary, a challenge in itself!

The mixing process was fun too, because engineer Frank and CdK had to avoid treating the music as background to the conversation. The equality of the sources was of primary importance.

The end result is 'I Have A Cat.'

Besides a radio presentation, Lucas & Co are investigating the possibility of live performances.

Please note that this was, in no way, intended to imitate or even approach Van Vliet's music.

This piece is in fact, an homage to a great man who showed us all that originality is a precious goal, tool and talent.

...or in his own words: 'If you want to be a different fish, you gotta jump out of school!' By the way, Gary Lucas and Co de Kloet think of the end result as a ballet.

KORTENHOEF/NEW YORK, MAY 2008

PART ONE

JAN [answering machine] This is Van Vliet at 707-677-04—

DON Co?

CO Don?

DON Yeah.

CO Hello.

DON [laughs] Who was . . . who was that talking?

CO I think it was Jan.

DON Oh.

CO On your machine.

DON [mocking] 7-0-7 . . . yeah. Sounds familiar.

CO How are you today?

DON Wunderbar.

CO All right. Shall we just start, or—

DON I thought we did, oh—well, tell me . . . prep me on what you're going to do.

CO I just have a couple of questions first, and then . . . I have just a small list of things that I would like—

DON Good.

CO That I would like you to give your first reaction on, like, your association with that.

DON Yeah.

CO Would that be ok?

DON Well, I don't see why not.

CO All right.

DON If I don't like it, I won't talk. [laughter]

CO OK, so . . .

DON How you doing?

CO I'm fine today.

DON How's your little fox terrier?

CO He's fine. Barking away.

DON I have a cat.

CO What's his name?

DON My cat, Garland.

CO Garland, I dig your tweed coat?

DON Right, that's what he's named from.

CO Is it ok if I start with my questions about the painting?

DON Yeah.

CO OK. Um, you've been active now for, for years as a painter, and in the recent past you've concentrated mainly on painting. But how is the climate in the United States now for, for contemporary painters? Do you find that a comfortable climate?

DON I don't go see them. I don't go there.

CO Mm hmm.

DON I just paint.

CO What is to you the difference in your work style—I mean, you've—you have a name for yourself both as a composer, a performer, a poet, a painter, a novelist—

DON All the same head. [laughs] The same head does all kinds of things. Tricky brain, I guess you might call it.

CO A tricky brain.

DON [laughs]

CO And are there any cross-references between the different disciplines that you do?

DON Mm . . . mainly, uh, sometimes I name the paintings after music that I've done.

CO Mm-hmm.

DON Quite different. Actually, I enjoy painting more than music.

CO Why?

DON More exciting.

CO In terms of what, is it more exciting? That interests me.

DON Uh, I get to do exactly what I want. Not as if I don't, anyway—but it's more just, on- the-spot.

CO Mm-hmm. Would—

DON It's just interesting. I don't have to think about anybody at all.

CO That's what I was saying. Would it have something to do—that you have a complete control over the end result without any other human beings interfering in it?

DON Yeah. There's sure that.

CO Because a composer always has to go through the musicians?

DON Mm . . . yeah, but it's sometimes difficult to go through somebody when they don't want to be gone through. But [laughs] they will definitely be gone through if I'm doing it.

CO [laughs]

DON I'm a stubborn man.

CO You go right through them, huh?

DON Right through. [swoosh noise] But, with painting, I can do what I want right then and there, can see it immediately.

CO Today, I listened to the tape of our conversation in 1980, which is almost thirteen years ago, and I asked you then about your development as a composer, and you told me then that you didn't really believe in any development as a, as a person who wrote music, and my interpretation then was that you were, uh very—

DON Lying! [laughs]

CO Yeah, but that you were very related to your way of writing, and very clear about that at that time, and . . . would you have the same feeling about your work as a painter.

DON Uh, definitely. Yeah, for sure. I'm still just as stubborn.

CO But does that mean that you are, are exploring the depth of a certain style more than trying to move from one style to another?

DON Mm, well, recently, I've completely changed, but . . .

CO In what way?

DON In—God, that's a difficult question. Let's see . . . let me think one second. Oh, I would say that I'm having better control now with my brushes. I mean, I'm getting better.

CO So, it's a change in—it's a moving forward in technique. Could I describe it that way?

DON I think that would be a good way of looking at it.

CO Do you have, as a painter—somebody who is very visually orientated—do you take a special interest in certain matters? For instance, nature?

DON Yeah, definitely. Animals help.

CO And how do you look upon what's happening right now in various parts of the world, in that perspective?

DON I try not to look at some of these horrible things that are happening. There's some horror stories out there. Does it bother you?

CO Yeah, a lot, I mean—

DON Me too.

CO [laughs] You dedicated the *Shiny Beast* album to the people—to all conservation and wildlife preservation organizations everywhere. I mean, they're—the need for them is even more than in the time that you put out that album.

DON It's getting worse. I don't think that it's improving that much. For instance, they're burning down the rainforest. Doesn't that bother you?

CO It keeps going on, day by day.

DON As we talk.

CO At this very moment.

DON Horrible. Human beings. It goes way back. I can think way back to when I wrote '*White ants running, yellow ants dreaming, Uhuru, ant-man-bee.*' It's scary to find the things you're saying acted out in front of your very eyes. I was right, and that's one time I'd like to be mistaken.

CO Yeah.

DON Yes, it's horrible.

CO Since there's people who are involved in the, in the decision-making side of those things, my next question would be how your views on the political situation in your country is. How do you look at that subject?

DON [laughing] I try not to. I think it's absurd. They don't know what they're doin'. It is like swinging a sponge on the end of a string.

CO I would like to talk about your lyrics for a moment. The very poetical content of the lyrics that you, that you made—also in association with your music. Did they find their origin in the sound of them?

DON Well, usually I would do the music with the words right at the time.

CO You mean simultaneously?

DON Yeah. Yes. That's a good word, isn't it? Simultaneous. Usually, I would do it right at the same time. Maybe I was a better musician than a poet. Usually.

CO But therefore, maybe, the—the way your poetry sounded always had a very musical tendency to it.

DON I think perhaps music has nothing to do with it. [laughs] Now I sound . . . that's ridiculous! [laughs] God, it's hard. Hard to talk. Hard to do music.

CO Well, let's talk about music. That'd make it a bit easier. This week when we talked on the phone, you asked me if I ever listened to the radio.

DON Yeah.

CO Do you?

DON No. [laughs]

CO Let's just take one of your albums. Let's take *Trout Mask*. I mean, what would you think the response or the reaction would be if that album was now being put out as a new release, the way the music situation is now. What do you think would happen?

DON What do I think they would think?

CO Yeah.

DON I'm not for sure they can think.

CO You're not for sure they can think at all?

DON No. I think most of the stuff they're doing now is reacting. A bunch of reactionaries.

CO Second hand.

DON I think . . . what do you think?

CO Well, people try to—like to re-act a lot of periods that are long gone, and that were, in most instances, the originals are better and always will be.

DON Yeah. Hmm. I wonder what Roland Kirk would think now.

CO What do you think he would think?

DON [laughs] The last thing that I'll tell you—that, I—he was playing at the beach, and he asked me, he said 'Where can I get something to eat this time of night, Don?' and I said 'Well, the only place you can get ribs in Los Angeles at this time of night, Roland, is in . . . the only place you can get ribs is in the Bible.' [laughs] . . . and he laughed. That's the last time I saw him. God, what a loss.

CO You often gave people that you worked with, you gave people your own names. I mean—

DON Yeah.

CO Why did you do that?

DON I didn't care about their names. And they seemed to be related to their mama and papa. And I don't think that I would get along with their mama and papa. So, I would get another name. You mean like 'Zoot Horn Rollo?'

CO For instance.

DON Yeah, was that what you were thinking?

CO Yeah. 'The Mascara Snake.'

DON [laughs] Yeah. That's a relatively true name. He is a snake, and he does wear mascara. There was no lie to that.

CO And where did the 'Antennae' from Jimmy Semens come from?

DON Just popped in my head. I thought it would sound better than 'Jeff.' I thought it would be better. Jeff 'and his surname.' Cotton. Jeff Cotton. I thought 'Antennae Jimmy Semens' would be better.

CO Would it be ok if I gave you now a small list of, of words and ask you to comment on those? Maybe also in one or two words?

DON I'll try.

CO OK, I'll just start with my list. Of course, my first one will be 'soprano saxophone.'

DON Let's see . . . a real skinny goose.

CO 'Roland Kirk.'

DON One of the best.

CO 'The desert.'

DON Hot and, uh—sandy.

CO Do you like the desert?

DON Yeah. Don't like it as much as I used to. Right now, I'm painting a group of burrs [laughs] called 'Goat Heads.' They'll actually blow out a tire. They're that strong. If you see 'em ...

CO No.

DON They're pretty, pretty good. Pretty good exhibit.

CO How about the old paint that you would get from Holland?

DON Marvelous. You mean the 'Old Holland?'

CO Mm hmm.

DON Fantastic. Some of the best I've found.

CO OK. Next on my list is 'Vincent van Gogh,' 'Van Go.'

DON Van Gogh, yeah. Should be put with Albert Einstein. I think he was one of the best. Another painter that I really like is Piet Mondriaan.

CO Yeah.

DON Yeah. How do you say that?

CO Piet Mondriaan.

DON Pi-et?

CO Piet. Like 'Pete.'

DON Piete?

CO Like 'Pete.'

DON Piet Mondriaan. Fantastic painter. He did 'Broadway Boogie Woogie.' You familiar with that?

CO Yeah.

DON And you can hear the horns honk! One of my favorite paintings.

CO 'Ornette Coleman.'

DON Ornette Coleman, hmm. It's hard to know. Do you like him?

CO Yes.

DON I liked 'Dee Dee.'

CO 'Frank Zappa.'

DON He's the only Frank Zappa I know.

CO The relation and friendship between you and him is probably one of the most discussed combinations of persons in the music history.

DON [laughs] Why?

CO I don't know why, but it's something that I see.

DON Yeah, then—I guess we fooled 'em.

CO I guess you did.

DON Maybe.

CO What was your first collaboration with him?

DON Years ago, at a place in Cucamonga. A studio he had. We just started playing. What's your favorite album?

CO By who? By you or by Frank?

DON Both of us. *Hot Rats*?

CO It's a hard question.

DON Not *Hot Rats*?

CO Well, it's obviously one of my favorites, but—

DON *Bongo Fury*?

CO I like that one, yeah.

DON Pretty funny.

CO It's a funny album.

DON [laughs]

CO But I think it's a hard question on your behalf to ask, because both you and him have put out such a 'various' catalogue, so much variation and so much different—

DON Yeah.

CO Approaches, and so much different styles and if—let me, let me ask you a similar question: if there was one album from your catalogue that you would advise me to broadcast completely in this program, which one would it be?

DON Hmm, it would be *Lick My Decals Off, Baby*.

CO Because I think it would be a good idea, in this program, to at least play one album completely.

DON Wouldn't hurt to do *Lick My Decals Off, Baby*.

CO OK.

DON Not bad.

CO No. And as we speak, in the meantime, I have that very album in my hands.

DON You just had that.

CO Yeah.

DON You didn't even ... oh, you knew that!

CO It was on the top of the pile.

DON [laughs] How convenient.

CO Why would you pick that album? Would that just be a—why that particular one in your catalogue, I'm interested in that.

DON Telepathy. Maybe because it was on the top of the pile.

CO [laughs]

DON Maybe.

CO Well, anyway—I think that would be the reason to do it, so we'll play that one completely.

DON Good.

CO How is your relation now to—to the music that you have put down, and that you have made? And also, why did you decide to concentrate on painting and let the music be what it is?

DON Well, I thought it was time for me to uh, let it live without my help. Besides, I like to paint more.

CO Mm-hmm.

DON I always have.

CO I've seen you sketching onstage.

DON Right. [laughs] I didn't want to waste any time.

CO And, are you still writing words? Are you completely painting now, or are you also still writing poetry or novels, or ...?

DON Well, mainly just painting. But, uh—I have to name the paintings.

CO Do you, do you feel a—I mean, you've written a lot of music and within your composition you've always been very demanding to the performance and very involved in the structure of it—

DON Yeah.

CO Is there—you said to me earlier, 'It all comes from the same head.' Do you see parallels in the way you treat it? Is the—the fact that you can—from nothing, you can create something—is it the same feeling and the same kind of satisfaction that you get from doing that, in painting, poetry, or music?

DON I get more out of painting than music.

CO Which, at first—it might be that people think that it is the other way around, because with the music—the, the contact with your audience is far more direct . . . or does it not have something to do with that?

DON No, the audience has nothing to do with it—nothing to do with what I did musically.

CO Mm-hmm. But as an artist in general, how do you see your relationship toward the audience?

DON Pff. [laughs] Very, very tedious. Should probably stay away. Don't you think that?

CO I don't know.

DON You don't seem like the sing-along type.

CO Uh, I like to listen.

DON [laughs] To who?

CO Well, basically to people who have something to say.

DON Few and far between.

CO Are you the sing-along type?

DON [laughs] No, oh!

CO You sure can sing.

DON You know I'm not. [laughter]

DON That's—that's good. [laughter]

DON Can you imagine that?

CO It depends on what you had to sing along to.

DON Perhaps. The whales.

CO Yeah.

DON Not really. They're too complicated. Lot of whales up here.

CO Are there?

DON Oh, yeah. One time, uh—four Easters ago, there were thirty-six whales in the bay. Trinidad Bay. Thirty-six of them! They must have been feeding on krill. I don't know. Probably. You know what krill is, don't you?

CO Mm-hmm. Yeah.

DON Little shrimp.

CO Mm-hmm.

DON Incredible.

CO So you—if you had to sing along, it would be with them.

DON Yeah. But they're very, very complicated. I mean, those things can do thirty-six-minute compositions without a repeat. Thirty-six minutes! It's amazing. [makes whale song noise, laughs] Mm, yeah—beautiful.

CO I sometimes find it melancholy.

DON Yes, I think so. Is that just human? Is that us? Because I do too.

CO Yeah. I some—

DON Beautiful blues.

CO That's right. It touches some parts that I very rarely have with music.

DON Indeed. I like Howlin' Wolf. Chester Burnett.

CO You sang a song once on a Howlin' Wolf background.

DON You mean with Frank?

CO Yeah.

DON It was what, was . . . ?

CO Pepsi? 'Why Doesn't Somebody Get Him A Pepsi?' I think that had the background of 'Smokestack Lightning?'

DON Yeah?

CO Yeah.

DON Kinda silly, huh? [laughter]

CO But still, it's a nice song.

DON Yeah.

CO Besides the—*Lick My Decals Off, Baby*, is there an album that you have a special relationship with? That you would see, like—a thing that you would cherish—that has a special feeling for you?

DON The thing that has a thing called 'Ink Mathematics.'

CO Uh, I—it's number two on the pile, as a matter of fact. It's *Ice Cream For Crow*.

DON That's it.

CO Yeah.

DON Two on the pile! You're kidding.

CO 'Ink Mathematics.'

DON Oh, you're not!

CO No, it's here. I'll let it—here it is! [smacks on LP cover] You hear it? [laughs]

DON Yeah.

CO 'The Past Sure Is Tense.'

DON Boy, is that frightening.

CO No, it's comforting.

DON 'The Past Sure Is Tense?'

CO No, that isn't. But the fact that it's number two on the pile is.

DON Well, that is! [laughter]

DON Let me say something to Jan real quick?

CO Of course. We'll take a little break.

DON [off mic] Jan?

PART TWO

DON What were those things you had—one and then two?

CO One was *Lick My Decals Off, Baby.*

DON [to Jan] *Lick My Decals Off, Baby.*

CO And the other one was *Ice Cream For Crow.*

DON Then, *Ice Cream For Crow*, that's just what I was thinking.

JAN [off mic] You mean your albums?

DON Yeah, I do like *Doc At The Radar Station*. Do you?

CO What?

DON [laughs] *Doc At The Radar Station.*

CO *Doc At The Radar Station.*

DON Yeah.

CO It's also here. But then again, it's a pile. But it was just so, so amazing that those two albums would come up.

DON Frightening.

CO No, it's relaxing.

DON No, I mean—in a good way.

CO Yeah.

DON [laughs] Some things are sacred, I guess. But, I didn't—I thought it was 'Pi-et,' not 'Piet.' That's even hipper, 'Piet Mondriaan.'

CO Yeah.

DON Ooh. Oh . . . [laughs] God.

CO If we were going—I'm going to ask you for your help now a bit about putting our program about you together. Of course, one of the albums that you are famous for is *Trout Mask*.

DON Yeah.

CO How do you feel about that album now? Because for me, it's still an album that is—is—that I play on a—well, not on a daily, but at least on a weekly basis.

DON Hit parade. Yeah, I love the album. I like it.

CO Because, that is what I was asking you before, is that—people tend to see albums like that to, to connect them with the period that they were released in, and with all the things that were around them then, but if you place that album in the day and age we live in now . . .

DON [laughs]

CO Do you think that it has gained a new role or a new meaning?

DON It better have. I think it would be good if it did. For them. Do you like 'Wild Life?'

CO Yeah.

DON Yeah, me too. I enjoyed doing that horn.

CO 'Veteran's Day Poppy.'

DON Yeah. [laughs] It's frightening. That's frightening. '*I cry, but I can't buy / Your Veteran's Day poppy / It don't get me high, it can only make me cry / Your Veteran's Day poppy.*' Ooh.

CO [laughs]

DON What about 'Dachau Blues?'

CO That's frightening.

DON Boy, it sure is.

CO But the thing I have, that—even though it's a collection of songs, uh—the thing that I have with that album is that I—I cannot pick and choose and play one or two songs from it. I think it is something that you, that you start and you finish. You go through it all the way.

DON [laughs] Thank you. Yeah. It's amazing they'd allow that.

CO Why?

DON It would hurt their little ears, they used to think.

CO Well, maybe even more now than then.

DON Maybe, [laughs] maybe. Let's hurt their little ears.

CO One of my favorites on that album is 'Hobo Chang Ba.'

DON I like that myself. Let's see, '*Strawwood claw, rattlin' m'jaw / You can't call it.*' No, '*I can't call it,*' No, wait a minute. '*I can't call it / Feather times uh feather / Mornin' time t'thaw / Strawwood claw rattlin' m'jaw / Hobo chang ba.*' Boy, that's been years since I've said that. God, I'm getting senile.

CO [laughs] But it's good that all these things are—are still there.

DON Helps. What a—what a wonderful floorplan.

CO One of the things that always—

DON [laughs]

CO Amazed me, or delighted me, or—I don't really know how to put it, is that—

DON Gimme a little more juice.

CO One of the things that I heard about is—

DON Can't hardly hear you.

CO Can you, can you hear me now?

DON Yeah.

CO All right. One of the things I always think of when I play that particular album is the story I once heard about the 'tree doctor' that you arranged.

DON [laughs] Oh, yeah. Do you know that when I went down to see the exhibit I had in Los Angeles, I went by and saw those trees. They're still living.

CO Those very same trees you recorded *Trout Mask* near?

DON Yeah, they're fine. A male and a female Eucalyptus. They're still getting bigger.

CO Must have done them good to be—

DON Yeah.

CO The witness of that.

DON I'm glad that I helped out. They're still there.

CO Yup. If we are going tonight to—obviously, we will play about—selections from each and every title that you released, each and every album that you released . . . do you think we should do them all? Or are there particular albums that you, looking back, think of as something that is not part of you anymore. Like, obviously, when we talk about *Trout Mask*, or about *Lick My Decals Off, Baby*, those things are so vivid and still—also to, to listeners, are vivid.

DON Is there anything that I wouldn't like you to play? Is that what you're asking?

CO Yeah.

DON Yes. Anything that had anything to do with the DiMartino brothers.

CO Like, uh—*Moonbeams*?

DON Yes. [laughs] Thank you, yes.

CO So, basically the two albums, uh—*Blue Jeans And Moonbeams*, and *Unconditionally Guaranteed.*

DON Right. They're wrong. They screwed with those.

CO I remember you once told me that on the track called—let me think now—'Party Of Special Things To Do,' that they took off Winged Eel Fingerling or something.

DON He, he was there.

CO But didn't they take that off later?

DON Yeah. They've ruined everything. Horrible fellows. Crooks.

CO Well, then on this program we will, on special request, not play something.

DON Get rid of the crooks.

[laughter]

CO Let's have a legal program.

DON [laughs]

CO Very legal.

DON Make it legal.

CO Yeah, legal show.

DON [laughs] Beautiful. Yeah, they—they've ruined those songs, everything. They'd lunched everything.

CO One of my last question is that the—the surroundings that you now live in, is that part of the inspiration for your work? What kind of atmosphere, what kind of surroundings do you work and live in?

DON Right on the ocean. Uh, I can look out my window and see a spout if I'm lucky. They breech out there, the whales. They're wonderful.

CO We've talked about so many things. Do you think there is something I didn't bring up, and that I should have? For now, that is.

DON Well, let's see. I'm trying to think of, uh—you brought up some pretty good stuff. You've amazed me quite a bit. [laughs] That's for sure. Do you like Phil Larkin?

CO Philip Largen?

DON Larkin. The writer.

CO I'm not really familiar with his things. I'm a listener, I'm not really a reader.

DON [laughs] Oh.

CO Well, you know people like that.

DON Yeah, I—I'm sort of like that myself. But he's awful good. I think, perhaps the best poet. Let's see, oh—God, that time went by so fast!

CO It did.

DON I'll tell you, I thought it was fifteen minutes!

CO Yeah.

DON I hope they like our program that much.

CO I think they will.

DON [laughs] You can only hope. I think that maybe I'm not senile.

CO Well, I—I never said that, you did.

DON I did. [laughs] It was me. [to self] What am I saying? Damn, what was I say, wha—

CO One of the things that amaze—well, it doesn't really amaze me, but one of the thing that I notice is that recently, so many young musicians, when asked about their influences—it seems that in the, in the recent past, so many people will name you—

DON [laughs]

CO But, but even more so than, for instance, ten years ago.

DON Yeah.

CO Would you consider it a possibility—or does it ever cross your mind that the music as composed by you, and as written down by you could ever be performed by other people? I mean, some people already did covers of your material—

DON Yeah.

CO But then mostly they would pick and choose, like—uh—'My Head Is My Only House Unless It Rains,' or stuff like that, but could you see a young group of young people, um—perform the *Lick My Decals Off* album, or *Trout Mask*?

DON I would like to hope that they would be willing to work that hard. I wish they'd try it. It would be funny.

CO Let me ask you something.

DON What?

CO Let me ask you something—are you familiar with the composer Gavin Bryars?

DON No.

CO He recently, released a remake of one of his older compositions, called 'Jesus' Blood Never Failed Me Yet,' and it's a recording of a man, a hobo—who was recorded in the streets with a small tape recorder, and he sang the line, the short traditional song 'Jesus' Blood Never Failed Me Yet,' and he made a loop out of it, and it goes on and on and on for about seventy-five minutes, and he did an arrange—

DON Wow.

CO I'll send you a copy of that because it's pretty amazing.

DON Never heard that.

CO I think you'll like it, it's very amazing, but one of the people who participated in that project was Tom Waits.

DON Ooh, ooh, ooh. Not a friend of mine.

CO He is, or he is not?

DON Not. To be perfectly truthful with you. No, he, uh—he just—he kind of is too slick, if you know what I mean. What do you think?

CO I don't know him personally.

DON [laughs]

CO I know that he did an album with a title that—I think, that was—thought up by you, that was made up by you.

DON It was, uh –

BOTH *Swordfishtrombone*.

CO That's right.

DON Guess what? He calls me and he told me that title, and I was in the desert visiting my mother, and he asked me, 'So, what do you think of that?' and I said 'Well, I don't know, should I think of that?' He said, 'Well, I just wondered.' That's kind of funny, that you got that comparison. Sounds like *Trout Mask*, right?

CO Yeah. Well, I like the—

DON And—

CO I like the word *Swordfishtrombone*, anyway.

DON Yeah, but the very idea of him calling me and seeing if that went by me. Right?

CO Mm-hmm.

DON Without a comment.

CO Mm-hmm.

DON It's kinda corny.

CO Would you say there's more slick people in the music world than in the painting world?

DON I think so. But it's quite a toss-up.

[laughter]

DON But, uh—this Waits character, uh—he . . . [off mic] what do you think, Jan? [on mic, laughs] She runs out. She doesn't like him.

CO Let's forget about him.

DON Wh—who? [laughs] I think why I got away quick, he had the nerve to think he could sing like me.

CO But you go higher and deeper than that.

DON Huh, indeed. I'll go as high as I need to go, and deep as I need to go to get by him.

CO [laughs] I think—

DON He's rich!

CO He's rich?

DON Yeah. Money. You knew that, right?

CO Well, I gather he is, but—but then again—

DON [laughs] Beautiful, yeah. Do you know Anton Korb [Corbijn]?

CO Yes, of course. I'm looking—

DON You've seen him?

CO I don't, I don't get to—I don't meet him, I don't know him personally, but of course I'm familiar with his work. As a matter of fact, I'm looking at one of his pictures right now.

DON [laughs] Fancy that.

CO Well, the *Ice Cream For Crow* picture is probably one of the fa—most famous pictures ever made.

DON He's good.

CO Do you get to speak to him?

DON Oh, yeah. Yeah, I see him . . . uh [off mic] how long . . . Jan? How long has it been since we saw Anton?

JAN [off mic] couple years.

DON A couple of years. Two years.

CO I'll send him a copy of the program.

DON Oh, would he like that. He's a good friend. Tell him, say to him, 'Cheesian Phips.' We were in England once and he was telling about 'Cheese And Chips,' and I told him 'Cheesian Phips.' He's funny. He's a hell of a photographer.

CO I will play, I will play this tape—I think, a lot of times, to, to find out what we talked about because right now I've just been concentrating on the moment and I really don't know what's, what's on the tape. But I think it's a lot.

DON Yeah, I hope—hope I sound all right.

CO Very clear.

DON Good.

CO Perfectly, I mean—

DON Good. [laughs] We love to talk, I think. I know I've enjoyed it.

CO So have I. I want to thank you very much for this conversation.

DON Thank you.

CO Yeah. And, before we're going to air this, I'll probably call you up and give you an idea how I'm going to put the four hours together, because right now I'm together with P.H. who will do the show together with me, we just—we just have piles and piles of material and we're going to have to make some choices here.

DON Yeah.

CO But maybe we can do four hours and then later in the year, we'll just do it again.

DON [laughs] Yeah. Well, I sure enjoyed talking to you.

CO OK. I'll be in touch very soon about all the material that I promised you, that I will prepare for you. And please say hello to Jan for me.

DON Yes, thank you. She enjoyed herself the other day. 'Course she had to be in the moment. You know that. She's worried about getting things set up.

CO And how will your day be today, after we hang up the phone? Painting?

DON Yeah. I have no choice. I have so many cities that I have to have paintings in. A.R. Penck. You don't know him, huh?

CO No.

DON Good painter.

CO But, I mean—even this conversation gives me a lot of new ground to cover. You—

DON Yeah.

CO You've given a lot of suggestions.

DON Good.

CO And now you know it's 'Piet,' and not 'Pi-et.'

DON Dammit, that helps. Tell me one time how you really say that.

CO Piet Mondriaan.

DON Piet Mondriaan.

CO That's right.

DON Good.

CO So, I'll give you a call in about a week or so to tell you how we have set the things up, and, um—

DON Thank you.

CO If there's anything else, I mean—you know how to reach me by now, because—

DON Yeah.

CO You have all my, my numbers and so on and so forth.

DON Yeah.

CO And if you say hello to Garland, I'll say hello to the fox.

DON [laughs] Definitely.

CO OK.

DON They will like that.

CO OK. OK, thanks again.

DON Thank you.

CO On behalf of all of us here, and we will be in touch very soon.

DON Tell 'all of us here' hello.

CO I will.

DON Take it easy.

CO OK. Take care.

DON Bye.

CO Bye, bye.

DON Bye.

Finale

This, as you might have gathered, is the end of the book.

Hope you enjoyed it.

Don't throw stuff on the stage!

Bye Don.
Bye Frank.
Thanks for everything!

CO

KORTENHOEF, THE NETHERLANDS

Acknowledgments

NEW FRIENDS

THANKS TO FRANK, I'VE BEEN FORTUNATE ENOUGH TO MEET SOME AMAZING PEOPLE, AND EVEN GOT TO MAKE GREAT MUSIC WITH A FEW OF THEM: Mike Keneally, Napoleon Murphy Brock, George Duke, Bruce Fowler, Jimmy Carl Black, Terry Bozzio, Denny Walley, and Dweezil Zappa. Susan Rubio is still a treasured friend.

My deepest and most spiritual friendship that I have Frank to thank for is with Steve Vai—as a person, and as a fellow professional. I'll write more about our friendship in another book. As Frank told me the very first time we met, 'The future lies ahead.'

THE CREW

This book wouldn't have been possible without my friends, who have been an enormous help and support.

The first mention must go to Menno Kalmann, my musical and business associate, and my friend since high school. Without intending or wish it, over time he's become a Zappa expert in his own right. Frank liked him a lot.

Dave Pearson is an artist and musician from Menominee, Michigan, a small resort town on the shores of Lake Michigan in the USA, where he lives with his totally bitchin' wife Heather. He became a hardcore Zappa fan at age fifteen, when he saw FZ for the first time on November 20th, 1980—a night that forever changed his life. When Dave is not painting at his easel or recording in the studio, he spends time with his daughters Allicia and Marcy, gardening with his dogs, and restoring classic Schwinn bicycles. Dave's artist page is yooperstudio.com. Music is the best!

Tom Trapp translated all the Dutch parts in this book for me. Tom is a highly talented composer, orchestrator (for Steve Vai and Adrian Belew, to name but two) and multi-instrumentalist who lives and works in Holland. He's received international acclaim for his work for the Metropole Orkest, and his recent solo project *The Cowboy* has met with wide praise. tomtrapp.net.

Ernest Potters is a Dutch photographer with a long track record in rock and jazz photography. Nowadays he presents his impressive work through Luycks Gallery in Tilburg, displaying his sharp eye for detail, rhythm, light, perspective, and color as he documents everyday life. He zooms in on idiosyncrasies that others miss, to highlight the beauty and poetry of the ordinary, the dull, the perishable, and the unsightly, but also the majestic and monumental. He adopts unusual points of view to turn reality into images of universal value. luycksgallery.com.

Mark van Schaick provided the photographs of objects and the portrait of CdK with the gasmask. Born and raised in Hilversum, Mark has been writing for Dutch music and musicians' magazines and periodicals for almost four decades, during which time he has interviewed multiple FZ alumni as well as a couple of Frank's siblings. Thanks to his Italian wife Barbara, he can now hold a real Zappa every now and then—although he still prefers cameras. Mark's first book *Why go*—a portrait of the Seattle scene in the 1990s—saw the light in 2018. His website, markstekst.nl, is under construction more often than not.

Thank you also to Steve Vai and Dweezil Zappa. Let's get to work!

ALSO AVAILABLE IN PRINT AND EBOOK EDITIONS FROM JAWBONE PRESS

Riot On Sunset Strip: Rock'n'roll's Last Stand In Hollywood Domenic Priore

Million Dollar Bash: Bob Dylan, The Band, And The Basement Tapes Sid Griffin

Bowie In Berlin: A New Career In A New Town Thomas Jerome Seabrook

Hot Burritos: The True Story Of The Flying Burrito Brothers John Einarson with Chris Hillman

Million Dollar Les Paul: In Search Of The Most Valuable Guitar In The World Tony Bacon

To Live Is To Die: The Life And Death Of Metallica's Cliff Burton Joel McIver

The Impossible Dream: The Story Of Scott Walker & The Walker Brothers Anthony Reynolds

Jack Bruce Composing Himself: The Authorised Biography Harry Shapiro

Return Of The King: Elvis Presley's Great Comeback Gillian G. Gaar

Forever Changes: Arthur Lee & The Book Of Love John Einarson

Seasons They Change: The Story Of Acid And Psychedelic Folk Jeanette Leech

Crazy Train: The High Life And Tragic Death Of Randy Rhoads Joel McIver

A Wizard, A True Star: Todd Rundgren In The Studio Paul Myers

The Resurrection Of Johnny Cash: Hurt, Redemption, And American Recordings Graeme Thomson

Just Can't Get Enough: The Making Of Depeche Mode Simon Spence

Glenn Hughes: The Autobiography Glenn Hughes with Joel McIver

Entertain Us: The Rise Of Nirvana Gillian G. Gaar

Adventures Of A Waterboy Mike Scott

Read & Burn: A Book About Wire Wilson Neate

Big Star: The Story Of Rock's Forgotten Band Rob Jovanovic

Recombo DNA: The Story Of Devo, or How The 60s Became The 80s Kevin C. Smith

Neil Sedaka, Rock'n'roll Survivor: The Inside Story Of His Incredible Comeback Rich Podolsky

Touched By Grace: My Time With Jeff Buckley Gary Lucas

A Sense Of Wonder: Van Morrison's Ireland David Burke

Bathed In Lightning: John McLaughlin, The 60s And The Emerald Beyond Colin Harper

My Bloody Roots: From Sepultura To Soulfly And Beyond: The Autobiography Max Cavalera with Joel McIver

What's Exactly The Matter With Me? Memoirs Of A Life In Music P.F. Sloan and S.E. Feinberg

Who Killed Mister Moonlight? Bauhaus, Black Magick, And Benediction David J. Haskins

Lee, Myself & I: Inside The Very Special World Of Lee Hazlewood Wyndham Wallace

Throwing Frisbees At The Sun: A Book About Beck Rob Jovanovic

Long Promised Road: Carl Wilson, Soul Of The Beach Boys Kent Crowley

Eyes Wide Open: True Tales Of A Wishbone Ash Warrior Andy Powell with Colin Harper

Eternal Troubadour: The Improbable Life Of Tiny Tim Justin Martell with Alanna Wray McDonald

Confessions Of A Heretic: The Sacred & The Profane, Behemoth & Beyond Adam Nergal Darski with Mark Eglinton

Seeing The Real You At Last: Life And Love On The Road With Bob Dylan Britta Lee Shain

The Monkees, Head, And The 60s Peter Mills

Complicated Game: Inside The Songs Of XTC Andy Partridge and Todd Bernhardt

Perfect Day: An Intimate Portrait Of Life With Lou Reed Bettye Kronstad

Tragedy: The Ballad Of The Bee Gees Jeff Apter

Becoming Elektra: The Incredible True Story Of Jac Holzman's Visionary Record Label Mick Houghton

Shredders! The Oral History Of Speed Guitar (And More) Greg Prato

Fearless: The Making Of Post-Rock Jeanette Leech

Shadows Across The Moon: Outlaws, Freaks, Shamans And The Making Of Ibiza Clubland Helen Donlon

Staying Alive: The Disco Inferno Of The Bee Gees Simon Spence

The Yacht Rock Book: The Oral History Of The Soft, Smooth Sounds Of The 70s And 80s Greg Prato

Earthbound: David Bowie and The Man Who Fell To Earth Susan Compo

What's Big And Purple And Lives In The Ocean? The Moby Grape Story Cam Cobb

Swans: Sacrifice And Transcendence: The Oral History Nick Soulsby

Small Victories: The True Story Of Faith No More Adrian Harte

AC/DC 1973–1980: The Bon Scott Years Jeff Apter

Keep Music Evil: The Brian Jonestown Massacre Story Jesse Valencia

Lunch With The Wild Frontiers: A History Of Britpop And Excess In 13½ Chapters Phill Savidge

Wilcopedia: A Comprehensive Guide To The Music Of America's Best Band Daniel Cook Johnson

King's X: The Oral History Greg Prato

More Life With Deth David Ellefson with Thom Hazaert

Take It Off: KISS Truly Unmasked Greg Prato

I Scare Myself Dan Hicks

I Am Morbid: Ten Lessons Learned From Extreme Metal, Outlaw Country, And The Power Of Self-Determination David Vincent with Joel McIver

Lydia Lunch: The War Is Never Over: A Companion To The Film By Beth B. Nick Soulsby

Zeppelin Over Dayton: Guided By Voices Album By Album Jeff Gomez

What Makes The Monkey Dance: The Life And Music Of Chuck Prophet And Green On Red Stevie Simkin

So Much For The 30 Year Plan: Therapy? The Authorised Biography Simon Young

She Bop: The Definitive History Of Women In Popular Music: Revised And Updated 25th Anniversary Edition Lucy O'Brien

Relax Baby Be Cool: The Artistry And Audacity Of Serge Gainsbourg Jeremy Allen

Seeing Sideways: A Memoir Of Music And Motherhood Kristin Hersh

Two Steps Forward, One Step Back: My Life In The Music Business Miles A. Copeland III

It Ain't Retro: Daptone Records & The 21st-Century Soul Revolution Jessica Lipsky

Renegade Snares: The Resistance & Resilience Of Drum & Bass Ben Murphy and Carl Loben

Southern Man: Music And Mayhem In The American South Alan Walden with S.E. Feinberg